On the Shadow Tracks

On the Shadow Tracks

A Journey Through Occupied Myanmar

CLARE HAMMOND

ALLEN LANE
an imprint of
PENGUIN BOOKS

ALLEN LANE

UK | USA | Canada | Ireland | Australia
India | New Zealand | South Africa

Penguin Books is part of the Penguin Random House group of companies
whose addresses can be found at global.penguinrandomhouse.com.

First published in Great Britain by Allen Lane 2024

001

Set in 12/14.75pt Dante MT Std
Typeset by Jouve (UK), Milton Keynes
Printed and bound in Great Britain by Clays Ltd, Elcograf S.p.A.

The authorized representative in the EEA is Penguin Random House Ireland,
Morrison Chambers, 32 Nassau Street, Dublin D02 YH68

A CIP catalogue record for this book is available from the British Library

ISBN: 978–0–241–62389–3

www.greenpenguin.co.uk

Penguin Random House is committed to a
sustainable future for our business, our readers
and our planet. This book is made from Forest
Stewardship Council® certified paper.

To Hen

Contents

Introduction

On 8 November 2015, my colleagues at the *Myanmar Times* newspaper woke before dawn and queued outside polling stations to vote, many of them for the first time in their lives. We had feared there would be unrest in Myanmar that day. But after casting their ballots, voters strolled calmly through the streets, displaying fingertips stained with purple indelible ink.

That night, crowds gathered outside the headquarters of the National League for Democracy, the political party led by Nobel laureate Aung San Suu Kyi, to watch the preliminary vote count flash onto an LED screen. As the scale of the party's likely victory became clear, people across the country spilled onto the streets to celebrate. They waved flags emblazoned with the fighting peacock, the symbol of their twenty-seven-year struggle for democracy. It rained that night, and from the heart of the celebrations, our photographers sent images back to the newsroom of exultant, rain-streaked faces turned towards the sky.

For three days and three nights my colleagues and I camped out at the office, editing stories filed from across the country. We crowded around a small television to watch the results being announced. When we realized that Aung San Suu Kyi's party would win an absolute majority in parliament, I watched my colleagues celebrate their own victory: for press freedom, for the right to tell the truth, to record, to remember, to see, and to be seen.

Outside the country, and particularly in the West, the election result was hailed as a triumph for liberal democracy in one of the world's most repressive states. At the centre of the story was Aung San Suu Kyi, the Oxford University-educated daughter of Myanmar's independence hero General Aung San. After emerging as the leading figure of the pro-democracy movement in 1988, she had endured fifteen years under house arrest, while her supporters had been thrown into colonial-era prisons, where many of them were tortured or killed.

With her calm resolve and mantra of peace, Aung San Suu Kyi appeared to stand in sharp and uncomplicated opposition to the military generals, who had brutalized Myanmar's people for half a century. Both in Myanmar and in the West, the struggle between the two had been reduced to a simple contest between good and evil.

It was this compellingly simple narrative and the exhilarating pace of change in Myanmar that drew me to the country from Hong Kong, where I had been working as a financial journalist. There, I had reported occasionally on the economic reforms that accompanied the political transition, after Myanmar's military handed power to a nominally democratic government led by a former general, Thein Sein.

From Hong Kong's financial district, where I spent my days interviewing bankers about share prices and interest rates, I had found the events unfolding in Myanmar intoxicating. In the spring of 2014, I packed up my tiny apartment and moved to Yangon, the largest city in Myanmar, and the former colonial capital. I was twenty-six years old and I had no commitments anywhere else.

But when I sat down at my new desk and began editing the business pages of the *Myanmar Times*, an English-language newspaper, I found myself grappling with what was, in fact, a formidably complex history. It was also, I would come to learn, one that was deeply entangled with that of the United Kingdom – my own country.

These two histories began to intertwine in 1824, when the British East India Company waged its first war against the Burmese Konbaung dynasty. The Company already ruled large parts of India and was looking to expand its control over the Asian sea trade. Within three decades, it had seized the long Indian Ocean coastline that stretches from modern-day Bangladesh to the Malay Peninsula on the sea route to Singapore, forcing the Burmese inland. Establishing a new capital at Rangoon (the same city, now known as Yangon, where I would live for the next six years), Britain waged a third and final war against the Burmese kingdom in 1885 and deposed its king. It annexed not only the Burmese heartland, but a much larger territory, including land inhabited by more than 100 other ethnic groups that live in Myanmar today.

At the centre of this diverse territory were the ethnic Burmese, who now make up an estimated two-thirds of Myanmar's population of 54 million (the data on Myanmar's ethnic makeup is considered so sensitive that it is not made public). Parts of the surrounding lowlands were home to rival kingdoms, including the Rakhine in the west and the Mon in the southeast. In the eastern mountains were the Shan States, whose hereditary rulers had paid tribute to the Burmese court. (The Shan are now Myanmar's second-largest ethnic group, comprising around 10 per cent of the population.) Encircling these territories were vast stretches of highland, where hundreds of tribal groups, including the Chin and Kachin (now smaller but sizeable minorities) lived in relative isolation, kept apart by the region's mountainous terrain (see map on p. 164).

This territory became known as British Burma. At independence in 1948, rather than dividing it back into separate states, as some ethnic minorities had hoped, the British simply transferred power to Burmese independence leaders in Rangoon. Aung San

Suu Kyi's father, General Aung San, had promised ethnic leaders that he would grant them autonomy. But he was assassinated six months before independence, and his promise was never kept. Instead, a year after independence, in 1949, the first separatist insurgency broke out. Myanmar has since become home to some of the world's longest-running civil wars.

As conflict erupted across the country, one of the Burmese independence heroes, a general called Ne Win, quietly consolidated power over the armed forces. Within just over a decade, he had staged a coup, and soon he established a socialist regime, centralizing the economy and isolating Myanmar from the rest of the world. From 1962, for more than half a century, the military ruled the country. In 1988, when Ne Win's regime collapsed during a national uprising, it was quickly replaced by another military government. By then, Myanmar's armed forces were no longer considered heroes; to hold onto power, they brutally crushed the pro-democracy protests, killing thousands of innocent civilians. Under Than Shwe, a strongman who would remain in power until 2011, they would rule by violent force.

More overtly nationalist than Ne Win's regime, the junta that Than Shwe would come to lead changed the country's name from Burma to Myanmar in 1989. It also changed the names of its cities, towns, rivers and streets, as if to erase all traces of British rule. It promoted Buddhism as the state religion, and it mythologized the pre-colonial past.

It also tried to reframe Myanmar's conflicts, propagating the idea that for hundreds if not thousands of years, the country (meaning the geographical territory demarcated by the British administration and claimed by the modern state) had been home to a fixed number of indigenous 'national races' – which did not include the Rohingya, a long-persecuted predominantly Muslim minority. These groups had lived together more or less in harmony, the junta claimed, until the British invaded, violently disrupting this peaceful union, and creating deep and lasting divisions. It was the responsibility of everyone in the country, it argued, to restore the nation to its former unity. The problem, of course, was that to the country's ethnic minorities, 'unity' meant submission to the Burmese military.

By the time I sat down at my desk in the cavernous, colonial-era *Myanmar Times* newsroom, the country was home to more than twenty established ethnic armed groups and more than 100 militias. Some of these groups had signed ceasefires with Myanmar's military, but none had given up their weapons. Their struggle was complicated by their involvement in the shadowy illicit industries that fund the war: the multi-billion-dollar narcotics, timber, jade and gemstones economies, which also function as money-laundering schemes for Asia's criminal gangs.

But these were the knotty, difficult subjects that I would find myself reporting on in the years to come. For now, as the newsroom hummed with the activity of young reporters, much of this complexity was occluded. Instead, my colleagues profiled their newly elected lawmakers, including former political prisoners, activists and poets, and wrote optimistic articles about the peace process, which Aung San Suu Kyi would soon make a priority.

On the business desk, we wrote about the sunny outlook for the economy, the lifting of Western sanctions, the opening up of the banking and telecoms sectors, and Myanmar's first stock exchange. During those heady months, it felt as if the country was moving into a new phase of history – and in that moment, the future for my colleagues had seemed bright and secure.

The city we lived in was already beginning to resemble any

other Asian metropolis. As the generals stepped back from direct power, people from around the world had flocked to Yangon in their thousands, attracted by what appeared to be vast new opportunities. New shopping malls, luxury condominiums and high-end hotels proliferated, obscuring the violence of the recent past. There were new nightclubs and bars, where guest DJs flew in from Asian capitals for one-night shows. There were pop-up restaurants, fast-food outlets, luxury spas, yoga studios and state-of-the-art gyms. The city was booming, and at the time I saw this as a further sign that Myanmar was leaving its troubled past behind.

As a young journalist, one who had not lived in the country for long and who had never experienced the darkness that in Myanmar is associated with military rule, it was easy to overlook the past. I hardly noticed that the legacy of the military's abuses lingered, exerting a power I could not see and did not yet understand.

I hardly noticed, either, that I was being drawn – imperceptibly at first, and then with growing momentum – into a journey that would eventually transform my understanding not only of Myanmar's modern history and its present, but also of my own country's past.

In the mornings, from my apartment, I could hear the horns sounded by train drivers as they pulled into Yangon Central Railway Station or left it again, to travel hundreds of miles across the country, to places whose names I did not yet know.

I would step out onto my balcony and look over the street, where men in short-sleeved shirts were sitting outside tea-shops on plastic stools, sipping sweet tea and smoking Red Ruby cigarettes, the military's brand. To the north, at the end of my road, I could see the station's distinctive white towers topped with golden, multi-tiered roofs. There were lines of carriages parked among a grove of trees. And if I watched for long enough, a slow train would roll into the station with its windows down.

The country's dilapidated railways were beginning to capture my attention. Within a year, I would find myself embarking on a 3,000-mile journey, by train, to the far reaches of Myanmar, to discover how the country had been shaped by these tracks.

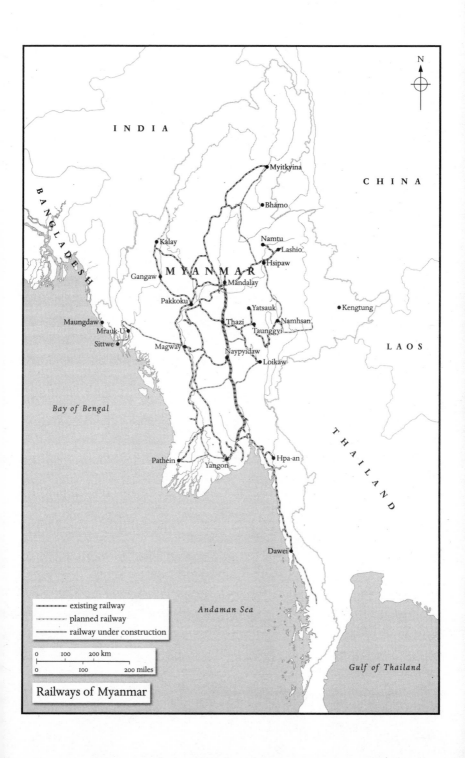

Railways of Myanmar

PART ONE

Q: What about the railway? SLORC says it will benefit the people.
A: What they say is all useless garbage. We gain nothing from it.

Interview conducted in a Mon refugee camp, 1995[1]

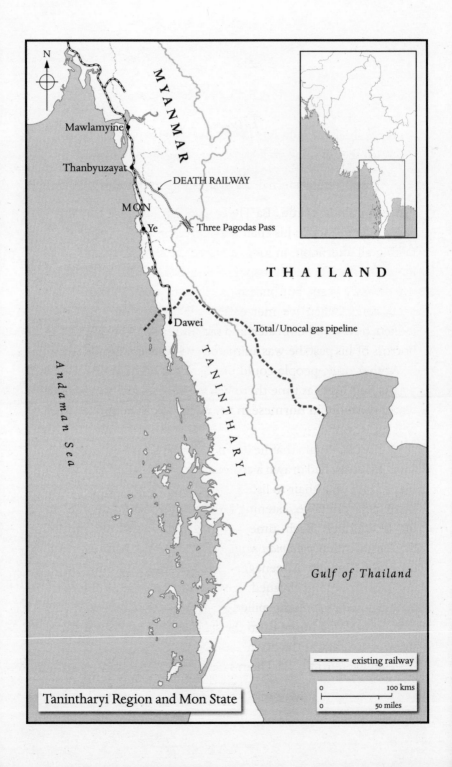

Tanintharyi Region and Mon State

I.

Dawei

'It was a pointless time,' Ba Thein spat. 'Brutality for nothing.'

He leaned back in his chair and closed his eyes. He had been talking all afternoon, in long, agitated bursts, punctuated with long silences. He had not spoken about these things for more than twenty years, but once he started, he couldn't stop. I had been struck when we met earlier that day by how tired he looked, how weather-beaten and sad. But now, as he dug up the horrors of his past, he was animated and we were captivated.

'At that time, people could not bear to live here,' Ba Thein was saying. 'At that time there was . . .' He seized my pen and wrote the word in Burmese in my notebook as he spoke: '*Khat bey*: catastrophe'.

During the hours that he had been talking in this village teashop, his story had drawn a crowd. The teashop owner was the first to pull up a chair to listen. Now, she was chopping onions at the adjacent table, listening intently, with her young daughter beside her. Each time we ordered another round of tea – rich, sweet *pote man saint* – the waiting staff lingered at the table. A group of teenagers was listening too, their bottles of Coca-Cola long finished. It was golden hour, in the early evening, and as sunlight spilled across the room, several of the farmers walking home from the surrounding paddy fields had stopped to listen at the door.

'They were rude,' Ba Thein said quietly. The teashop owner

looked up from her onions and nodded vigorously. 'They did not treat us fairly. They were extremely rude.'

We were in Dawei, the capital of Tanintharyi Region in Myanmar's deep south, a strip of land that extends from the body of the country like the tail of a kite. I had arrived there several days earlier on a propeller plane that was the only vehicle in the local airline's fleet. From Yangon International Airport, we had risen above the sprawl of Myanmar's largest city, before swinging east over the brown waters of the Gulf of Mottama and the Thanlwin River delta. As we veered south, for hundreds of miles I could see nothing beneath us except jungle and the Andaman Sea.

On the flight there had been a military officer, identifiable by his sunburned skin, the camouflage hat clenched in his fist and his rings set with gemstones – a reminder of the immense personal wealth that Myanmar's military officers have amassed since the 1990s. This soldier's journey south hinted at what I would discover when I landed: that the military was everywhere in Tanintharyi Region. Unlike in Yangon, where I lived, the army's presence here was conspicuous, from the trucks that rumbled through the villages to the sprawling, fortified barracks, and the soldiers on the streets.

It had not always been this way. As Ba Thein was explaining to us, this tropical southern peninsula had once been a relatively peaceful backwater, inhabited by fishermen and farmers. Soldiers from Myanmar's military and groups of insurgents had intermittently passed through the villages here, but they never stayed for long. (Myanmar's military calls itself the *Tatmadaw*, using the royal particle 'daw'. Opposition groups call it *sit-tat*, which translates simply as 'military'. In this book, I will use the neutral descriptor 'the military'.)[1]

But one morning in the summer of 1993, a group of soldiers

turned up at Ba Thein's village in rural Dawei township and for the first time that he could remember they showed no signs of leaving. Instead, they called a meeting, telling him and the other men in his village that one person from every household was required to leave their village and clear a route through the forest. They were building a railway line, they said, the first railway to have ever been built on the Myanmar side of this peninsula. Many of the people at the meeting had never seen a railway before in their lives.

Ba Thein reiterated with quiet bitterness how forceful the soldiers had been. The request for workers was in fact an order, given by men who appeared to see civilians as subordinates. The soldiers put a price on freedom: anyone who wanted to stay behind to work on their farms would have to pay an exorbitant tax. Ba Thein couldn't afford it, but neither could he afford to leave his farm behind. He was a toddy-palm farmer, and the palm-sugar harvest was his only source of income.

But what choice did he have? The soldiers were armed, and were already renowned for their brutality. For several years they had been abducting young men from villages further north to work as porters in their campaigns against ethnic armed groups. Horrifying stories had spread south, of young civilian men being conscripted, starved, beaten, tortured and left in the jungle to die.

So when the soldiers told Ba Thein and the others in his village to pack their tools, they reluctantly went to get their machetes and tree-cutting saws. They packed their own food, too, enough rice, oil and fish paste to last them for a month. They piled into trucks that were sent to collect them and were driven north towards the mountains at the top of the peninsula, where they were dropped in an unfamiliar village that was surrounded by jungle. There, a group of military engineers told Ba

Thein that the route for the railway had been marked on the ground among the trees. All they had to do was clear it.

'But the local people told us it was not a good place to start,' Ba Thein told us. 'It was the rainy season, there was a lot of water flowing, and it was very difficult to find the route.'

His group of workers had no guide or map, and no idea where they were going, which had a profoundly disorientating effect, made worse by the perpetual rain.

'Sometimes it took two or three days to find the next mark,' Ba Thein said.

They would climb trees, or chop them down, just to create a line of sight. When they found each mark among the trees, they would build a crude shelter to sleep in, and spend their days felling the ancient hardwoods and cutting away the undergrowth, creating just enough space for a train to pass through, before moving on.

When they had been working in the jungle for almost three months, a new group of soldiers turned up and told them that the route had changed. Someone high up in the military command had decided the route they had been working on was no longer strategically useful. They ordered them to start again, but in another direction, beginning at a place about 9 miles to the west. The casual abandonment of the work he had sacrificed so much for proved to Ba Thein that the soldiers placed no value on his life, nor on the lives of the people who were working beside him, which outraged him so much that twenty years later his anger was still raw.

'So we searched again, and for a second time we cut down the trees,' he said, shaking his head as if he still could not believe it. 'And this time they built the railway.'

When he returned to his village, he found that in the space of just a few months four people that he knew had died while working on the railway. One was crushed by a tree and three other people had caught malaria while sleeping without cover in the jungle.

Malaria was a constant threat in Tanintharyi and even now, at the teashop, mosquitoes swarmed around our table as the light faded. I slapped at one that had landed on my arm. The teashop owner jumped up to fetch us swats from behind the counter, and then crouched beneath our table to light an incense coil.

Her movements broke the spell of Ba Thein's story, and as the heat of the day lifted, we each realized that we had stayed longer than we'd intended and that, enthralled, we had hardly noticed the daylight waning.

In that moment of quiet intimacy, Ba Thein turned to me and asked how I would have felt if I had been born here. His question surprised me and I looked at him for a long time in silence, before finally managing to say that I would have been heartbroken. As I stumbled over my words, the teashop owner came to my rescue, telling us that her father had also been forced to clear part of the railway route.

Like Ba Thein, he had been ordered to provide his own tools and food while he was away from home, and he had never been paid for his work. When he left, her entire family of eleven worked as hard as they could to raise money, so that they could pay for a replacement worker, but they couldn't raise enough. They eventually decided to flee across the mountains to Thailand. Recalling the suffering the military had inflicted on her family, her voice shook as she spoke. 'The army made so much trouble for my life,' she said.

Many of the older men and women in the room were visibly moved, because none of them had escaped the military's violence. While these were not things that were easily forgotten, it was rare that anyone talked openly about what had happened here.

Hundreds of thousands of civilians[2] had spent four years building a 100-mile railway connecting Tanintharyi Region across the mountains that divided the southernmost part of Myanmar from its centre. With hoes and knives they had hacked through jungle and bamboo forest. They worked on mountains and in valleys, in dense forest and on paddy fields, in rubber and betel-nut plantations, moving everything in their path. In the years it had taken to clear the path and build the railway, everything on Myanmar's southern peninsula had changed.

In fact, everything in Myanmar had changed. A decade before the railway was finished, in 1988, nationwide demonstrations had toppled the socialist government of ageing military dictator Ne Win. The protests, which brought Aung San Suu Kyi to prominence, marked a rare moment in Myanmar's modern history when the armed forces were not in power. Soldiers and police killed thousands of civilians before they were able to crush the uprising towards the end of that year, and the end of the protests marked the beginning of a more overtly martial, corrupt and cruel regime: the State Law and Order Restoration Council, or SLORC.

The end of the protests also marked the beginning of a decades-long reign of terror that would disproportionally harm the country's ethnic minorities, but would leave nobody unscathed. Violence was the means by which the military regained power, and violence would come to define its rule.

In the years that followed, the SLORC dramatically expanded the size of the armed forces, transforming a relatively small and poorly equipped national army into one of the largest in Southeast Asia. The generals had been profoundly shaken by the scale of the popular resistance in 1988, and the protests – coming on top of decades of economic mismanagement – had pushed the country to the brink of bankruptcy. Fearing fresh protests in the towns, and in reaction to intensifying guerrilla operations in the jungles, they sought out new weapons and defence technology. They paid for these with soft loans and barter deals, granting foreign access to the country's natural resources for the first time in decades, and importing billions of dollars' worth of aircraft, tanks and armoured vehicles.[3]

But they also needed money. One of the most obvious sources was Myanmar's untapped gas reserves. So the generals signed a lucrative deal with French oil major Total and its American partner Unocal to develop offshore gas fields, and to build a pipeline across Tanintharyi to Thailand, passing close to the village where Ba Thein lived.

This would become the regime's largest source of foreign currency.[4] But there was just one problem: Myanmar's far south, where I was now talking to Ba Thein, was barely controlled by the state at the time. Not only was the jungle home to multiple insurgent groups, but there were hardly any roads in the region. Even the infrastructure that connected the peninsula to the rest of the country was so dilapidated that the journey south by land could take days.

To protect the new pipeline that would pump gas across the peninsula to Thailand, the regime and its troops needed reliable access, which meant they needed new infrastructure. But there was little available labour in the south, where most people worked on their farms or at sea, and the state had no money to pay competitive wages.

So, at the same time as overrunning rebel bases deep in the jungle along the border with Thailand – capturing the headquarters further north of Myanmar's oldest ethnic armed group, the Karen National Union – and brokering a ceasefire with another, smaller ethnic armed group called the New Mon

State Party, the regime also sent troops to round up civilians like Ba Thein to work.

When the railway was finished, the regime celebrated its success in establishing control over the region. Its foreign minister told the United Nations General Assembly that 'peace reigns like never before'.[5] In reality the junta had driven out entire communities of ethnic civilians and many of the villages along the railway route were abandoned. More than 100,000 people had fled the military's broader offensives in the region, crossing the border into Thai refugee camps, and tens of thousands more were believed to be hiding in the jungles of eastern Myanmar.

But this hardly mattered to the junta because the twin aims of its military campaign in Tanintharyi Region, Operation *Nat Min* or Spirit King,[6] had been accomplished, aided by the railway's construction. First, the military had ended the armed resistance in Tanintharyi. By forcing most of the region's adult population into labour camps, the junta had prevented many of them from joining the resistance and had driven others to flee, helping to consolidate its hold over Myanmar's south. Second, it had secured the new pipeline that would pump gas from offshore reserves, past Ba Thein's village, across the border to Thailand.

The entire river valley that contained the railway had been flooded with government troops.[7] Extending to either side of the railway itself there were sprawling military bases, built at gunpoint by local people, identifiable by their identical rectangular buildings, the high walls surrounding them and the guard stations that prevented unauthorized entry.

A decade of destruction followed as the regime plundered Tanintharyi's other natural resources on a scale that hadn't been seen in southern Myanmar since the days of British colonial rule. Dividing up the land that had been abandoned by ethnic people, the generals awarded more than one million acres to their cronies, telling them to grow enough palm oil to supply the nation. But these businessmen had no experience growing palm oil.

Instead, they simply logged large areas of hardwood forest, which was then home to some of the most endangered and vulnerable species on earth: tigers, clouded leopards, tapir, sun bears and hundreds of species of rare birds. As the trees were felled and exported, poachers killed the fleeing animals, stripped and skinned them, and sold them to merchants at markets along Myanmar's borders with Thailand and China.

The people of Tanintharyi did not benefit from this destruction, just as they did not benefit from the extraction and sale of natural gas. Today, this peninsula remains the only part of Myanmar that is not connected to the national electricity grid. Instead, communities pay a premium for power supplied by diesel generators, or rely on firewood and charcoal for cooking and candles to generate light.

Sitting beside Ba Thein in the village teashop was a young man who wore an Adidas zip-up jacket over his *paso*, a traditional wrap-around sarong. This was Min, a prominent local human-rights campaigner, a friend of one of my colleagues in Yangon, and my connection to Ba Thein and the others. We had met the previous day, at the dilapidated guesthouse where I was staying. For hours, as we sat in the lobby watching the monsoon rain beat down into the courtyard outside, Min described how he had been forced to work on the railway when he was just a child.

'All of Dawei Region had to work,' he told me. 'Forced labour was very familiar to us.'

In the year that Ba Thein was clearing a path through the jungle, young Min was living nearby with his family at a resettlement camp on the other side of the river from the village he called home. They had moved there after a group of government soldiers arrived at their house and shouted at Min's mother, accusing her of supporting insurgent forces. Ordering the family to leave their home, the soldiers threatened to shoot them if they returned. So they left, with only the things they could carry, leaving behind their wooden home, the small store where Min's mother sold oil and onions, and their betel-nut plantation. Min at the time was just eight years old.

At the camp, which was guarded by government officials and patrolled by soldiers, forced labour became part of life. Min and his family, along with thousands of other people who had been forcibly relocated, were made to carry rocks to build a road, and to work on the army's rubber plantations.

His uncles and the other adult men were made to work as porters, which was worse than regular forced labour, because they had to walk for miles every day during the military's counter-insurgency operations, carrying rations, weapons and ammunition. They were hardly fed, and without food they became weak. When they stumbled they were beaten, and if they fell behind, they were left in the jungle to die. If the soldiers advanced into an area where there were landmines, they forced the porters to walk ahead of them, sweeping the ground with branches. When the landmines exploded, it was the civilians, not the soldiers, who lost their limbs or were killed.

When Min's mother was ordered to work on the railway, she took Min with her. They packed clothes and enough food to last them for a month. They were forced into a truck, along with thirty other people from their relocation camp, and driven to another camp known as '21-mile', because it was 21 miles north of the railway's southern terminus in Dawei. Already well-established, the camp was organized around a central longhouse made from bamboo and palm leaves, where hundreds of people slept together, the men on one side and the women on the other. There were groups who took care of the cooking, and others who cleaned.

Every morning they lined up in front of the longhouse to be counted by a government official, who Min referred to as 'the boss' and who supervised their work.

'We had to dig and carry the soil – it was poor work,' Min said. It was exhausting, and the boss watched them all the time, shouting at them to hurry up.

'It was the rainy season, like this,' he added, pointing towards the open door of the guesthouse lobby, where the rain slammed into the courtyard. 'It was a bitter experience.'

Even when they were soaked and shivering with cold, they were forbidden from sheltering beneath the trees. Min quickly became sick and his memories of this time are feverish and imprecise, but he could never forget the savage beatings inflicted on workers who tried and failed to escape from the camp. Worse was the treatment of prisoners at another camp 6 miles along the line, whose job it was to smash rocks into ballast.

'They were thin and unhealthy, and hungry all the time,' Min recalled. These men and women were convicts, on loan from a nearby prison, and they wore chains, carried heavy iron bars across their shoulders, and were often beaten as they worked.

There was a day, towards the end of their time on the railway, when the boss shouted at Min and his mother because they were unable to finish their work on time. That evening, his mother cried. She told Min she was crying for him and for all their people. Holding him close, she told him that the only chance he had to escape from this worthless existence was to study. Education, she repeated, was the only chance he had.

Now, in the café, as dusk fell, Ba Thein asked the teashop owner to clear the table. He wanted to take me to see his village, before it was dark. Hundreds of years earlier the village had been a city, whose history was now all but forgotten. This city was inhabited by Ba Thein and Min's people, the Tavoyans, who are native to this part of the country, but are not recognized by the state as a distinct ethnicity, despite numbering half a million people. Instead, they are considered a sub-group of the Bamar, the country's largest ethnic group. Their national identity cards describe them simply as 'Bamar'.

Min said he wanted to come with us, and as we walked along a dirt path flanked by wooden houses, he told us that the world around him felt safer now. The previous year, in November 2015, the country's democracy icon and former political prisoner Aung San Suu Kyi had been voted into power, marking a seminal moment in the country's history: the start of what appeared to be a transition to democracy after half a century of military rule.

'Aung San Suu Kyi is leading the government and we believe in her, so I hope we can have a good future,' Min told us, as we walked.

Min was much younger than Ba Thein and he had more energy for politics. As an active member of civil society he thought a lot about what could to be done to improve life for his people.

'But I can't believe it one hundred per cent,' he added, quietly. The most important challenge Aung San Suu Kyi faced was to end the country's civil wars, which were some of the longest-running domestic conflicts in the world. They were also immensely complex, involving dozens of armed groups, which fought not only against Myanmar's military but also among themselves. Aung San Suu Kyi had made the peace process a priority, but there was no guarantee she would succeed. Until there was peace, Min believed there would be no sustainable development, by which he meant things as basic as stable jobs and affordable electricity.

But the main thing he worried about was that at seventy Aung San Suu Kyi was growing old. 'I worry about the unity of our people if she is not there,' he said. 'We must work together for peace while she is alive.'

When we reached the old village, Ba Thein led us to an ancient well and bent down to rub away a film of moss, revealing lines of script inscribed into the stone. Nearby, a group of women and their children were washing, drawing buckets of water from the well, which they decanted into silver-coloured bowls and poured over their heads. The women were wrapped in strips of fabric and the children were naked. They jumped and shrieked as the torrents of cold water cascaded across their shoulders.

Standing at a safe distance from splashback, I asked Min and Ba Thein if they knew of anyone who was recording Tavoyan history. Neither of them did. There were no historians here, they said, no writers, no artists, no filmmakers. But there was one more artefact to see, a ruined portion of a wall at the edge of the village. It was important to Ba Thein, in particular, that I saw it. He wanted me to understand there was more to the story of his life than the abuses he had been subjected to. This was his place and his history. The old well and the crumbling wall were symbols of the legitimacy and the resilience of his people. As a village elder, it was his responsibility to show them to the outsiders who occasionally passed this way. These ruins had existed for hundreds of years, and they had continued to exist despite the military's invasions, its atrocities, its attempts to assimilate and to erase.

As we walked on in search of the wall, my phone rang. Just a year earlier I wouldn't have been able to receive the call, but now even remote parts of Myanmar were being connected to the national network.

It was a friend in Yangon who was calling with important news: US President Barack Obama had removed the economic sanctions on Myanmar that had been in place since the late 1990s, when the railway here was built.

My friend was overjoyed because, while the sanctions had been imposed in response to the military's abuses, they were also a blunt instrument that had contributed to keeping ordinary people in Myanmar in isolation and poverty. It was finally over, he was saying, with infectious optimism. Decades of isolation under military rule were finally coming to an end.

Contemplating this new sign of hope, I scrambled after Min and Ba Thein up a hill to where the top of the old city wall was visible above a patch of dense foliage.

As we looked out across a football pitch to a pagoda, where families had gathered to pray, I told them the news.

'It is good, it is the right time,' said Min.

Then he showed us the wall, rubbing his hand along the top of it. 'It makes me sad to think about our people who once lived here,' he added. 'Time has taken this place and it will take us too. We fear it will take Aung San Suu Kyi, at any time, and then our country will disappear again into darkness.'

On my return to Yangon, I typed 'Tanintharyi railway' into Google's search engine. Thousands of results came back, but very few of them mentioned the abuses that accompanied the construction of the railway that Ba Thein and Min had helped to build.

In Burmese, there were articles about train services being suspended, scheduled upgrades to railway lines, and plans to build a new railway connecting Tanintharyi with Thailand's Kanchanaburi Province. There were Facebook posts about train crashes, the delivery of new carriages from China, and freight contracts signed with the railway ministry. Further down the results, there were several Wikipedia pages in Burmese, many of which contained misleading information, including a page about Dawei, the railway's southern terminus, which claimed there was no railway there at all.

The same search in English brought up a Wikipedia page about the railway in Myanmar's south. Entitled 'Tanintharyi Line' it included information about the railway's gauge (metre gauge), its operator (Myanma Railways) and the dates it was built (1994 to 1998). But there was no reference on the page to the forced labour performed by hundreds of thousands of people during the railway's construction, or to a subsequent report by a United Nations International Labour Organization (ILO) Commission of Inquiry that found Myanmar had violated its obligations under the Forced Labour Convention 'in a widespread and systematic manner, with total disregard for . . . human dignity, safety and health'.[8] There was nothing on the Wikipedia page about the sanctions that were subsequently imposed on Myanmar's junta, or anything else that indicated this railway was anything other than an unremarkable line in a little-travelled part of the world.

The fact that I was shown so few results relating to forced labour suggests that Google's algorithms did not consider this information relevant to the search, which indicated that other people were not interacting with it. Very little had been written about forced labour on the railway since it happened. The reports by the United Nations and other groups like Amnesty International that exist online were published in the late 1990s, when almost nobody inside Myanmar would have been able to read them, and no testimonies appeared to have been collected since.[9] Every time new content was posted online about the railway in Tanintharyi it inevitably related to accidents or railway operations (in Burmese), or tourism (in English), and each engagement pushed those results to the top of similar searches. The truth about the violence that attended the railway's construction had thus slid further into obscurity.

But the problem was not just that information about the railway's construction hadn't been compiled and posted online. What happened in Tanintharyi was hardly known beyond the region itself, which even today remains isolated from the rest of Myanmar by its distance from the country's largest cities and the poor quality of the connecting roads. This railway, like military-built railways in other parts of the country, was constructed at a time when people in Myanmar were largely cut off from each other and from the wider world.

Under junta rule, there were no mobile networks in the country, except in the largest cities, and SIM cards were prohibitively expensive, priced at $1,500 or more. Media was heavily censored, physical movement was restricted, and even the spread of information by word of mouth was limited by poor physical infrastructure and the fear of arbitrary punishment. The military's stranglehold on information meant that most of its abuses were never documented, let alone collectively discussed and remembered. Not only was there no attempt to secure justice, but the abuses never even became part of the national imagination.

Impunity had been the price of the political transition in 2011 to a partially elected civilian government, with the military writing a guarantee of non-prosecution into Myanmar's new constitution, approved at a sham referendum a few years earlier.[10] Aung San Suu Kyi had accepted this deal, making it clear she would not pursue transitional justice. Retribution was a red line and it extended to the collection of evidence, which included reporting on historical events. Since the political transition began there was an increasingly free press, but journalists wrote about current events, rather than digging up the past.

And so there had been no retelling of the story of how hundreds of thousands of people had been forced to build a railway in Tanintharyi Region, except perhaps in the places where the events took place. Even this did not usually happen publicly, which is why Ba Thein's story captured everyone's attention in the teashop that day. Beyond a handful of testimonies published in obscure reports by the United Nations and others, which never made it into Myanmar's national consciousness, these stories were unwritten, existing only in the memories of the people who were there. And when those memories disappeared, it would be almost as if the events had never taken place at all.

It's a reflection of just how obscure Myanmar's military-built railways are that, two years after moving to Yangon in 2016, I still believed that all the country's railways dated to the colonial period. I even lived beside Yangon Central Railway Station and often took a detour through the station buildings and their sprawling grounds on my walk to and from work. As an editor at the *Myanmar Times* I worked long hours, and at night, to unwind, I would climb onto the empty tracks to walk home, savouring the darkness and the silence after the last train was in its depot.

On some nights I took a detour through the living quarters for railway staff, where thousands of workers and their families lived in a warren of single-storey houses. The narrow streets were always packed with people, squeezed around televisions to watch a Korean drama, or spilling out of beer stations, and I loved the feeling of community there. At weekends, I travelled by train whenever I could, at first on the metropolitan railway to the outskirts of Yangon, and later on overnight trains to other cities.

But I might never have realized there was anything unusual about Myanmar's railways, if it wasn't for my work. I was a business journalist, and part of my job was to write and edit stories about infrastructure – including railways. So when the Asian Development Bank published a policy paper on Myanmar's railway network in the summer of 2016, I read it from cover to cover.[11]

This document made many of the railway ministry's paper records available for the first time. It showed that the military regime had spent billions of dollars building new railways, many of which it had since abandoned, at a time when the country desperately needed investment in health and education. This was interesting enough for an article, but what really captured my attention was a map of the railway network that illustrated the scale of the problem. Myanmar was covered with new railways, from the southern Tanintharyi peninsula to the embattled mountains of Kachin State in the far north, and from the western Rakhine State coast to the restive, militia-controlled towns along the Chinese border in the northeast.

The report divided the railways into four categories. 'Existing railways', mostly built by the British colonial government, formed the backbone of the network and also appeared on other maps I had seen. Most of the railways in the other three categories – 'newly open railways', 'railways under construction' and 'planned railways' – I had never heard of before. Many of these newer railways were only partially open, and even on the completed lines it was not clear if trains were still running, or if they had ever run.

Before long, I found myself calling one of my contacts in Myanmar, a railway expert. 'Yes,' he said, when I asked him about the new railways. 'There are services to all sorts of places.'

I asked him if he thought it would be possible to travel on them. He wasn't sure, but he didn't think it would be a good idea. 'The services are not good,' he warned. 'They are slow and bumpy and you'll find yourself turning up at stations at 3 a.m.'

He also warned that few of the railway staff spoke English. 'Many of them are ex-military,' he said. 'Myanma Railways is a retirement home for veterans.'

I asked what else he knew about the new railways. 'From 1990 they started building these lines,' he told me. 'Terrible. Volunteer labour. Bad tracks.'

'Volunteer labour,' I echoed.

'Better not to dig too deeply, it happens all the time,' he said. 'In China, I saw blokes working like mad on road construction. I thought: this is a bit strange; they're wearing stripy uniforms . . .'

Towards the end of the call, I asked him to recommend a written history of the railways in Myanmar, expecting him to list at least one or two titles.

'I have been searching for many years and haven't yet found one,' he replied. 'There are bits and pieces, including a handbook that contains dates and details of locomotives, but you would have to piece together the story of how they developed yourself.'

For hours after we spoke, I trawled through Google's search results for information about 'volunteer' labour. I found and read the report published by the ILO Commission of Inquiry in the late 1990s.[12] It was compelling and disturbing: pages of testimony about the extortion, physical abuse, rape and murder that attended the construction of large-scale infrastructure projects across the country, including testimonies by refugees about abuses linked to the railways.

There was a tension between the raw violence that filled these pages and the optimism at the time in Yangon. As I read the interviews detailing the horrors of life under the regime, I began to understand what everyone in Myanmar who had experienced junta rule already knew. The military was brutal, uncompromising and immensely powerful. The generals had partly relaxed their control, but they were still, ultimately, in charge. The military held a quarter of the seats in parliament, giving it veto power over amendments to the constitution it had written, and it controlled the key ministries of defence, border affairs and home affairs.[13] Most civil servants even in the civilian-run ministries had been appointed by the junta, and many of them were former soldiers. What choice did anyone have but to agree to the military's terms, to invest in the progress that appeared to be unfolding, and to hope that the worst of the atrocities were over?

After reading the ILO Commission of Inquiry report, I went to see the organization's representative in Yangon, who explained how the system of forced labour had worked. The practice was entirely legal, she said, under British colonial-era laws that remained on Myanmar's books. The Towns Act of 1907 and the Village Act of 1908 provided for the exaction of forced labour and services, requiring local headmen to help government officials in their public duties, and anyone who refused without a 'reasonable excuse' could be fined or imprisoned.[14] When Britain ratified the Forced Labour Convention, which prohibited the practice, in 1931, it didn't extend the ratification to cover British India, of which Burma was then a part. Soon after Myanmar's independence, the country did ratify the convention, but despite repeated requests from the ILO, it never amended the British legislation.

The ILO representative introduced me to one of her Burmese colleagues, whose father had worked on the railway in Tanintharyi Region. R— was a shy woman who sat with her hands folded in her lap, as she recalled how a convoy of military trucks had rolled into her village when she was six years old. Soldiers looted the houses and farmyards and detained the men, including her father. They took them to a camp and forced them, just as they had forced Ba Thein, to clear a path for the railway through the jungle. After three months, having survived malaria, her father escaped and her family fled to Thailand across the mountains.

'Forced labour was a common scenario for all people in Myanmar,' the ILO representative told us. 'Everybody in Myanmar suffered.'

In the days that followed I thought of almost nothing else. I spent most of my free time pulling together the information that existed online and scouring the internet for anything I might have missed. As I searched, it struck me for the first time just how little had been published. The problem extended beyond forced labour – there was almost no information about the railways themselves. Most of what I found was contained in a digital archive of state newspapers, where propaganda pieces were published about generals inaugurating portions of track, or opening bridges, and making long, rambling speeches about the importance of development.[15]

But there was almost no independent media coverage, no blogposts, not even any surveys or technical reports. I spent days browsing bookshops near my apartment, which sold everything from bound photocopies of the junta's yearbooks to budgets and military histories written by retired generals, but I found hardly anything there either. Conversations with my friends and colleagues revealed that they knew very little. Most people I spoke to, including Burmese journalists, knew nothing about the military's railways, and the discussions we had raised more questions than they answered.

As a journalist, it was the absence of information, more than anything, that got me hooked on the story. In the world I inhabited and thought I knew, the idea that thousands of miles of railway could be built without any national attention or scrutiny was unimaginable. Outside the country, and even in transitional Myanmar, major public projects were usually written about extensively even before they were built, and they were reported on, analysed and documented at every stage in their construction.

More importantly, the silence that surrounded the railways in Myanmar raised a bigger question: if something as substantive as a nationwide rail network was not widely known about, what else was not being recorded?

The more I thought about the railways, the more obsessed I became with the idea of travelling on them. I imagined the tracks like a narrative thread, connecting plot points in a history that Myanmar's military had tried its best to conceal. In a country where rumours routinely assume the power of facts, they were a rare historical text that could not be easily erased.

By physically following the military's railways I could chart the regime's physical expansion since the uprising in 1988. I would learn about how the junta had governed the country in the decades leading up to the political transition, illuminating, by extension, the political dynamics in the country now that the military finally seemed to be stepping back from power. At the time, there was a feeling in Myanmar of progress, a sense that long-hidden secrets would eventually, inevitably come to light, and I saw my journey as a way to reveal another small part of the truth.

When I told my colleagues about my plan to leave the newspaper and follow the junta's railways across the country to find out why they were built, in a journey that I estimated would take me several months, they laughed and told me I was crazy. They recounted harrowing stories about trains being blown up by landmines, or old bridges falling apart and carriages plunging into ravines. One of them advised me to carry chili spray as protection.

'If anyone wants to take something from you, you will need to scare them,' she said, adding ominously, 'You should also take a knife.'

My colleagues also advised me to travel in traditional Myanmar clothing, sarongs known as *htamein* which are worn with matching blouses, telling me that it would improve my reception in remote villages. These clothes are made to measure, and as I waited to collect mine from a tailor, I stepped into a nearby antiques shop. I knew the owner, a former geologist, and I told him about my plans to travel around the country.

'Please sit down,' he said, as he rummaged through the drawers in his desk. After a while, he pulled out a brass pendant the size of a large coin, with the words 'One Hundred Years of Myanma Railways' inscribed in Burmese script around a blue ceramic band. It was a commemorative medal from 1977, made to mark the centenary of the year the country's first railway opened, which he insisted on giving me as a gift.

With the pendant stowed in the strap of my backpack, I flew to Dawei, in Myanmar's far south. This seemed like the natural place to start my journey, because most of the information I had found related to this southern railway. Its proximity to the Thai border had made it relatively easy for refugees and their stories to reach the outside world. There was also a thriving civil society in Dawei and I was already in touch with Min. I imagined I would meet other activists, historians and writers there who had documented the events of the 1990s, and who would be able to introduce me to their counterparts in other, more closed, parts of the country. From Dawei, I would follow the railways north and then around the country in a clockwise direction, through Yangon, into the delta, across the dry zone in Magway and through the country's ethnic states, ending my journey at the military's new capital, Naypyidaw.

The drive into Dawei from the airport revealed a faded town, whose delicate wooden villas were encircled by verdant gardens that blended into the jungle. The sprawl of ramshackle houses grew denser as we neared the centre, and here they doubled as shops, whose dusty shelves were crammed with tinned and packaged goods, as if the people of Dawei were anticipating a siege.

The capital of Tanintharyi had officially opened to foreign visitors three years earlier, for the first time since the Second World War. But few tourists had made it this far south, and I was the only guest at my hotel. Soon after I arrived, the hotel's owner introduced me to a slim man with boyish features called Thein Htaik. He told me that he had become the town's first registered tour guide, and offered to take me that afternoon on the back of his motorbike to see the local attractions.

As we drove along streets lined with decaying wooden houses, many of which were propped up by poles to prevent their collapse, it was clear that the town had suffered from a long period of isolation and neglect. But there were signs of development too; beyond the town we navigated winding roads lined with betel and coconut palms, where women were repairing the tarmac, hunched beside heaps of stones, with their heads wrapped in scarves to protect themselves against the dust.

Thein Htaik soon parked his bike beside a field, which we hiked across to reach a reclining Buddha statue. He proudly explained this was the second-largest statue of its kind in the country. As we walked around its vast body, I asked him about the railway, and to my astonishment his eyes filled with tears.

'The second Death Railway,' he replied, placing his hand on my arm.

The first railway he was referring to, the Burma–Siam railway, was built at the top of this peninsula, just north of Tanintharyi Region, during the brief Japanese occupation of Burma during the Second World War. It is widely known as the Death Railway because it killed almost a quarter of the Allied prisoners of war who built it. The story of their struggle for survival has been told by hundreds of survivors, writers, filmmakers and historians. What is less well known is that most of the workers on the railway were Asian civilians, including tens of thousands of Burmese men and women, and that between a quarter and half of these Asian civilian workers are believed to have died.

Few Burmese labourers feature in the body of tributes paid to the prisoners of war who worked and died on the railway – and the war cemetery maintained by the Commonwealth War Graves Commission at the railway's terminus in Thanbyuzayat, a scrappy trading town near Myanmar's border with Thailand, does not honour the Burmese dead. After the Second World War, the British closed the railway and sent teams along the tracks to exhume the bodies of Allied prisoners, to identify them and to bury them with dignity. The Burmese workers remained where they died, in unmarked pits beside the abandoned track.[16]

A local man in 2016 had opened a small Death Railway museum in Thanbyuzayat, but rather than remembering the Burmese who died building the railway, the museum is instead a reminder of how thoroughly they have been forgotten. Most of the exhibits there only describe the Allied experience, because this is the only experience that has been recorded.[17]

In the years I have spent searching for information about the Burmese who died on the Japanese-built Burma–Siam railway, the only source of any significance that I have found is in the National Archives at Kew in London.[18] Contained in four slim brown folders packed with typewritten pages, the Burmese declarations made before the British War Crimes Investigation Team describe conditions that are depressingly similar to those endured by the workers in camps run by Myanmar's military half a century later. Security forces abducted civilians and transported them to the worksites against their will. Workers slept together in crowded longhouses without beds or bedding. The settlements were squalid and there was very little food. The workers quickly became ill, but there were no doctors or hospitals. The Burmese labourers were civilians, not prisoners of war, yet they were held captive, and many of them were beaten, tortured and left to die.

'I can help you,' Thein Htaik said, responding to my question about the junta's railway, as we completed our second lap of the Buddha. 'You will have no problem finding information. Many people here suffered for this railway.'

That evening, he added me as a friend on Facebook, and I saw that at the top of his profile page there was a bilingual post. 'Feeling excited,' the English portion read. 'Retrospective Study of past event of Railway line construction between Ye and Dawei. Someone who wish to share of bitter experience then, you are invited.' The next day, we visited the people who replied.

We met a gold trader and his wife at their small shop beside the town's central roundabout, a shop hardly more than a counter, open to the street and protected from the rain by a tattered green tarpaulin. As rain dripped from the tarpaulin, the gold trader recalled how he and his wife had run a store at one of the larger railway construction camps, selling cheap imported products from Thailand to thousands of workers.

'It was a good opportunity to sell clothes, food, snacks, whatever they needed,' he said. Many of the workers were sick, because they were malnourished, overworked, or had caught mosquito-borne diseases.

'Many people died,' he told us. I asked him to estimate how many and he considered the question carefully.

'There may be sixty wards in Dawei District,' he said, referring to just one of the districts where people had been forced to work. 'From each, at least three or four died.'

'It was terrible,' his wife murmured. She said she had seen the bodies of two men dragged out from the mud, after they were buried alive while digging soil from the base of a cut slope.

Across town at Dawei General Hospital we visited a vaccine storekeeper, who we found in an outhouse, wrapped in an anorak and surrounded by deep freezers. A dishevelled man with curly, greying hair and a mouth stained by years of chewing betel, he greeted us gently and guided us past the stacks of boxes and brown-paper files that littered his office.

As we sat opposite one another, the man spoke to Thein Htaik in Burmese, hesitantly at first, and then with increasing energy, as he recalled being sent to a railway construction camp in the jungle. Although he was not a doctor, he was expected to work as one, equipped only with mild painkillers.

I asked how he felt when he was sent there and both men laughed at my question.

'He had to go,' said Thein Htaik. 'He was government staff and it was a government order.'

The vaccine storekeeper had been shocked by the living conditions, telling us how the workers drank, washed and defecated in the same stream. The food they had brought from their villages was insufficient, so they foraged what they could from the forest, but this was never enough, and they were always hungry. Worst of all, he said, there were people there with malaria who were being forced to work, even though they were dying.

As we talked, he often returned to the subject of corruption. He said there was a budget to pay the workers, but junta officials had taken it, becoming rich at their expense. I asked him if he knew who was responsible for building the railway, or why it was built.

'It is beyond my knowledge,' he replied. Was he given any information at all? 'No information,' he said.

I would hear echoes of this answer in the subsequent months, almost to the top of the chain of command.

The next day we visited more people who had replied to Thein Htaik's message, including a group of weavers in a wooden house on the outskirts of town. One of them described her work on the railway as 'a bitter feeling, a bitter time'. The railway to her, and to others I would later meet, was not a method of transport or even a physical road, but a painful experience. Everyone had to help build it, she told us. Men felled trees to clear a path through the forest for the track and women chopped the wood into smaller pieces. I asked her if many women had worked on the railway.

'Men worked, women worked and children worked,' she replied.

Everyone we spoke to remembered a small part of the story – the part that they had personally experienced. They spoke eloquently and passionately about what had happened to them and what they had witnessed happening to others. But when I asked about the bigger picture or anything beyond the personal, their answers were always vague. Why was the railway built? Who ordered its construction? What was the human cost of building it? How many people were forced to work? How many fled the camps into the jungle, to other parts of Myanmar, or across the border to Thailand? How many were injured? How many died?

Of course there was no reason why anyone would have answers. There was no independent data on the number of people who had worked on the railway, or how many had been injured, or killed. There were no civil-society groups or human-rights organizations here at the time it was built. To collect and keep information about the military's abuses would have been too dangerous, because there were *dalan*, or informers, everywhere.

But while the people we met recounted experiences that were clearly traumatic, there was also a casualness to many of the stories we heard, as if there was nothing particularly unusual, for example, about selling snacks to a group of enslaved people, as the gold trader had done. There was anger, but the abuses the people here had experienced and witnessed on the railway were consistent with the types of abuses they had been exposed to all their lives.

'The military abused their power, but we thought at the time it was normal,' explained Su Su, an activist with long dark curly hair, who ran a civil-society group called the Tavoyan Women's Union. She had been sent to a railway construction camp aged thirteen, because nobody else in her family was available to work. Still a child, she had been frightened of everything, from the animals that inhabited the forest, to the toilet in the camp, which was a festering pit filled with flies.

'We didn't know it was forced labour, we didn't know it was a violation,' she told me. 'Also, because of the Unlawful Associations Act we didn't have the right to complain.' The law, introduced by the British colonial government, was used to prosecute civilians who dared to speak out, stifling collective resistance – the right to protest.

'I would not have dared to say that before today,' the vaccine storekeeper told me, after he recalled the conditions at the camps. Aung San Suu Kyi's civilian government had only been in power for a few months, but the political climate was already improving. 'We have been afraid,' he said.

There were, as I had expected, plenty of civil-society groups in Dawei that had sprung up since the political transition began, but like their national counterparts they were more concerned with documenting contemporary problems than quantifying the abuses of the past. This was made clear to me during a long discussion one morning with a prominent local activist. A softly spoken man who wore black-framed glasses and a ponytail, he met me at his office, where dozens of young men and women reclined on the floor, and in low chairs, working on laptops to the sound of quiet music. Theirs was a formidable task: holding powerful interests to account in a country that ranks near the bottom of global corruption indices. Just five years earlier, their work would have been unthinkable. But now, as restrictions on freedom of speech were being relaxed for the first time in their lives, they were recording the new problems that attended the country's economic opening. He wanted to talk about their work: there was a new industrial zone being built on land inhabited by indigenous people near the Thai border, and there were problematic logging and mining concessions, as well as a special economic zone and an oil refinery that threatened miles of white sandy beaches.

It was only at the end of our meeting that he gathered up the research papers he had been showing me. 'But you're here to talk about the railway,' he said, clearing his desk. 'I can tell you what I know. There is a famous mountain range on the state border. Every year, landslides blocked the road from here to the mainland. Tanintharyi is a strategic area, and the military wanted to build bases from Ye in Mon State, to Dawei. In the 1990s, one person from every household was forced to help build a railway. It was a huge burden. We don't know the exact number of deaths, but we know it was thousands of people. We call it the second Death Railway.'

During the years the railway was built, there was an exodus of people to Thailand, he said. But he knew nothing more. Nobody here knew anything more. Even a former soldier and *dote-kai*, or stick-holder, who had been responsible for beating prisoners as they worked, was unable to tell me much. The only people who had access to information, he said, were those at the very top.

Compounding the problem was the fact that both within Myanmar and on the international stage, members of Myanmar's military had lied. As the allegations of forced labour became increasingly serious, the junta's denials had become more detailed – and more implausible. Accusing its detractors of cynicism for framing its efforts to establish law and order as acts of repression, it claimed to the ILO that on the railway in Tanintharyi Region, there had been no forced labour at all. 'The use of labour was purely voluntary, and it was remunerated equitably. No coercion whatsoever was involved,' it said.[19]

As evidence continued to emerge showing the pervasive use of forced labour throughout Myanmar, the ILO in June 2000 took action against a defaulting state for the first time in its history.

Whether it was because of this, or because the junta around this time was tentatively beginning to re-engage with the international community, releasing political prisoners and initiating direct talks with Aung San Suu Kyi, it quietly ended its practice of systematic forced labour on national infrastructure projects. Even when the regime's position hardened once more and Aung San Suu Kyi was put back under house arrest in 2003, widespread forced labour by the government, as distinct from the military, never really started up again.[20]

Yet the official position, that there had never been any forced labour, had endured during the transition to quasi-civilian rule. One afternoon I went to see a former soldier and village administrator, who had been responsible for recruiting workers for the railway in Dawei. I found him reading a newspaper in his clean, orderly general store, surrounded by sacks of sugar and rice. He wore a white vest that revealed the body of a soldier who had evidently once been fit and strong, although he now had trouble breathing and he clasped an inhaler in his left hand. Standing up and retying his *paso* across his broad stomach as I introduced myself, he avoided my eyes, but agreed to answer my questions.

He told me the same thing that junta representatives had always claimed: that the government had built the railway 'for the people' and to develop the region, which at the time was a remote area divided by mountains from the rest of the country.

'This railway was essential to connect the mainland to our region,' he said. It was the duty of every household to send one person to help build the railway, and compassionate leave was given to those who needed it. Everyone else worked fifteen-day shifts, on rotation. He claimed to have visited the worksite almost every day.

'Sometimes I motivated the workers by participating,' he

told me. 'We should not call it forced labour, because we all took responsibility for our own segment.'

Noting my cynicism, he explained, 'There are two groups of people. One wants to develop the region and believes he needs to participate. The other believes it is the responsibility of the government. These are two ways of thinking. It is not the same as forced labour.'

I asked him if anyone had been paid for their work.

'They had an allowance,' he said, and puffed on his inhaler.

Before leaving Dawei, I went to see the stationmaster while he waited, as he waited every day, for the arrival of the evening train. Dawei Station, like everything else about the railway, was decrepit. Its paintwork had faded and peeled. The roots of trees that encircled the main building had split the foundations and outer walls. Doors had been wrenched from their hinges and several windowpanes were smashed. The stationmaster's office was in a tower at one end of the deserted platform that leaned dangerously to one side.

As we sipped green tea, the stationmaster told me that with just a single daily service, there was nothing for him to do here except worry about the risks of flooding and derailments, as the train meandered south along the peninsula. This railway was unusually dangerous, because the men and women who were forced to build it had rushed to complete the work, so they could return to their farms. They had built hollow embankments from long grass, branches and plants, and covered these piles with earth to make it look as if they were formed of solid mud. Every year, parts of the earthwork collapsed during the monsoon, and had to be rebuilt. The railway urgently needed investment, the stationmaster said. Accidents could be deadly, and on the portion of track under his control he handled these accidents alone.

But there was no money for repairs. This route had never made a profit, and today hardly anyone travelled by train. Earlier in the year, Aung San Suu Kyi's new government had slashed the ministry's railway budget and was closing routes. He wasn't sure if this railway would stay open, he said, because inside information from the ministry rarely travelled this far south.

Lowering his voice and pushing his glasses up the bridge of his nose, he explained that he only felt able to speak to me because Aung San Suu Kyi's party was now in power. 'Now there is a new government, we dare to say a little more, because there is more freedom,' he said. 'Last year, under the previous government, I would not have dared to answer your questions, even in my own office.'

But when I asked him about the history of the railway, and the use of forced labour, his eyes darted to one corner of the room, where in the shadows there was another man, pretending to be engrossed in his mobile phone. There was a story that the stationmaster wanted to tell me, and which he began to tell – about how the regime had confiscated land from his family and other local people to build the station and a sprawling military base that extended into the hills.

But he was visibly nervous and we both jumped when a voice blared into the room, followed by bursts of crackling. 'It's the wireless,' he explained, regaining his composure. The evening train was running on time.

I asked who would be travelling on the train. 'Poor people and soldiers,' he said. 'If a soldier needs to travel and there is an option to take the train, his first priority must be to take it.' He didn't know why, he said, that was just how it was.

He led me out of his office and onto the platform, where he cautiously returned to his story: One morning, when he was a young man, he had been walking with his mother to their paddy fields, when they saw their land was staked out by red flags fixed to bamboo poles.

'When we saw the flags, we wept, because we knew our land was lost,' he said.

His mother did not dare to complain and anyway there would have been nobody to complain to. His family never farmed again. When the railway ministry advertised for young men to train as stationmasters, he signed up, and was sent to central Myanmar. This decision saved his family from the railway construction camps.

'They were free because of that,' he said.

He led me along the platform to a stone tablet that was shaped like the back of a throne and carved with scrolling acanthus leaves. Scraping away layers of moss, he revealed lines of Burmese script.

'The track from Dawei to Ye runs for 84.76 miles,' he read. 'The carts can turn by up to 16 degrees. There are 275 corners and 347 bridges . . .'

What might have been a tribute to the people who built the railway was instead a monument to the railway itself, revealing the pride the generals had taken in this feat of engineering, at the expense of their people, whose suffering they had erased from Myanmar's recorded history.

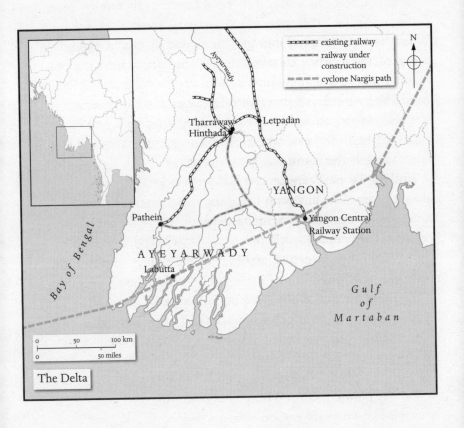

existing railway

railway under construction

cyclone Nargis path

N

Ayeyarwady

Tharrawaw
Hinthada

Letpadan

YANGON

Pathein

Yangon Central
Railway Station

Bay of Bengal

AYEYARWADY

Labutta

Gulf
of
Martaban

0   50   100 km
0   50 miles

The Delta

2.

The Delta

When I set out to travel into the Ayeyarwady Delta by train, I expected the journey to take a long time. I imagined trains might be late, that I might miss a connecting service, that there would be long delays between stations. But all these imagined scenarios were just versions of the type of difficulties I had encountered in the past while travelling on other railways in other parts of the world.

Nothing I'd ever experienced had prepared me for what lay ahead. More than anything I've done in Myanmar before or since, the journey into the delta by train revealed the chasm between the fictional world the generals were trying to create through their propaganda, and the reality of life under their rule.

The ticket seller at the booking office at Yangon Central Railway Station was asleep when I arrived at his desk. I woke him and told him that I wanted to travel to Pathein, the capital of Ayeyarwady Region. He stared at me with bleary eyes.

'No,' he replied. 'No Pathein.' He advised me to take the bus.

On my phone I showed him an article published in a state newspaper two years earlier, announcing the opening of the railway into the delta.[1] Unfolding my map of the railway network on the counter, I pointed to the new line.

As I held up the map and traced the railway with my finger, his colleague came over and told us that I was right, there was a new railway into the delta, but it left from Hlaing Tharyar, an industrial township on Yangon's western outskirts.

It's a quirk of Myanmar's railways that you can only buy a ticket from the station you're travelling from, and only in person, so the next morning I took a two-hour taxi from my downtown apartment across the city to Hlaing Tharyar.

It was the first time I had visited the township, which is separated from the rest of Yangon by a river. On the other side of the bridge, it felt like we were in a different city. The rutted roads were jammed with trucks and motorbikes. There was a factory on every corner and between the factories, on every available scrap of land, were huts fashioned from woven bamboo and tarpaulin sheets. There were thousands of these huts, crammed beside the roads and scattered across the fields. Built on stilts, they were sinking into the mud. Some of them had collapsed altogether, and the fields beneath them were clogged with plastic waste.

The sprawling miles of industrial estates and the encompassing shanty towns that mark Yangon's western fringe are inhabited by the city's poorest residents. Many have been pushed from the centre by rising land prices and a succession of state-led resettlement programmes. Around half have moved here from elsewhere in Myanmar, drawn by economic opportunities or driven from places that have been made uninhabitable by conflict, land confiscation or natural disasters.

A large portion of Hlaing Tharyar's population arrived after 2008, when the deadliest cyclone in Myanmar's history devastated the Ayeyarwady delta, the country's largest rice-producing region. Cyclone Nargis left at least 138,000 people dead or missing, and displaced or destroyed the livelihoods of two million more.

On the city's fringe, its dispossessed people eked out a living, as the military and its cronies built new factories and industrial zones. Now that foreign investment was pouring in, they were being pushed further and further from the city centre. Many people lived here without electricity, water supply or sanitation, instead sharing hand-powered pumps that drew saline groundwater for washing, and relying on expensive bottled water to drink.

Hlaing Tharyar Railway Station was not marked on Google maps, and my taxi driver stopped several times to ask for directions. Several times we were told that Hlaing Tharyar didn't have a railway station, but eventually a teashop owner explained the way. Following his instructions, we turned along a narrow road that led to an overgrown field, finding nothing there except a barrier and a sign bearing the Myanma Railways logo that warned against trespassing. Pointing towards an abandoned concrete building on the other side of the field, my driver hitched his *paso* around his waist, and indicated that I should roll up my trousers. Reluctantly, I followed him into the field, and we arrived at the station soaked through and covered in mud.

As we banged on a grate that was pulled across the doors, there was a bark, and then a round of barks, and a gang of dogs emerged from the gloom. Behind the dogs, I could make out a blanket on the floor, which stirred and then was flung into the air to reveal the broad shape of a man, who stood up, stretched and lumbered towards us. Unlocking the doors and drawing back the grate, he ushered us inside, through a cavernous passenger hall, to a platform. There, he showed us where we could wash the mud from our legs with fresh rainwater that he had collected in buckets. He gave us each a strip of fabric to dry ourselves and then welcomed us back into the abandoned station concourse, which he had made his temporary home.

In a makeshift kitchen, our host boiled a kettle and made us cups of tea. He told us to sit down on plastic stools, beneath a line of laundry strung from the pillars that held up the roof.

Handing around the cups, he sat with us, and as we drank, he recounted parts of the railway's short history. It was built, he said, beginning in 2009, shadowing the route taken by Cyclone Nargis when it tore through the region the previous year, flattening everything in its path.

The cyclone made landfall the week before a scheduled referendum on a new constitution that would enshrine the generals' powers, safeguard their assets and secure their impunity – the same constitution that remains in place in Myanmar today. When the cyclone hit, rather than postponing the vote, the country's dictator Than Shwe, who led the junta for almost two decades until 2011, did not appear in public until after the constitution had been approved with what the junta claimed was a 92 per cent vote in favour. As the world appealed for the removal of restrictions on the delivery of humanitarian aid, state media reports claimed the 2.4 million people who had been affected by the cyclone did not need foreign help.

'Myanmar people can easily get fish for dishes by just fishing in the fields and ditches,' one article in the *New Light of Myanmar* read, several weeks after the cyclone hit. 'In the early monsoon, large edible frogs are abundant. The people of Ayeyarwady Division can survive with self-reliant efforts, even if they are not given chocolate bars from [the] international community.'[2]

But the fields and ditches were clogged with corpses, the groundwater was undrinkable, the crops were destroyed, and the people of the delta were starving. To rebuild their villages, they needed natural materials including bamboo, but these too had been swept away. The landscape was devastated, and while local organizations and individuals had rushed to the delta to help, they were not equipped to handle such a major disaster. As well as needing food and shelter, survivors were suffering from the trauma of the cyclone, the loss of family members and the prospect of rebuilding their lives when they had been left with nothing.

As they blocked a large-scale international aid operation, the generals instead asked foreign donors for billions of dollars in funding for the 'reconstruction' of the delta, and drew up plans to build new infrastructure projects.[3]

During multiple tours of the region, Than Shwe, accompanied by a cohort of generals, assigned development tasks and construction projects to regional officials. These included a new hydropower dam, irrigation networks, 'life-saving hillocks', roads and bridges.[4] The regime awarded construction contracts to its cronies, and several of these companies were hired to build a new railway to Pathein, the regional capital, across 87 miles of marshland and mud.

Than Shwe personally oversaw this work, and he was pictured in state media inspecting blueprints for the stations and bridges and viewing the proposed railway route.[5] He had already built a reputation for his love of infrastructure back in the 1980s when he was the head of the Southwest Command in Pathein, where he regularly met with other officials on his tours of the delta, giving long speeches about the need to build more bridges and roads.

Like Indonesia's dictator General Suharto, Than Shwe took pride in infrastructure development, and he often travelled to see how the construction of his projects was progressing. Forced labour in the delta was widespread under his command even before he became the country's leader, and he expanded the practice to infrastructure projects nationwide. Ten years before he consolidated power, the state-run *Working People's Daily* was reporting on 'volunteer' labour in areas under Than Shwe's control.[6]

When Cyclone Nargis hit, the era of widespread forced

labour was over, but Than Shwe's fondness for new infrastructure projects had not dwindled. The opening of the first section of his new railway into the delta, in 2010, was marked by an article in the state mouthpiece, the *New Light of Myanmar*, entitled 'Glorious days in Ayeyarwady Division'.[7]

Only 16 miles of track had been finished, but the newspaper reported that local people were already excited about being able to get from the delta to Yangon in just three hours; the journey on the old colonial-era railway took an entire day. At the time, media was heavily censored in Myanmar, and there was no social media, so the generals could paper over reality.

'In the future, Ayeyarwady Division will be the most developed region in the nation as it can link with various regions of the Union through waterways, railroads and motor roads,' enthused the state media report. 'The government spent a large sum of money and labour on building infrastructures. Local people have been witnessing and enjoying the fruits of progress of Ayeyarwady Division.'

By the end of 2011, the bridge across the river at Nyaungdon, the main piece of engineering needed to connect the line to Yangon's outskirts, was open.

'May Ayeyarwady dwellers serve interests of region and nation with heart of gold like mighty white elephant appeared in the region' proclaimed the headline on the front page of the state newspaper.[8] Once a symbol of royal authority, white elephants in Myanmar represent fortune and power. Beneath the headline there was a photograph of Thein Sein, the diminutive former general who had recently been appointed Myanmar's president as Than Shwe stepped back from power.

These were the early days of Myanmar's opening to the world. As the ageing Than Shwe disappeared from public view, his former prime minister, Thein Sein, an unassuming general who was seen as relatively clean, had become the face of the military-led reforms. On the newspaper's cover, he was waving and there were crowds of local people waving back. He was flanked by the generals-turned-ministers that the world would come to see as his fellow reformers, including Aung Min, who had been minister for railways under Than Shwe and was one of the few cabinet members to retain his position after the handover. There was a stone inscription beside the bridge, which the president and his ministers sprinkled with scented water, before posing for a documentary photograph on the bank of the river.

In the end, the bridge did turn out to be a white elephant, but as the phrase is more commonly understood in English: expensive and useless. The road was hardly used because it was just a few miles upstream from another road bridge, which had opened a decade earlier. The railway bridge was briefly operational for about a year in 2014, when a portion of the track connecting it with Yangon opened.[9] Four carriages were assigned to the route and a train ran every day, but there was never more than a handful of passengers.

Hardly anyone wanted to travel by train, our host at the station's abandoned terminus told us, as he poured out fresh cups of tea. I asked him why, and he explained that there were buses from here to the delta that ran every fifteen minutes, and the journey by bus was twice as fast, and just as cheap.

The main problem, though, was that the railway's embankments had been built with silt from the delta that wasn't suitable for construction, and they collapsed almost as soon as they were built. Within a year of its opening, the entire route was destroyed by flooding, and the railway had closed.

It was a total waste of money, in a part of the country that had just experienced the worst recorded natural disaster in Myanmar's history. Parliamentary records later put the cost of the new railway at 65.7 billion kyat, or about £50 million at the exchange rate of the time.[10] That was £50 million that could have been spent on providing the families in the delta with new homes and clean water, rebuilding health centres, schools and community buildings, strengthening livelihoods, providing psychosocial care, or replanting trees and mangroves to protect the coast against future storms.

Why had the railway been built? I asked him. Had the challenges of the relief effort revealed a need for better infrastructure? Were the contracts awarded to cronies as a reward for helping the junta in the aftermath of the cyclone? Had the railway been abandoned simply because the generals underestimated the challenge of building across the delta, and then had no money to repair the line, when it collapsed? Or was it simply an opportunity for the generals and the cronies to take millions of dollars for themselves?

He shrugged. He didn't know, he told me. He had never asked these questions. All he knew, he said, was that there had been orders from above.

Back at Yangon Central Railway Station the next day, I tried again to persuade the staff to sell me a ticket to the delta. The new, direct line to the delta was closed, but I believed a much older route was still open: north on a British-built railway to a town called Letpadan, then west to a place called Tharrawaw, and across the river by ferry to a town called Hinthada. From there, my map indicated that I could travel on another colonial-era line to the delta capital of Pathein.

I wanted to take this journey to understand the opportunity cost of the new and now abandoned railway into the delta. The reports in state media had pointed to a problem it was going to solve: that the old colonial-era route between Yangon and the delta was so dilapidated it was hardly usable, and the journey of around 100 miles took a whole day, which the junta claimed the new railway would cut to just three hours.

Opening my map of the railways on the counter, I pointed to the old line that meandered through the delta and that appeared to require two connections to reach Pathein, including at a place called Tharrawaw.

There was a train to Tharrawaw, the ticket seller said, but it was only possible to buy a ticket from Kyeemindaing, another station in the west of Yangon. I thanked him and was about to leave, when he called me back.

'Pathein?' he asked, with some urgency.

'Yes,' I replied.

'No train,' he said, firmly, in English. 'Because . . . over floating.'

'Over floating?' I echoed him.

'Yes,' he said. 'Over floating. Ayeyarwady.'

The Ayeyarwady River had broken its banks, flooding the tracks. He took my notepad, which was open on the counter, and wrote 'Yangon to Hinthada bus' in large clear letters, and then 'Hinthada to Kyangin train'.

I had no idea where Kyangin was. We looked together at the map – it was nowhere near Pathein. I thanked him and decided to go to Kyeemindaing Station early the next morning to try my luck.

In a warren of backstreets in western Yangon, my taxi driver the next morning edged between market vendors who were setting up their stalls. He parked outside a red-brick building whose entrance was guarded by a band of dogs. Newspaper sellers squatted among stacks of papers, organizing their morning deliveries. A young army officer who had been watching them from the shadows rose to his feet when he saw me, and escorted me in silence along an empty platform to the stationmaster's office.

In the centre of the room, the stationmaster stood with his back turned. 'No,' he said, waving his hand dismissively, when I asked to buy a ticket to Pathein. 'Bridge broken.'

A boy in the corner of the room sat up, stretched, and lit a cigarette. The stationmaster agreed to sell me a ticket as far as Letpadan.

'Sit down,' he said. A policeman came in, as the stationmaster filled out a large form with my seat number and passport details, then the policeman walked me to the waiting train.

In the carriage, I wiped a pool of filthy water and the discarded husks of sunflower seeds from my allocated seat, as mosquitoes swarmed around my ankles. Several seats away, young men were playing electronic music on their phones. The walls and windows of the carriage were stained, parts of the ceiling were caving in, and it was in a mood of mild gloom that I began my journey. It had been difficult that morning to leave my apartment, after a meal the previous evening with friends, which had been comfortable and relaxed. I would be on the road now for weeks, at least, and I had almost no idea what lay ahead. The railways to the north of the delta passed through some of the most isolated territory in Myanmar – places where foreigners rarely travelled – and the presence of security forces at Kyeemindaing Station had reminded me that because of this, my movements were likely to be monitored.

The railway that I would travel on that morning is the oldest in Myanmar, built in 1877 by the British colonial government, to serve a thriving rice-export industry. As the train pulled out of the station and swayed through the suburbs of western Yangon, I could see into military compounds, where soldiers were washing, or standing around open fires. At Insein near the British-built prison in the northwest of the city, farmers waded through fields beside the track and children clambered over the swampy ground, collecting litter that had been cast from train windows.

It was a wet, green morning and despite myself, I found that I was enjoying the opportunity to see the city from a different perspective. My mood improved further at Danyingone, when the vendors came aboard.

Their faces and arms smeared with *thanaka*, a yellow cosmetic paste made from ground bark, they shimmied through the carriage, singing, chanting and shouting the prices of their goods for sale: pickled roots and leaves, coconut jelly and quails' eggs, or strings of tamarind sweets and sachets of instant tea-mix that were draped across their bodies like bandoliers. Within an hour they were gone, and as the train rolled north, our carriage was transformed into a shuttle for farmers, who jumped on and off again, as it edged through the fields.

The slow pace of life in this part of the country was reflected at Letpadan Station. I got off the train to find a group of men sitting around the stationmaster's office, just to pass the time. They gathered to listen as I asked about the train running to Tharrawaw, the next stop on my journey. There was a train running, the stationmaster told me, despite the floods I had been warned about, but it wouldn't leave for another four hours. The journey would be slow, because a bridge had collapsed, and the stationmaster told me that I wouldn't reach Pathein for at least another twenty-four hours, even though the city was less than 100 miles away.

The men argued over the train times and how long the journey would take, and managed to agree on just one point: that the railway was no good. They pointed along the platform to the waiting train: two converted goods wagons that had no doors, telling me the journey would be not only slow but dangerous.

They advised me to take the bus, and then they insisted on it. But there were passengers already boarding the train, and so I argued with them, until eventually the stationmaster sold me a ticket.

My behaviour was clearly suspicious, because a policeman who had been listening to the conversation escorted me to his police station at the other end of the platform. Sitting me down on a chair, he recorded my name, age, nationality and marital status in a ledger. When he was done, he closed the book and stared at me, as if daring me to escape.

The sky darkened and I could hear the crackle of rain on the town's tin rooftops. Within minutes, a storm had rolled along the platform and was smashing into the police enclosure, and rain was pouring in through gaps in the roof.

Resigning myself to the four-hour wait, I moved my chair out of the rain and opened a book. As the hours passed, the police officer settled in for an afternoon of drinking with his colleagues, and when I was finally rescued by an older police-man, he was so drunk he could hardly speak.

Examining my passport, my new minder led me to the wait-ing train, which was now heaving with passengers and cargo. Hands that clasped cooking pots, jerry cans, suitcases and foli-age extended from every window and there was a scrum at each of the doorways. The policeman took my wrist and dragged me through the crowd. We had almost wedged our-selves into a doorway when a guard appeared from inside the train, grabbed me by the arm and hauled me into the engine room, whose corroded walls were slick with diesel and rain.

A driver's seat was fixed in the centre of the room and two windows at the front revealed the track, which extended into a deep fog. We piled around the engine: my escort, two other policemen, the driver, his spare, three guards and several pas-sengers. The driver's wife squeezed onto a bench beside me, forcing my head and shoulders through an open window. The driver, whose view was almost completely obscured, shouted instructions, pushed a quid of betel into his mouth and revved the diesel engine to life, engulfing us in a plume of black smoke. Then we pulled out, at last, into the delta.

Rain drove through the windows and dripped through a dozen holes in the roof. We rattled through the storm for an hour, and then two, over innumerable bridges that I imagined were bowing under the weight of the train. This railway had always been dangerous – it was built by a British company before this part of the delta had been mapped, and even before it opened in 1903 the embankments had subsided, leaving parts of the track suspended all along the route. The earthwork was made of soft, unstable silt, just like the junta's railway through the delta. It also lacked adequate drainage, so the tracks flooded every year. As waterways changed course, and bridges were washed out, the embankments repeatedly failed. Severe speed restrictions were imposed, and at one point several years after the railway opened there were so many accidents that staff stopped reporting them.[11]

Now, fog obscured the view from the front of the train and the driver kept his hand on the horn. With my head half-out of the window, I could see why. The track ahead of us was busy with pedestrians, who used the railway to walk between villages. It might not have been much of a railway, but in this land of endless mud and paddy fields, it was the best road around.

Then, without warning, the driver stopped the train. We were not at a station and there was nothing around us except fields, but the other passengers began clambering down from the carriages into the rain and passing down pots and pans, suitcases and baskets filled with clothes. Then they walked along the track, with the young supporting the old, some of whom were too frail to walk alone.

My police escort latched onto my wrist, pulling me down from the train and into the thick mud beside the track. Before long, we came to piles of steel girders, abandoned cement mixers, and then a mountain of gravel beside a small stream, where I realized at last that we had reached the collapsed railway bridge. Families lingered beneath umbrellas on the bank, waiting for their turn on a motorized canoe. When the policeman tried to strong-arm me to the front of the queue, I resisted his grip and slipped. A hand grabbed the strap of the satchel around my neck, but I lost my balance and slid down the bank into a boat, spraying the women who were sitting in it with mud, as they roared with laughter and helped me to sit down.

On the opposite bank of the stream there was an eight-carriage train, whose size alone was comforting after the previous leg of the journey. My police escort and I walked through the carriages, whose benches had been torn from their fittings and were scattered like heaps of firewood on the floor. In the fourth carriage we found a bench that was partly intact and sat down next to a group of women and their children. As the younger children played and fought around us, the afternoon turned to evening and the train went nowhere.

We had been there for several hours, when a younger policeman swaggered through the carriage. He cleared two children from the bench beside me with his baton and sat down. 'Where will you sleep?' he barked and mimed the act of sleeping. I told him that I would find a guesthouse to sleep in at Hinthada, on the opposite bank of the Ayeyarwady River.

Even then, I didn't understand. There was no chance that I was crossing the river tonight.

'No Hinthada,' the policeman said. 'Go, yes. Forward, no. No, Hinthada.' He took my pen and tried to explain the situation by drawing a train, then a boat, on his hand. 'No,' he said, pointing at the boat. Then in frustration, he went away and returned with another man who introduced himself as Myo Myint, a merchant seaman.

'This train is broken,' he said in fluent English. 'You cannot sleep in Hinthada.'

Myo Myint was a slim man with a wide, kind face and teeth that had been stained red by years of chewing betel. He was travelling back to his village, to visit his elderly mother and father, a trip that he described as his duty. He sat down opposite me, and soon he was telling me about his childhood in the village. Like most people who have been through the state education system in Myanmar, he felt he did not have a proper education, and so he had left the delta as a young man to study business management in Yangon. But when he tried to start his own business, a small shop, he quickly went bankrupt.

'There was profit and loss,' he told me ruefully, 'but mostly loss.'

Like many young men in Myanmar, he realized his best hope of making money was to leave the country. He went to sea, landing illegally in Malaysia, where he could earn a salary four times the average wage in Yangon.

But he couldn't stay there for long, he said, because, 'They are not like us. They are Muslim and we are Buddhist. If we stay in their country for too long, they will kill us.'

I was surprised to hear this, and told him so.

'Yes,' he replied. 'A little here, a little there. They are killing our people.'

There were frequent reports in the Malaysian press of killings in Penang, where there is a large Burmese community – of throats being slashed, bodies dismembered and occasional stories of beheadings. Malaysian police usually attributed the deaths to disputes between migrants, but whoever was responsible, it was clear that life overseas for undocumented Burmese migrants was dangerous, much as it was back home.

As we spoke, the train groaned and then shuddered. There was the unmistakable sound of the engine, and at last we pulled away from the riverbank and began edging through fields that were etched out by water.

'In England,' Myo Myint said as we picked up speed, 'you are proud. In Myanmar we are scared.'

I asked him if he thought this would change now that Aung San Suu Kyi was leading the country.

'No,' he replied, and looked furtively at the policemen, who were pretending not to listen.

I asked him why.

'You know why,' he replied, crossly.

I told him I didn't know what he meant. He looked around again. The policemen were all watching us now.

'We cannot speak. In ten years maybe it will be different, but now, still, we cannot speak,' Myo Myint said. 'Some people can say whatever they want,' he added. 'They are the army.'

His evident discomfort indicated that police informers on railways are nothing new in Myanmar. In a Government of Burma Railway Police Manual from the 1920s, that I would later read, the rules are set out for a railway police force in British Burma that was paid for partly by the government and partly by railway companies. The police force was organized into train patrols, detectives and surveillance staff, whose primary job was to memorize the faces of well-known criminals. But they were also expected to spy on the passengers, to help keep the government 'informed of the political attitude of the people towards measures initiated by it, or towards events of the day'.[12]

Railway surveillance staff formed the backbone of state intelligence networks, because from the colonial period right up until the 1990s, before Myanmar's roads were improved with the use of forced labour, most long-distance travel in the country was by train. Confined in crowded carriages for hours and sometimes for days, passengers shared news. They talked about politics, crime and even planned uprisings. And plainclothes surveillance staff sat among them, listening and taking notes.

On Myanmar's railways today, methods of surveillance are largely unchanged. The trains have no closed-circuit television, reports are still written by hand, and the duties of the railway police officer, as I was quickly finding out, remain more or less the same. Headed by a police colonel and answerable both to Myanma Railways and the Myanmar police force, the railway police are tasked with upholding law and order on trains and at stations. As well as general policing, the curriculum at the railway police school apparently includes railway-specific combat training, security and intelligence.

Today, the railway police are part of a much wider network of informers who during the decades of military rule became a critical part of the state intelligence system. Some are professionals, others are employed part-time. At its peak, the military intelligence apparatus had a mandate to spy on the entire population. But even with its vast network of informers, Myanmar's military, like the British colonial government before it, repeatedly failed to predict the reactions of its citizens. Incompetence played a part, but also corruption and the fact that by granting themselves exclusive power and privileges, members of the military had become increasingly disconnected from the population they sought to control.[13]

Myo Myint spoke quickly and earnestly with the policemen, then finally he sat back, satisfied. 'They voted for the National League for Democracy,' he said – Aung San Suu Kyi's party.

The light faded as we talked. Myo Myint explained that he

was unhappy about his prospects. As a merchant seafarer he wasn't paid much, but he didn't feel he had any other options. Life in Yangon was too expensive, and there was no work for him in the delta. He pointed from the train window to where three emaciated men were standing in a flooded field.

'Those men are catching fish,' he said. 'Very small fish. There is nothing else for them to do.'

At each station the train stopped for at least twenty minutes, and it also stopped briefly every few minutes between stations, which infuriated Myo Myint. The generals had not only impoverished Myanmar's people, he said, they had also robbed them of their time.

'Our time here is always wasted. If anyone wants the train to stop, so they can talk to a friend, the train stops.'

It had not been like that in Malaysia, where trains had automatic doors and ran on schedule. In Myanmar, to get anywhere, you had to walk, or rely on boats and railways that were so dilapidated they continually broke down, or risk your life travelling by bus on dangerous roads.

Soon the train was stopping even more regularly, and I realized that the villages in this part of the delta had been built around the track and that our train functioned as a travelling emporium. Vendors were reaching out of the train windows to sell medicine and food into the candlelit houses as we passed.

By contrast, we were now travelling in total darkness. I asked Myo Myint why there were no lights on the train.

'I also do not know,' he said.

I knew that there was no point in asking anyone else, because they wouldn't know either. The lights had broken and nobody had mended them; that was just how it was.

When the young policeman returned from one of his patrols, he wedged his torch into an overhead luggage rack, casting a spotlight on his baton and the blade of his knife. Glancing at the knife, Myo Myint told me that he was leaving at the next station and asked the policeman to make sure I ate a meal that evening.

'Sis, you are our guest,' he told me. 'You have been travelling all day. You must wash, eat and sleep.'

As the train pulled into the next station, he said, 'This is my native village. It is very poor, very small, very dark.' He was angered and depressed by his government's ineptitude and having lived elsewhere, it was hard for him to come home.

After another hour, the train ground to a halt inside a mass of houses and sheds that pressed against the sides of the carriage, as if this hamlet was its depot. My police guards picked up their batons and radios. '*Thwa*,' they said, which means 'Go'. This was Tharrawaw, the end of the line, on the eastern bank of the Ayeyarwady River.

We jumped down from the train into a swamp, colliding in the darkness with groups of men from the village who were unloading sacks of freight into cargo sheds.

Fixing my eyes on the policemen's legs, I followed him to the end of the train and into a small, cosy house. As my eyes adjusted to the light, I saw that a dozen people had gathered there. On receiving news of my arrival by radio, they had prepared cake and tea. Insisting that I sit on the floor and eat, they began to discuss my fate.

Throughout my journey, the railway police had gone out of their way to help me; now, they even wanted to make sure I had somewhere to sleep that night. This level of kindness would never have been shown to a Burmese traveller, unless a bribe had swapped hands. But police were under strict instructions to 'Warmly Welcome and Take Care of Tourists' – as signs across the country proclaimed. If anything happened to me on their watch, there would be serious consequences.

There was, of course, no ferry to Hinthada that night, and there was no guesthouse in Tharrawaw. Nobody ever travelled on this train except the people who lived on the line. This village, like most places in Myanmar, except its cities and designated tourist sites, was isolated and insular and completely unused to the arrival of strangers.

They were all concerned because it is illegal in Myanmar to host a foreigner overnight without a hotel licence, and there were no hotels for miles around. There was talk of sending me to a monastery, but an elderly man, who appeared to be the village head, decided that because I was a woman, this would be inappropriate. He pointed to the only other woman in the room.

'You can stay with her,' he said. 'She lives alone.'

This was Daw Myat, a middle-aged woman with a stern expression, whose hair was pulled back tightly from her face. She was obviously considered respectable, and the men were turning to her for help in this moment of crisis. I tried to turn down the offer, because it had not been her idea, suggesting I could instead sleep on the train, which wouldn't leave until the next morning. But Daw Myat walked over to me, placed her hand on my shoulder, and nodded.

'Come,' she said.

We left the house and walked back through the train, which now occupied the main thoroughfare between the houses. At the other end of the train, Daw Myat leaned from one of the carriage doors to remove a metal panel, revealing what seemed in the darkness to be the entrance to another cargo shed. We stepped down from the train, and she fixed the panel back into place behind us, drawing the lock. As she switched on a lamp, I saw that we were inside a spacious wooden teashop. Handing me a length of fabric, she led me to a deck at the back of the shop, where she indicated that I should wash, using a barrel of water. Removing my wet, muddy clothes, I wrapped the fabric around my body, and poured the icy water over my head.

Inside, Daw Myat had prepared a bowl of instant noodles. The wooden floorboards were warm against my feet and as I ate, I realized that I was exhausted. In a corner of the shop, an old television was playing a review of that day's developments in the national parliament. From this simple teashop in the delta, the halls of Myanmar's new capital Naypyidaw seemed impossibly grand. I realized that there were farmers who would have been dazzled by the spectacle, and that this was no accident.

As the hours passed, Daw Myat and I spoke to one another sporadically in Burmese and English, testing the limits of our shared languages, and before we went to bed, she showed me photographs of her children.

Her son was a soldier in Myanmar's military, garrisoned in Yangon, near the city's famed Shwedagon Pagoda. She raised three fingers to her shoulder in a gesture that I took to mean his rank – she was proud to have a son in the army, which in Myanmar was the easiest way for a family to escape poverty. Over decades, the military had consolidated control over every avenue of social mobility, and those willing to enlist in the military and pledge allegiance to its leaders had a chance not only to rise through the ranks, but to become rich. President Thein Sein embodied this mobility; born to a family of landless farmers in the delta, he had risen to be head of state.

We slept beside one another on the wooden floor. Daw Myat threw rugs over two straw mats, and strung a mosquito net from the ceiling that was wide enough to cover us both. After a day in the company of men it was a pleasure to spend a moment of quiet intimacy with her. Before she climbed into bed she unfurled her hair from its tight bun. It fell to her waist and as she pulled at it with a comb, it fanned across her back.

On one wall of our improvised bedroom was a Buddhist shrine, lit by small orange and red lights, whose glow suffused the room. Daw Myat sat down on the mat beside me and intoned her prayers until I fell asleep.

The next morning, the flooded fields behind the teashop shone golden in the dawn light. From the deck, I watched the mist rise until Daw Myat woke. She removed the shutters at the front of the shop to reveal the train, which sounded its horn and set off back towards the broken bridge. Its departure revealed my police escorts from the previous day, who were drinking tea outside the local police station, underneath a bilingual sign, which in English read 'MAY I HELP YOU'. They took my photograph with their phones. Daw Myat embraced me and asked me to visit her son at his barracks when I was back in Yangon. We walked together to the edge of the village, where a boat woven from wooden planks and rope was moored on the bank of the Ayeyarwady, a river so wide that it stretched to the horizon.

On the boat, Daw Myat laid out a sheet of newspaper for me to sit on. Once the other villagers and their cargo were on board, she waved us off from the shore. The sun rose over the river as we chugged west, and within an hour we were pulling up in the port at Hinthada, alongside dredgers loaded with sand and gravel. The boat moored and I ran up the slipway, past a disused railway line, in search of a motorbike taxi. I had been told in Yangon that the daily train for Pathein left Hinthada at 8 a.m., which meant I had fifteen minutes to get to the station. When I found a driver, I asked him to hurry and he raced us into town, attempting back routes and reversing from dead-ends, arriving at the station with one minute to spare.

But as I ran onto the platform, I found it was deserted. The train would leave in an hour, perhaps two, the stationmaster told me. He introduced me to the resident policeman: a young, plump man, who wore conspicuous gold jewellery and who he said would protect me on the train; from what, it wasn't clear.

Later that morning, we boarded the train, which was sun-bleached and almost empty, and the policeman sat beside me as we travelled further into the delta, watching miles of paddy fields pass. In each field, there were dozens of farmers, most of them women, who stood in knee-deep water and had to bend almost double to farm the rice. They wore bamboo hats and scarves around their faces to shield them from the sun, but the heat must have been oppressive and the work was repetitive and tough.

The policeman watched me watching them, until a book-seller came through the carriage, and the policeman picked out a book entitled *Current English Dialogue* and flicked through its pages. Referring to the translations in the book, he wrote carefully in my notepad. 'My name is Thiha Aung. I live in Aye-yarwady Division, Wakama Township. I weak English language. Why do you visit Myanmar? Please! Your answer! On business or on duty? Do you come here to work?'

This method of communication was not completely eccentric. While school textbooks are published in English, there are limited opportunities to practise conversation, so many people in Myanmar read and write English better than they speak it. I wrote back to the policeman and he wrote more questions, probing me gently about my reasons for taking this train, and my subsequent plans. If it was an interrogation, it was an unusual one, because he also asked me several questions from the book on English dialogue, which he pointed at, such as 'Have you arrived in Singapore?'

I didn't tell him the truth about what I was doing, or where I was going, saying instead that I was a tourist, on the way to the beach. I had been under police guard since the previous morning and was worried that it might become a permanent feature of my journey. Eventually the policeman ran out of questions and we sat together quietly, leafing through the bookseller's other titles. When we finally pulled into Pathein, the capital of the delta, I had been travelling for thirty-six hours; the journey by road would have taken just four.

Like other regional capitals in Myanmar, Pathein was a functional but dilapidated city. From the station, I walked through the town centre, past a large colonial-era prison that was surrounded by high walls fitted with watchtowers. Beyond the prison, past the downtown shops that sold hardware and religious paraphernalia, I turned along a narrow street lined with wooden houses. At the end of the street was the small, family-owned motel where I would stay that night.

At the guesthouse, I searched online for translators based in the city, and found the profile of an English-speaking tour guide called Soe Moe. He replied quickly to the message I sent him, and met me that evening in the motel lobby.

An enthusiastic man who wore wrap-around shades and a moustache, Soe Moe told me that he had trained as a lawyer, but had never practised law because the courts were corrupt, and he was ashamed to take bribes. So he worked instead as a guide, and ran bird-watching tours. By chance, he also had an old friend who worked for Myanma Railways.

'He knows everything,' Soe Moe said, when I asked whether his friend could tell me about the history of the junta's ill-fated railway into the delta. So we called his friend, who agreed to meet us for breakfast the next day at a teashop near the railway station.

Lucky One was a typical, busy Burmese teashop, a wide roadside café fitted with low tables and plastic stools. Soe Moe's friend was sitting alone at a table in the far corner, and we had to push through the crowds to reach him. Squeezing onto a stool opposite him, I ordered tea and a plate of paratha, an Indian-style flatbread that is widely eaten in Myanmar for breakfast. Around us, the other customers, mostly men, were shouting over one another; with cigarettes hanging from their mouths, they gossiped and bantered. Others were quietly reading the papers, or holding hushed conversations over rounds of tea.

Soe Moe's friend, who I will call Tun, was an earnest man in his mid-thirties, who made me promise not to use his real name. By talking to me he risked incurring a 'black mark', he said, which could result in him being sent away from his busy urban station in Pathein to an isolated outpost on one of the junta-era railways, miles from any town. Or, worse: to one of the country's ethnic states, where there was hostility to Burmese officials, and where insurgents occasionally attacked the railway stations.

I promised I wouldn't use his name, and in return he agreed to tell me the 'real story' behind the abandoned railway through the delta.

But first he wanted to explain the hierarchy of the railway department, which he said was essential to understanding what had happened. At the top was the minister, based in Naypyidaw. At the bottom, several ranks below Tun, were the clerks at rural railway stations. Everyone, at every level, he said, was complicit in a system that was designed to make money for civil servants at the expense of the public, and above all, to enrich the minister and his immediate subordinates.

A senior official, such as the district mechanical engineer, would approach the railway minister with a proposal to build a new railway in a region under the senior official's authority. The minister would agree, and procure the budget. Then the minister and the engineer would 'share the cake' – Tun moonlighted as an

English teacher and punctuated his speech with English idioms. They would pass whatever was left down the chain of command. This process continued 'all the way down, until there was not much left. And that is what they used to build railroads,' Tun said. He spoke with an American lilt and called railways railroads. 'You can say it is corruption. There are many new railroads in Myanmar. Did you ever see trains running on them?'

'Corruption,' he continued, taking a bite of his paratha, 'is a deep habit for the people of Myanmar.'

It was not just the money intended for building new railways that had vanished. Just as the generals stole from the people, civil servants took everything they could from the state.

Ballast disappeared from the tracks. So did the wooden sleepers, which were eventually replaced with concrete ones that were harder to steal. The railway staff siphoned diesel from the trains and sold it at night. They used the budget to order new engine oil for the locomotives, as well as new tools and brake parts, and they sold these too. Nothing was sacred: indicator lamps, starter magnets, even seats, were removed and sold.

Tun believed the main reason for this was that railway staff weren't paid enough. Most of them earned around £2 a day, which at a stretch was enough for one person, but not for an entire family. Staff were given free housing, but had to pay for their own electricity and water. Like Tun, everyone had another job on the side, running small shops, or motorbike taxi services.

There were two distinct phases of railway building in Than Shwe's Myanmar. The first, in the 1990s, was attended by brutality and the widespread use of forced labour. The second phase, which began in the early 2000s, after international scrutiny had mostly brought the practice of forced labour to an end, was characterized by corruption. Corruption in Myanmar's railway ministry, like in all its ministries, was not new, but until the 1990s the country was bankrupt and there was not enough money for anyone to become really rich.

It was only in the following decade that the railway budget began to increase, coinciding with the appointment as railway minister in 2003 of a general called Aung Min, who would lead the ministry for almost a decade. He would later become known as one of the most forward-thinking ex-generals driving Myanmar's transition to democracy.

Appointed to the Ministry of the President's Office in 2012 and given responsibility for the country's peace process, Aung Min was lauded by Reuters as a 'top reformer', by the *Financial Times* as part of a new 'super cabinet', and by an *Economist* correspondent as 'very open-minded' and 'refreshingly honest'. *The New Yorker* was more cautious, with reporter Evan Osnos writing after meeting Aung Min that he 'couldn't figure out how much of what he said was pabulum, for international consumption, or how a man who had spent eight years in the Cabinet of one of the world's most vicious dictators could think that his people had forgotten'.[14]

During Aung Min's eight years in Than Shwe's cabinet, he had overseen an exponential increase in spending at his ministry. Throughout the 1990s and early 2000s annual capital investment by the junta into Myanma Railways was less than K5 billion. It doubled when Aung Min took over the ministry and it continued to rise.[15] During Aung Min's last full year as minister, by the time the junta prepared its final budget for the 2011–12 fiscal year, some K200 billion (around £150 million at the time) was allocated to the railways, or 3.3 per cent of the total state budget – almost as much as was spent on education.[16]

This in itself was not necessarily cause for concern. But

Aung Min was a lifelong soldier, and he had no experience that qualified him to run the railways. Rather than spending the money on upgrading and repairing ageing rolling stock, track and signalling equipment, and rebuilding bridges and tunnels on existing lines, in the decade that Aung Min was in charge of Myanmar's railways he spent some 90 per cent of the money on building new railways like the one through the delta, most of which had since closed.

While money was being ploughed into ill-considered railways, other parts of the network were falling further into disrepair. Railways typically have two main functions: to move passengers and freight. Their usefulness can be measured in passenger and freight density, which make it possible to accurately compare one year to another on a single railway network, regardless of the route length.

One academic found that passenger density on Myanmar's railways peaked at 1.4 million passenger miles per mile of route per year, in 1987. By 2015 it had fallen by almost two-thirds, to a level not seen since the mid-1960s. In other words, despite spending hundreds of millions of pounds on the railways during his time as minister, when Aung Min was done with them, their efficiency was no better than it had been fifty years earlier. The trend in freight density was even worse: at the end of Aung Min's term in office it was around 50 per cent lower than it had been fifty years earlier.[17]

By almost any measure except the total length of track, Aung Min left the railways in a worse state than he found them. All of Myanma Railways' assets, from the track to the rolling stock and the signalling equipment, urgently needed upgrading. Financially, the railways were also struggling: losses had ballooned and the operating ratio, an indicator of financial health, was twice as bad as the operating ratio of other railway networks in the region. All of this came at a cost: while the creation of railway infrastructure often led to a higher quality of life in other places, the opposite had happened in Myanmar.

Several years after I travelled into the delta by train, I met the former general Aung Min for the first time. A contact of mine in Yangon put me in touch with his personal assistant, who invited me to a nondescript housing estate at the edge of the city's downtown area. He met me in the carpark and accompanied me into a second-floor office, where Aung Min was waiting for us. As we sat facing each other across a conference table, Aung Min quizzed me, through his assistant, who also worked as his interpreter, about the railways in England. The interpreter referred to Aung Min throughout our meeting as 'the general', even though he had long since retired from the military.

Aung Min was immaculately dressed – his dyed black hair was oiled and neatly parted, his white shirt was fastened with a diamond stud, and his fingers sparkled with gemstones. On his right hand was a nine-stone *nawarat* ring, an amulet that is popular with members of Myanmar's military, because they were once worn by members of the Burmese royal family.

'If Myanmar had the same amount of funds that you do in the United Kingdom or elsewhere, the railways would be much improved and much advanced,' Aung Min's interpreter translated.

'When the general became Minister of Railways it wasn't out of good luck,' he continued. 'In fact, it was very bad luck for him, because he had to work with very limited resources.'

This was the start of a speech that was hardly disturbed by my questions. Aung Min repeatedly returned to the subject of thrift and he spoke as if the lack of money in the state budget was unavoidable, and had nothing to do with him and his cabinet, or the dictator he had served.

In fact, there was plenty of money. Myanmar's jade industry alone is valued at tens of billions of dollars a year, its rubies and sapphires are the world's most valuable, it has forests of teak and other hardwoods, large oil and gas reserves, and a huge array of mineral resources including gold, copper, tin, tungsten and rare earths. But most of the money from these industries never reaches the national budget.

Nevertheless, Aung Min tried to illustrate his point with a selection of stories that were designed to elicit sympathy, including one in which he had dared to ask Than Shwe for $6 million to pay for new railway tracks. Instead of giving him the money, he claimed that Than Shwe scolded him. 'He said if there was that much money, he wouldn't need me to work, he could hire the French company Alstom to do it instead. The work of a minister was to find solutions, despite the constraints,' he said.

The ministry had no foreign exchange, and no access to foreign loans, so Aung Min went overseas to beg for discarded equipment. It was humiliating, but he was proud of his resourcefulness. 'It was not as if we didn't want brand-new equipment,' he said, with a rasping laugh that triggered a coughing fit.

He told me about his vision, when he became minister, of building new railways that were as efficient as planes. There would be bullet trains, and integrated subways providing a door-to-door service.

'But of course,' he said, 'since Myanmar is a poor country, these were just my dreams.'

He was charming, and inscrutable, and he seemed genuinely convinced that he had done his best, with the limited resources that were available to him. He denied that money had been wasted, claiming that not only was his budget tiny, but he was expected to stretch it to build hundreds and hundreds of miles of new track.

The country was already well connected along its large river valleys that run from north to south, fertile regions that support large populations, where towns had sprung up along the British colonial railways. The problem was that the colonial railways all led towards the ports in the old capital of Yangon. His task, as he saw it, was to do the same thing, only from the east of the country to the west, creating new economic channels with the purpose-built new capital of Naypyidaw at their centre.

There are two different theories of nation-building, he told me, apparently referring to two early theories of political geography that were developed in Britain and America: the 'rimland theory', which he said was used by richer countries, and the 'heartland theory'. Myanmar had adopted the heartland theory, Aung Min said, moving its capital city to the country's centre, and building transport links that connected the capital with every state and region.

This was a formidable challenge because of the mountain ranges that extend south from the Himalayan foothills, separating the country's river valleys, and it was made much harder by the junta's lack of engineering expertise.

'We did not have access to modern tunnel or bridge technologies, as in other countries,' Aung Min said. 'So when building lines in mountainous regions, we had to build around the mountains.'

But plenty of Aung Min's railways that were no longer operational were built over flat ground, like the railway through the delta, and the line south of Dawei. When I asked him about these railways, he initially tried to shift the blame.

'The railroad to Pathein was built by Senior General Than Shwe,' he told me. 'He was a dedicated road builder.' Aung Min claimed he had told the Senior General that the railway through the delta did not make any economic sense, but nevertheless it went ahead. Aung Min snapped when I told him that the project made no sense at all.

'If you appoint me the lifetime minister of railways, I will complete it,' he retorted. 'Where does the fault lie? With the person who built these lines, or the one who couldn't make them economically viable?'

He meant Aung San Suu Kyi's government, which had been closing the railways he had built – those that were not damaged beyond repair – because it was too expensive to run empty trains on them.

When I left Aung Min that day, his assistant asked me to send over more questions by email, if I wanted to continue the conversation. The next time we met, at the same housing estate, Aung Min wasn't wearing any jewellery. He arrived at the second-floor meeting room carrying a stack of hand-written answers to my questions, which he gave me, telling me to get them translated.

He had read an article, published by an investigative magazine called *Frontier*, where I would work for several years, that had evidently troubled him. It was about the abandoned railway in Pathein, and it pointed to corruption as one of the reasons the project had failed. Most of the notes he gave me, which he summarized during our meeting, reiterated what he had already told me: that railway-building was an essential part of nation-building, that even the colonial-era railways in Myanmar initially made a loss, that he had advised against building the railway through the delta, that there wasn't enough money to do everything that was needed, and that it was ultimately the new parliament's fault that so many of his railways had closed.

On the final page of his notes, he had written me a challenge, in his spindly Burmese script: 'If Aung Min, who built railways, commits corruption, do take action against him,' it said. Of course, I had no means of taking action, and I never met the old general again.

How much money, if any, had Aung Min taken for himself? A large amount of money – £50 million on the railway through the delta alone – had disappeared, or been wasted. He was a minister at a time when everyone in Than Shwe's cabinet was getting rich, and it was unlikely that he had resisted the temptation entirely. But regardless of how much had been stolen, and how much had been misspent, the effect was the same: nothing in the delta had changed.

Travel time from Yangon to Pathein by train had not been cut to three hours. The poorest people in the delta, who couldn't afford to travel by car or bus, were still wasting entire days waiting for the train. The delta was still recovering from Cyclone Nargis, almost a decade later, and was still highly vulnerable to weather and climate shocks. Without money to rebuild, many villages were abandoned. Others were still waiting for the government to build cyclone shelters, to protect them against future storms.

On the other hand, Myanmar's bureaucracy presented endless opportunities for corruption. There was no incentive not to steal, as Tun had explained to me, back in the teashop. The railway police were supposed to report on theft and corruption, but they were corrupt, too.

'Everyone turns a deaf ear,' Tun had told me. 'Everyone takes care of himself.'

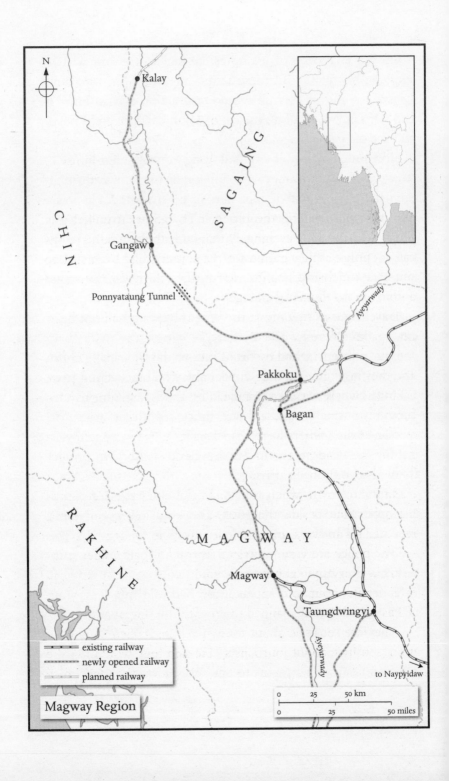

Magway Region

3.

Magway

Sunlight spilled along the platform as our train pulled into Magway in the early evening, illuminating the epaulettes of the railway police as they monitored the new arrivals. A tight group of police had formed at the eastern end of the platform around a man whose round, gentle face was framed by thick-rimmed glasses. This was Nay Aung, the Magway correspondent at the newspaper where I worked.

Four policemen had escorted me on the train to Magway, and they now greeted their colleagues, who blocked our path, asking us where we were going. Unflustered, Nay Aung handed them his business card, and we walked together out into the tree-lined yard, where he retrieved his motorbike, handed me a helmet, and told me to jump on the back.

We had only been driving for a few minutes on the track leading into town, when Nay Aung's phone rang. He parked his motorbike beside the road, answered a few questions, repeated his answers, and when he was done, he turned to me.

'The police are very interested in you,' he said. 'They want to know everything about you – your name, age, country, and even details about your appearance.'

I asked what they planned to do with this information.

'They are sensitive about foreigners,' he replied, 'and even more sensitive about journalists.' He said they would use the information to file a report to Special Branch, the local office of the police intelligence department run by the military-controlled home affairs ministry in Magway.

'They are scared of journalists,' Nay Aung added with a grin. 'They want to find them, catch them, and put them in jail.'

He was only partly joking. Even though censorship laws had been lifted and journalists in other parts of the country had more freedom, Magway was a military stronghold, and the police here still routinely intimidated reporters.[1]

I asked Nay Aung if they wanted to put him in jail.

'They want to kill me,' he replied. 'They do not say so directly, but they show it in other ways.'

When I told him he was brave, he laughed. 'I am not brave,' he said. 'I'm scared. But I'm still alive, so I keep writing.'

We drove north along the Ayeyarwady River's wide coast, where couples walked across the sand to watch the sun set at the water's edge. It had taken me two days to travel the 300 miles north from the delta capital of Pathein to Magway, the capital of Magway Region in central-western Myanmar, and on the journey I had watched the landscape change. The endless miles of mud had become fields of rose bushes and sunflowers and then wide, parched riverbeds, which was alarming because it was the end of the monsoon and the rivers should have been full. Here in the dry zone, at the height of summer when the temperature can reach 45 degrees Celsius, deep fissures would form in the earth as drought set in.

At tables set out along the riverbank, men convened around bottles of whisky, and teenagers slurped milkshakes. There were families, who shared tea-leaf salads and deep-fried beans, and who tossed their plastic waste over the railings onto the beach. There was an imposing hotel with extortionately priced rooms, owned by a former general called Phone Maw Shwe who had run Magway Region for the junta like a fiefdom, and who still controlled the local economy.[2] There was only one other place in town that accepted foreign guests, a filthy hostel on the central roundabout, which rented rooms by the hour. A teenager at the reception had given me a heavy lock to use on my door.

We had dinner on the promenade at a table overlooking the river, where we were joined by Nay Aung's friend, a broad-chested Muslim man with a ready smile called Olar ('like a Spanish hello'), who told me when he introduced himself that he was half-Afghan.

He was sweating profusely, and immediately after sitting down he reeled off the names of the new civil-society groups he was involved with – a novelty in a region that the military had always kept under tight control.

He and Nay Aung were working together to investigate community complaints, of logging in the nearby Bago Mountains, and illegal mining. Their work was dangerous, so they worked in a group. In Magway, a city of several hundred thousand people, there were only four journalists, Nay Aung claimed – one of whom couldn't really be considered a journalist because he blackmailed his sources.

'I am so sad that my country is like this,' he said.

Because there were so few journalists here, everyone knew who Nay Aung was, which meant there were topics he couldn't write about.

'This is a very closed region,' he said. 'Phone Maw Shwe owns everything: mining, charcoal, oil, construction. His companies get all the contracts and build all the roads; they even built your railway line. He opens his pockets and everyone from Magway puts their money inside.'

To the north of where we sat, a monstrous steel and

concrete bridge spanned the river. We would cross it the next morning to the opposite bank, where the railway minister, Aung Min, had overseen the construction of a 320-mile railway traversing the flat, sandy western edge of the Ayeyarwady River, from Kyangyin in the southern delta region, to Pakokku in Myanmar's northwest. There, it connected to a town called Kalay in neighbouring Sagaing Region near the Indian border. Or, at least, that had been the plan. Parts of the line were still operational, but most of it was now abandoned and Nay Aung referred to it as the 'bush railway' because of the undergrowth that covered the tracks. Construction began in 2007, around the same time as the railway from Yangon through the delta, and it was built in nine stages, with the completion of each stage marked by a separate opening ceremony.[3]

Aung Min attended most of these ceremonies, as did Phone Maw Shwe and a handful of other generals. They made speeches, saying things like, 'Local people have already realized that such goodwill of the government towards them is huge and profound.'[4] They cut ribbons, they unveiled plaques, they posed for documentary photos, and they handed out gifts.

State media reports claimed that the railway in Magway would put the impoverished western bank of the Ayeyarwady River on a more equal socio-economic footing with the relatively prosperous eastern bank.[5] The problem was that the railway had two large gaps in it, and even the parts of track that were operational had already fallen into disrepair.[6] An Australian academic called Lindsay Stubbs, who tried to travel the full length of the railway several years after it was built, reported that the journey took three days, and he had to make large parts of it by road. A landslide in the south had blocked part of the track, and another large section was not open to the public. At one point, Stubbs wrote in his PhD thesis, the train started rocking so violently that the driver had to slow it down to walking speed. Stations were unstaffed and run down, if they weren't already abandoned.[7]

It was only in late 2015, about a year before I travelled to Magway, that any problems with the railway had been reported publicly, and this only happened when a group of sesame farmers began demanding compensation because the junta had seized their farmland to build the track.[8] They hadn't dared to speak out under the junta, but since the reforms began, there were stories everywhere in Myanmar about people seeking redress for land that had been taken from them during the decades of junta rule.

Nay Aung picked me up the next morning in his friend's car, and we drove across the bridge to Pwintbyu, a township on the railway route, where everyone we met seemed angry about the project. The junta had taken 4,000 acres of land to build the line, as a parliamentary memo would later reveal,[9] most of which local people had been farming for generations.

We visited Moe Moe, a small woman with light-brown eyes and golden hoops in her ears, who told us the story of how she had been working one day in her field when a bulldozer drove in and began to dig up the ground. Terrified, she ran back to her house. She didn't know what to do, she said. She had inherited this land and had always been free to farm it. The paddy, sesame and beans that she grew were her family's main source of income.

She had paid little attention when a few government officials turned up with measuring equipment a couple of weeks before the bulldozer arrived. But when they began to dig up her land, she realized they had taken it, just as they had taken millions of acres of land from other people across the country.[10]

'I was afraid and I cried, but I still said nothing, because I was afraid,' she told us. 'They took our best land. Now we will have to struggle for our whole lives.'

Nay Aung and I were sitting under a tree in the yard of Moe Moe's wooden house, surrounded by her children and an assortment of other people from her village. Nobody here had been warned that the railway would be built. After the bulldozer came, there were construction workers and more machines that operated day and night.

'The railway line was built very fast,' Moe Moe said. 'They were loading and unloading earth, for two weeks – that's all.'

During the next monsoon, her fields flooded and she realized, just as many other people up and down the railway route were also realizing, that the track was acting as a dam, blocking the flow of water to the Ayeyarwady River.

'The canals were blocked up, there were floods, and the crops were destroyed,' Moe Moe explained.

The people here had become the latest victims in a long history of railway building by contractors who had little understanding of the landscape they were carving up, or concern for the people who inhabited it. Ever since the 1850s, when the first railways were built in British India, companies had failed to build enough tunnels, culverts and drains to allow water to flow beneath new railway embankments. Indian railway history is filled with accounts of disputes between contractors and communities who lost their homes and their land to flooding. In some cases, gangs of farmers would even venture out at night to wreck sections of earthwork to protect their crops.[11]

Unable to make any money that year from farming, and with her son's student fees waiting to be paid, Moe Moe took out a loan.

'We got money from someone who was rich, a stranger,' she said. The interest rate was 10 per cent a month, and she had struggled ever since to make the repayments. 'All our extra money goes to repaying the debt,' she said.

Land matters everywhere, but that is particularly true in Myanmar. Farming underpins the economy but also the Burmese way of life. More than two-thirds of the population are employed in agriculture, mostly on smallholder farms that depend on manual labour. Myanmar's economy has always been agrarian, and for most of the country's history the rural economy has centred around the dry, central plains – areas like Magway Region – where most people have always been subsistence farmers.[12]

Before it was annexed by Britain, the area now known as Myanmar was a collection of smaller territories ruled by kings and princes. At its centre, occupying what is now the country's heartland, were a succession of Burmese kingdoms. The wealth of these kingdoms was contained in their labour and their irrigated paddy land, which was governed by customary agreements between villagers: verbal contracts that were de facto law. The Burmese kings invested in agrarian infrastructure, particularly the construction and repair of irrigation works, because they recognized the importance, both to the economy and to their own legitimacy, of making sure that the paddy fields were fertile.

After independence in 1948, as the country's new ethnic Burmese leaders searched for a national identity that had nothing to do with the humiliating experience of colonial rule, they looked back to the agrarian, pre-colonial past. During the British occupation, which saw the arrival of millions of Indian workers from British India, large numbers of Burmese farmers had become indebted to Indian moneylenders. Many of them lost their land in the Great Depression (1929–39) when rice prices crashed. They later found that they couldn't compete with Indian daily-wage workers, even on the land they once owned.

After independence, the government sought to redistribute land, through the Land Nationalization Act. When Ne Win seized power in 1962, he took this further, forcing hundreds of thousands of Indians to leave the country, and cutting Myanmar off from the global economy. Like the rulers of many other newly decolonized states, he understood that without economic independence, political independence would remain a distant dream. Because most of the Burmese people were subsistence farmers, this meant reorienting the economy away from industry and manufacturing for export, towards agriculture.

Ne Win's Burma Socialist Programme Party, which governed the country until the 1988 uprising and claimed to be the party of the working people, created programmes that focused on the peasantry, who the party saw as the custodians of Burmese tradition. It created a nation of subsistence farmers by buying up excess rice (just as the Burmese kings had once done), which prevented land being traded again on a large scale.

The problem with building an economy on land managed by smallholders is that any land claimed by the state must always be at the expense of the farmer. And it was not long before Ne Win introduced a new constitution that made the state 'the ultimate owner of all natural resources above and below the ground, above and beneath the waters and in the atmosphere, and also all lands', in wording that remains in the country's charter today.[13]

After Ne Win's experiment with socialism failed and the

junta embarked on a nationwide programme of development, it seized more and more land for the state and for private companies, introducing the same dynamics of dispossession and capital accumulation that had once fuelled the Burmese struggle for independence.

Land is one of the most contentious issues in Myanmar partly because it reveals the military's hypocrisy. The generals claimed to be making serious attempts to improve the country's irrigation systems, in the tradition of the kings, building and renovating dams, reservoirs and weirs, paying particular attention to developing the central plains of the dry zone.

But rather than upholding tradition, they took advantage of the ancient tradition of land governance by customary agreements between villagers, confiscating land from people like Moe Moe who had no title deeds. While claiming to be investing in irrigation systems for the benefit of farmers in the central dry zone, they instead built a railway that blocked hundreds of waterways, preventing water from draining into the Ayeyarwady River and destroying thousands of acres of fields, demonstrating in the process how little they understood or cared for the land and the irrigation systems that sustained it.

In the country's heartland, in villages like Moe Moe's, where life revolves around agriculture and where the junta had supposedly focused its development efforts, smallholder farmers felt increasingly abused, abandoned and afraid. The junta had failed the peasantry, and now, ruined by drought and floods, the heartland was emptying, as the land became increasingly difficult to farm, and the rural population inched closer to destitution.

In some villages, only children and the elderly remained, as men and women migrated to the cities or overseas to work. The farmers who stayed behind faced labour shortages and children were being roped into the harvest. Robbed of security, the fears of Myanmar's rural population were boiling over into anger. The only people who benefited from the railway, Moe Moe said, were the owners of the companies that built it.

'They are rich,' she shouted, throwing up her hands. 'They are working only for their own richness.'

The section of the railway that destroyed her land never opened, Moe Moe said, because the quality of construction was so poor. The contractors sold half the cement that was intended for the sleepers, and without proper foundations the track had sunk into the earth. Bushes had sprung up on former farmland, and then trees, which were now almost as tall as she was.

None of the people in the village had ever taken the train, she said. Even if the railway had opened, the stations were a long way from the villages.

'Their system was to avoid the villages,' Moe Moe said, and it struck me how absurd that sounded. 'The railway stations are very far away, so the transport charges are very high.'

Stripped of their farmland and struggling for survival, people here had lived for years in resentful silence.

'We were afraid of the army government, because they had guns,' Moe Moe said.

All across the region, people put up with the military's confiscation of land, its cruelty and its complete disregard for them – but they never accepted it.

In the 2015 election the people of Magway had voted unanimously: Aung San Suu Kyi's National League for Democracy, the NLD, won every seat in the region. The people here had not voted for the party so much because of its policies, but because it was the only viable alternative to military rule. In their eyes, a vote for Aung San Suu Kyi was a vote for freedom from arbitrary cruelties, from an exploitative economy, from instability, and from fear.

It was also a vote for protection against large-scale development that under the junta had profited outsiders, while harming local people. It wasn't just in Magway; all across the country, communities had mobilized against land confiscations and were demanding redress.

Leaving Moe Moe in her garden, Nay Aung and I stopped in to visit the nearby house of one of the new NLD parliamentarians. Officials who took questions from journalists were still a novelty to Nay Aung, and on the way there he showed me a photograph on his phone of him and the other reporters in Magway sitting on the floor of the regional parliament, between rows of seated representatives. This level of access would have been unthinkable a year earlier, he told me with a grin. But as we pulled up to the politician's house in our car, he warned me against asking too many difficult questions.

'NLD politicians might have been activists and political prisoners in the past,' he said. 'But now they have to sit in parliament and they want peace.'

The lawmaker was waiting for us under his house, which like others in Magway was raised on stilts, to protect it from the annual floods. He was surrounded by an entourage of party members who all wore the party uniform of white shirts and salmon-orange jackets decorated with badges that featured the party's logo (a fighting peacock), its flag, and the faces of Aung San Suu Kyi, and her father, General Aung San. I was struck when I saw the party members by how vulnerable they were in this region that was still controlled by soldiers and their cronies. The women held hands with one another, sitting a few metres from the men, who had convened around a small wooden table.

They told us they didn't know much about the railway. It had been built almost ten years ago, they said, and the military and its proxy party, the Union Solidarity and Development Party, hadn't shared any information during the handover about the railway – or about anything else. The lawmaker could only tell us that residents of his village had been 'worried and depressed' since it was built, because it had destroyed their livelihoods.

As in Moe Moe's village, the embankment had blocked the flow of a large stream from the western hills into the Ayeyarwady River, flooding the fields every year and ruining the crops.

'They are afraid,' he said, 'that there will be a big flood one year and their houses will be swept away.'

There were plans to build a new embankment to protect the village, and the lawmaker had started compensating people for their lost land, but there wasn't enough money to pay everyone. He said it was possible that at some point in the future the railway might be rebuilt, but he spoke as if someone else might build it. It was as if he could not believe that he was in power, or else that there were limits on this power, confining him to small, immediate actions, and preventing him from imagining himself as the agent of real change.

He and the other party members here had been activists, and for decades they had risked jail, torture and even death as they fought for democracy. Yet there was no feeling of victory here. After all, Myanmar's constitution had been written by the military, which held veto power over any amendments.

Stuck between military rule and genuine democracy, the party members were uncomfortable in their new position of power, and afraid of losing it. The lawmaker was nervous about answering my questions, and visibly relieved when a minibus pulled up outside the house, and another group of people in orange jackets stepped into the yard, bringing our interview to an end.

As the party members posed together for a photograph, a slight man in a white short-sleeved shirt offered to take Nay Aung and me to his village. He said he would call ahead to ask the village elders if they were willing to share their story with us, and we agreed to meet him there.

His village was a group of wooden houses that clung to the main road, and the elders were already waiting for us when we arrived, sitting around a table on a platform that was covered by a tin roof. They had laid out packets of cake and sachets of instant tea-mix. As they passed around a thermos of boiling water, so that we could all make tea, the head of the village, an old man with sun-beaten eyes, told us that not long ago this place had been remote and travel was only possibly by boat, or by foot. When the villagers learned that a railway was being built, they were so excited that many of them helped to build it, working for the contractor crushing stone to make ballast and digging earth. They were told they would be paid, but the contractor disappeared before the project was finished and they were never able to track him down.

'Many contractors go away like this,' Nay Aung explained to me. 'It's always the same problem.'

Instead of bringing development to the village, the railway and the road that was built soon afterwards brought 'big problems', the village head said. Morosely, he asked if we wanted to see what had happened to the village, and we all climbed down from the platform and walked towards the cluster of houses.

I could see before we got there that the entire village had been split in half by a fissure, six or seven feet deep and almost as wide. Having blocked the natural drainage channels, the railway contractors had bored a hole in the embankment so that water could flow through the village to the river.

'But they built the drain opposite the village, so that in the monsoon the water comes in so fast that the ground disappears,' the village head told us. 'When it rains at night we cannot sleep because we are so worried.'

He pointed to the eastern end of the village where the gorge narrowed between two houses that were balanced precariously on its edges. It then curved out of sight into a copse, where the roof of another house was visible among the trees. This was the path to the village school.

'Every year our children have to walk across the water, which is strong, and they cannot swim,' he said. 'It's very dangerous. We are worried that our babies will drown.'

I asked if there had been any accidents.

'Yes,' he replied, pointing to the house whose roof was just visible among the trees. 'Last year, one boy, he died.'

The boy had been trying to get home from school. I imagined him in his standard-issue green-and-white uniform, struggling against the current.

'Nyan Lin Maung, seven years old,' the village head said sadly, as we all stood there, looking towards the place where the boy had drowned. 'We lost our treasure.'

And this was not the worst of it, he told us. There were others who had drowned too, many people all at once. He advised us to visit Yaw Su, a village further along the line, whose residents, he said, had lost everything.

In the centre of Yaw Su village there was an expanse of packed earth that was partly being used as a volleyball pitch. We parked the car beside it and walked towards a small public library at one edge of the field, where books were stacked high on trestle tables, and people were reading on plastic stools, in the sparse shade of palm trees.

The library's owner, who had been arranging his books into piles, waved us over and began setting out three chairs for us in the sun. As we walked across the field, Nay Aung explained that the previous year, in July, a cyclone had struck Myanmar's western coast, bringing with it torrential rains and the worst flooding the country had seen in a century.[14] I remembered it well, I told him. I had reported from the delta, where entire villages were underwater, and relief was distributed by community groups in fragile wooden canoes. In Magway, a state of emergency had been declared, Nay Aung said.

'We are talking about the flooding,' he told the librarian, as we reached him, and sat down.

The librarian laughed.

'For the last one hundred years there was flooding every year of just one foot,' he said, lowering his palm to just above the ground. 'Last year, the floods were six or seven feet high.'

In early August, after weeks of torrential rain, government officials had driven through the village in a pick-up truck, announcing through megaphones that everything was under control. There were two dams near the village that were close to capacity but water was being released, and there was nothing to worry about.

'They went around shouting the same thing, all day until 6 p.m.,' the librarian said.

By that time, the water level in the village was so high that all the roads had flooded, and the pick-up truck sped away. Within two hours, the water the government had released from the dams was 'all over town'. They had released it into a nearby stream, assuming that it would drain into the river. The problem, of course, was that there was a railway in the way. 'This is a very funny story,' the librarian said – or it would have been if there had not been so much destruction.

As the water rose, he and his neighbours piled their possessions into the troughs they used to feed their animals, and tried to haul them to higher ground. But the water was rising too fast, he said. 'It was not normal water, it was very strong and travelling at high speed.' So they dropped everything and ran for their lives. They came to a military cantonment on a hillside, where they stayed for four days until the floods receded, and then they returned to the village to assess the damage. Most of the houses had disappeared, and their crops were buried beneath several feet of silt. The few buildings still standing were filled with debris, including trees and furniture from other houses, which had been swept through the village and deposited there by the floodwaters, and there were snakes and scorpions everywhere.[15]

The librarian asked if we wanted to see what had happened to the railway, and he hurried away and came back ten minutes later with another man, and two motorbikes. We jumped on the back, and they drove us through the village, then along a rough track that led into a wood. We drove on, through clouds of flying insects that filled the hot, still air. After a while we reached a grassy bank and parked the motorbikes. The librarian laughed again.

'This is my country's railway road,' he said, pointing to the bank, which was overgrown with bushes several feet high. Scrambling to the top, he dug around in the roots, revealing parts of the track. Ahead of us, two cows walked along the side of the railway, as if it was a road, stepping neatly around the bushes that blocked their path. But this was not what we had come to see, and the librarian soon led us back down the hill again. We drove alongside the railway for a while, across fields that had once been fertile but were now caked in sediment. Nothing could grow, in this thick, baked silt.

'How can we clear it away, when we have no money!' the librarian shouted.

We turned along a narrow, rutted track between fields where watermelons, beans and tomatoes had once grown on vines, and towards a wide, dry riverbed that stretched out to the horizon. Soon, the silt was too thick for the motorbikes, so we parked and walked, and then waded through it. When our shoes filled up with silt, we took them off and walked barefoot. We tramped through fields that looked from a distance as if they had been ploughed, but up close turned out to be covered in more baked sand.

'The crops are dead,' the librarian said, as we trudged across them. The beans and cow peas that had been planted there were no more than yellowing shoots.

Turning a corner, he pointed into the distance, where a twisted length of railway track was suspended in mid-air. Framing it, the ruined piers of a bridge were capped by masses of protruding rebar. The bridge and the railway track across it had been ripped apart by the force of the water released from the dams.[16]

Beyond the bridge, there were pools of brown water surrounded by pampas grass. Clouds of smoke billowed from trash piles on the horizon.

At the edge of the fields, we jumped down onto the dry riverbed, then walked out across the sand. When we were near the railway, the librarian bent down and drew a map in the sand with his finger, showing us how the floodwater had surged towards the Ayeyarwady River.

'It is our dream,' the librarian said, as we all looked up at the bridge and the suspended track, 'that the whole railway will be destroyed in this way, so that the water can find its way between our villages again.'

That evening, Nay Aung told me that a small section of the railway that had been ripped apart by floodwater was still in use, connecting several munitions factories beside the river.

'There are five or six gun factories, and they are all beside the railway line,' he said. 'Almost all the military's gun factories are on the Ayeyarwady west bank. That is why the government and officers are so sensitive about this area.'

Just beyond the factories, he said, at a place called Malun, there was a railway bridge connecting this otherwise isolated portion of track to another line that ran directly east to Myanmar's capital, Naypyidaw.

'A lot of people here believe the military built this railway so they could easily transport their guns,' he said.

This was not a complete surprise – I knew that Myanmar's defence industries had been based on the western bank of the Ayeyarwady River since the 1970s, when the military moved them from Yangon to sites it considered more secure.[17] At first there were just a handful of factories here, producing small-arms ammunition and copies of submachine guns, but this all changed after the nationwide uprising in 1988. Immediately after reasserting their control, when the generals ramped up defence imports, initiating an unprecedented expansion and modernization of the armed forces, at the same time they launched a major defence import substitution programme, building up the country's domestic arms industries.[18]

By the mid-2000s, around the time that the railway along the western bank of the Ayeyarwady River was being built, there were unconfirmed reports by foreign diplomats about new weapons factories in Magway, where North Korean technicians were allegedly spotted unloading large crates and heavy equipment from trains at stations on the military's new railway.[19] There was a rumour that Myanmar was building underground facilities and tunnels, and another that the generals had launched a nuclear and long-range missile programme – an allegation that the regime repeatedly denied.

Despite, or perhaps because of, the lack of evidence either way, international speculation about Myanmar's nuclear ambitions intensified throughout that decade. Capturing the mood of the time is a 491-page document entitled 'A sourcebook on allegations of cooperation between Myanmar (Burma) and North Korea on nuclear projects', which collates content published mostly in 2009, when the question was being discussed at the highest levels of the US government. It contains media articles and op-eds, diplomatic cables released by WikiLeaks, transcripts from US State Department briefings, policy notes, blogposts, directions from a colonial-era gazetteer, regime directives, maps, satellite imagery, photographs, and even schematic diagrams and sketches of machine parts, all aimed at figuring out whether Myanmar was developing banned weapons.[20]

Shipments were being analysed at the time, too, with the Institute for Science and International Security in 2010 asking why the regime had procured extremely high-precision, expensive dual-use industrial equipment from companies in Switzerland, Germany and Japan. Was it intended, as declared on the shipment, for building train engines, or was it part of a nuclear programme?[21]

That same year, an exiled Burmese media organization called the Democratic Voice of Burma published an investigation, based on information provided by a military defector.

Drawing on extensive testimony, as well as leaked documents and photographs, it seemed to prove beyond doubt that Myanmar had embarked on a programme to develop nuclear weapons. The generals wanted a deterrent against foreign intervention, and saw North Korea as a useful model to follow. They built facilities, imported equipment, and conducted some basic experiments, but a combination of poor management and a lack of resources and expertise meant they were unable to get much further – the sophisticated machine tools they had imported from Europe were so badly maintained they had become unusable.[22]

Rather than exposing the junta for having a nuclear weapons programme, the investigation appeared to have exposed it for not having one – at least, not one that could act as a serious deterrent. Instead, all the evidence pointed to the fact that although the generals might have wanted to build weapons of mass destruction, they had no idea what they were doing. As the intelligence company Janes concluded, after analysing the new evidence, 'Myanmar is vastly out of its depth in terms of nuclear pursuit.'[23]

But still, the rumours persisted. Veteran Swedish journalist Bertil Lintner, who has written extensively about Myanmar's relationship with North Korea, claimed in 2012 that a new factory in Magway near Malun and another factory on the railway line further north were both producing advanced weapons, based on North Korean designs. And the railway through Magway Region that connected the entrances to these factories, Lintner wrote, could 'only serve one major purpose: to transport heavy goods relevant to producing Scud-type missiles or supplying a nuclear programme'.[24]

Was he right that the railway was built to supply the military's factories? It's certainly possible. Of the estimated twenty-five defence industries in Myanmar, at least ten are believed to be in Magway, with another cluster further south at Pyay, where the railway connects to the delta.[25] Most of the stations on this railway are miles from population centres, and the railway was referred to in state media as a 'strategic railroad', a term usually reserved for railways built primarily for military use.

We also know that the railways carry military supplies, because the data, or at least part of it, is published in the country's statistical yearbooks. The railways transport some 23 million ton-miles each year of military accoutrements and stores. The numbers were much higher in the early 1990s, but they fell significantly at the same time the 'miscellaneous' category in the yearbooks ballooned, indicating some degree of reclassification. The railways also transport explosives and other dangerous goods, as well as materials for heavy industry, including iron, steel and machinery, and there are dedicated goods trains for military use.[26]

I asked Nay Aung if we could drive back across the bridge the next day to the part of the railway that was still operating. I wanted to see if we could find evidence that what he had told me was true – that the railway was not, like almost every other railway in the world, built for civilian use. Instead, if Nay Aung was right, it was built to strengthen the military, helping it to produce weapons and transport them to other parts of the country where it would use them, not against a foreign enemy, but against its own people.

Of course, as we had seen the previous day, parts of the track were unusable, and evidently weren't transporting anything. But that didn't mean they weren't built to supply the factories, only that the junta had struggled to build them. It also sounded like the factories were still connected by a functioning portion of track to the country's new capital in Naypyidaw. From there, weapons and ammunition could be easily supplied to wherever they were needed.

Nay Aung agreed to the trip, but said he didn't want to stop outside the factories because it was too dangerous. Instead, we could follow the railway south, to Malun Junction Station, where the line veered east towards the new railway bridge over the Ayeyarwady River that connected the weapons factories to Naypyidaw.

The next morning, we crossed back over the river to Minhla and headed south, speeding past the heavily guarded gates of two factories, one of which I later identified as the same factory that Bertil Lintner believed was being supplied by the railway with heavy goods to produce advanced weapons, and which he claimed covered no fewer than 100,000 acres of land.[27]

But looking at the decaying railway that ran past the gates, which was covered with mud and overgrown with weeds, it struck me how unlikely it was that these factories were producing sophisticated weapons. While Myanmar's military has never revealed details of its indigenous arms programme, there are clues elsewhere as to what might be being produced behind the heavily guarded walls. The condition of the railways is one clue, and the military's chronic mismanagement of state-owned factories is another; there is no evidence, in fact, that Myanmar's military has ever been able to produce advanced products of any kind.

At a state-owned rubber factory in southern Myanmar, which supplies the military with tyres and other products, I was told that production had almost stopped, because most of the machines were broken and nobody knew how to fix them. At Myitnge, the country's central workshop for railway-carriage repairs, a worker told me that operations were held back by what he called 'disqualification'. 'Nobody is qualified, including me,' he said.

Unable to reproduce imported parts domestically, Myanma Railways either had to keep paying foreign suppliers, or abandon the equipment. The head of the workshop had told me that Myanmar was unable to design its own railway carriages.

'We have access to design software,' he said, 'but we cannot use it.'

It's possible that the military's own factories are more sophisticated than those run by other parts of the state, but that seemed unlikely to me too. Some of their joint ventures with foreign companies have been profitable. But I had visited the headquarters of both of the military's conglomerates in Yangon, where clerks processed piles of paperwork by hand, much as they did in any other government office. Shielded from competition, and deriving much of their income from rent-seeking, there was nothing to suggest the military's businesses were much more sophisticated than any other state-owned enterprises.

Chronic underspending on education, a curriculum that actively discouraged independent thinking, a deep mistrust of foreign technocrats, and a national budget decimated by systemic corruption meant the military was unable to build anything of high quality, or even useful. Instead, it built things that were large. This meant new infrastructure projects like bridges, roads, railways and hydropower dams. It meant a vast new capital city, Naypyidaw, three times the size of London, but home to a population just a fraction of the size, with a twenty-lane highway that is hardly used outside the country's parliament. It meant sprawling new barracks, and military factories built on plots of land covering tens of thousands of acres, surrounded by high walls and defended by armed guards.

The problem was that while investing so heavily in creating an illusion of power, the generals had let everything else wither.

Leaving the factories behind us, Nay Aung and I passed the village where Nyan Lin Maung, the seven-year-old boy, had drowned. Soon afterwards Nay Aung parked the car.

On a ridge in the distance, a guard stood outside a building that otherwise appeared to be abandoned. This was Malun Junction Station, a wide empty place where the heat was so intense that as we crossed the field, sweat quickly pooled in the small of my back.

'This place is no good,' said Nay Aung as we came to the building, which had once contained accommodation for railway staff. Parts of the ceiling had fallen in and the floor was strewn with litter. The same words were scrawled in black spray paint on every wall.

'What does it say?' I asked him.

'If you trespass,' he read, 'you will go to jail.'

He took photographs of the graffiti and then he asked the guard, who had been watching us in silence, where the station was. Something about the place had made me nervous, and once again I found myself admiring Nay Aung's bravery. He had told me the previous evening that he wanted to be a photographer, but he was afraid because the job was too dangerous. Yet here he was, photographing a place where we were clearly not meant to be.

The guard, an employee of the railway department, set off across the baked earth beyond the buildings to the wide valley below, signalling that we should follow him. We scrambled after him down the hill, dislodging chunks of dry earth that tumbled ahead of us towards a small building that had been built into the bank near the bottom of the valley.

Long before we arrived I could see it was deserted. Inside,

the ticket-office window was boarded up, and the station sign lay discarded on the concrete floor. There were more signs warning against trespassing, and others that banned throwing stones. We asked the guard if the station was abandoned and he said no, a train came through here once a day or so. Trains came from the east, across the steel bridge over the Ayeyarwady, or south from Minhla, through the wide, dry river valleys that were choked with silt and past the weapons factory gates.

Leaving the guard beside the track we ran up the bank and across the field. Looking back, Nay Aung said it was a 'zombie' station – a place for the living dead.

Back in the car, as we scrolled through his photographs, he told me there were more weapons factories beside the railway, in Magway Region's mountainous north, more than 100 miles away. It was too far for him to come with me, but as we talked about the logistics of getting there, I remembered I knew someone who lived at the railway's northern terminus. An ethnic Chin man who went by the English name Dustin, he worked for a telecoms infrastructure company in Kalay, a town in the foothills of the Chin State mountains that border north-eastern India.

'In my opinion, the railway is for the army,' Dustin said, when I phoned him that evening. I asked what he meant. This wasn't a regular development project, he said. In his view, the regime had never done anything for local people, and this was no different.

'Look, if the railway is not for local people then it must be used by somebody,' he explained. 'It goes through a place called Kyaw, where there is a railway tunnel, and a very wide concrete road was also built there more than ten years ago. Nobody goes there, it's restricted. We think they're making chemical weapons – one journalist went out there to the road and took photographs and he was arrested.'

I asked him why he thought chemical weapons were being produced there.

'I have friends in the army and they know about the place,' he said simply.

When he hung up, I opened Google Earth on my laptop. Kyaw was 30 miles north of a place called Pauk, where the previous year a local journal had reported that the military was building a secret chemical-weapons factory. I found the article, which claimed the facility was built by top-ranking generals and Chinese technicians, beginning in 2009, on the orders of Than Shwe. The government had denied the report, saying it was just a standard ordnance factory, but it also confiscated copies of the magazine and sentenced five journalists from the publication under the colonial-era Official Secrets Act to ten years' imprisonment with hard labour.[28]

Another flurry of international articles had ensued, analysing the journal's claims, with two non-proliferation experts concluding that the site was 'clearly a high-value defense facility, as suggested by features such as the security perimeter, barracks-style housing, and helicopter pads', but that it was impossible to say, from an examination of satellite imagery alone, whether it was producing chemical weapons.[29]

Intrigued by what Dustin had told me, I searched online to see if I could find any articles that linked the northern part of the railway to the alleged chemical-weapons facility. Most of the information I found was in state media, about the construction of the railway itself. Work had started from both ends at once, the idea being that the two sides would eventually link up. Separating them was the Ponnya mountain range, and it was in the foothills of these mountains that the junta had run into problems.

'Personnel of Myanma Railways with the help of experts are building a 5,700 feet long tunnel,' announced the railway minister Win Sein in 1997, at the opening ceremony of a section of track between Kyaw, where Dustin claimed there was a restricted-access road, and Zee Pyar, the station nearest to the alleged chemical-weapons factory at Pauk. 'About 35 per cent of the work has been completed', on a key bridge along the route, the minister said, adding optimistically that the entire project would be completed 'soon'.[30]

So far, this was all fairly standard state media fare, but something in the article about the opening ceremony caught my eye. The short section of railway between Kyaw and Zee Pyar was built by the Tactical Operations Commander of the 101st Light Infantry Division, based in nearby Pakokku. LIDs are Myanmar's most battle-hardened units, deployed on special missions, and they report directly to the commander-in-chief of the army. The fact that such an elite division had been tasked with building part of a railway whose construction was otherwise entrusted to civilians seemed unusual. A week after this section of track opened, Than Shwe himself turned up to visit, and was briefed on tunnelling through the Ponnya range.[31]

But I was getting ahead of myself – that was 1997, and the weapons facilities that Dustin had spoken about weren't built until more than a decade later. Throughout this decade, with the rest of the railway now open, all efforts were focused on building the tunnel.

Horrifying stories reached northeast India about the working conditions, with one Chin refugee in Mizoram telling a human-rights group that soldiers had forced local people to carve out the rock face while hanging from ropes, saying that if they died their families would receive K10,000, or the equivalent of £5.

The Chin refugee said the local people were told, 'You are poor and have nothing. How could your family ever get such an amount of money? We are only concerned about completing the railroad, not about your life!'[32]

Railway minister Win Sein inspected the tunnel several times, as did his successor Pan Aung, and then Pan Aung's successor, Aung Min, the general who I would meet in Yangon. It was only in January 2007 that Prime Minister General Soe Win gave a speech, aired on national television, from the small railway station at Kyaw.

'Ponnyataung Railroad Tunnel is the longest of its kind in Myanmar,' he announced. This was the final piece of a railway connecting the country's northwest with its centre, completed with 'a great deal of tenacity' over a period of fourteen years. Soldiers, officials, and local people had all helped, in a monumental effort that had finally paid off.

'Humans conquest the nature after all,' the prime minister said, in a long speech that ended, like so many other speeches by Myanmar's generals, with a warning to resist foreign interference.[33]

Soon after it opened, a landslide blocked the Ponnyataung railroad tunnel. Around this time, a local news outlet published a story, citing unnamed military sources, which claimed the regime had almost finished building three nuclear reactors in the north of the country, including one at Ponnyataung. Local people in Kyaw were quoted, with one resident saying they were forbidden from going anywhere near the facility.[34]

Opening Google Earth again, I zoomed in on the tunnel. On the western approach, the railway from Kalay meandered over mountainous terrain, before disappearing into the side of the Ponnya range. Emerging from the other side of the tunnel it curved north for several miles before curling back around to meet the wide, new concrete road. The road and the railway then diverged, meeting again just south of Kyaw, and then crossing several times as they both continued south, to Zee Pyar. Nearby, I could see the weapons facility, with its helipad, security fencing and barracks-style housing, and just beyond it, the road came to an end at a small stream. It was just as Dustin had suspected: the road led to a weapons factory. But where did it originate? I scrolled up, following it back in the other direction, north past the railway stations at Zee Pyar and Kyaw, and then the turning to the Ponnyataung tunnel. It continued due north, further into the mountains, and after a while I came to more barracks-style housing, at a place called Kanthet, and then a high-security gate, and behind it a sprawling facility with features that were almost identical to those at the other end of the road – unusually large buildings with green ventilated roofs, security fencing, barracks and helipads, all set into the mountains.

By the time I closed my laptop that night, I was convinced that at the tunnel I would find the evidence I was looking for, that – just as Nay Aung and Dustin had claimed – this railway in western Myanmar had been built for military use. My anticipation only intensified on the journey north towards the mountains, partly because getting there was so difficult. Most of the new line between Magway and the tunnel was abandoned, so I crossed the Ayeyarwady River by train to a place called Taungdwingyi, and then spent a sleepless night travelling to the ancient city of Bagan on an express train, which travelled a little faster than a regular train, so that each time its carriages collided with the rail joints I was thrown into the air.

There was a train the next morning, back across the Ayeyar-wady River to Pakokku, the largest city in Magway Region. There, I was told that trains were only running north on isolated parts of the track, connecting villages and small towns where there were no guesthouses licensed to accept foreign guests.

'Train hard, bus easy,' the stationmaster at Pakokku told me. So I took the bus to Kyaw, at the southern end of the railway tunnel, where Dustin believed the military was making chemical weapons.

I was hoping there would be people in Kyaw whom I could interview, but when I was actually there, in the village teashop, watching the owner toast bamboo sticks filled with sticky rice, I realized that anyone I spoke to would be at risk. These were dangerous questions, of a type that had already landed local reporters in jail. Foreigners almost never came to Kyaw, and my arrival in the small village had already generated significant interest. Everyone had wanted to know what I was doing there, and so, reluctantly, I told them I was just passing through. I hired a car to take me to Gangaw, the town on the other side of the Ponnya range, where there was a guesthouse, whose owner agreed to let me stay, and told me she had friends who could drive me to the railway tunnel.

'They are Seventh-Day Adventists,' she said. 'They will be glad to help you.'

When the two men arrived, they were both wearing sunglasses, white shirts and grey, knee-length shorts. One of them, Kap Khan Mung, told me he could translate for me, and the other, Kam Do Mung, was his driver, who cackled when I told them their price for driving me there was extortionate – we all knew I had no other options.

As soon as we left the town, Kap Khan Mung began telling

me stories about how dangerous the road was, and how often it flooded.

'The road is very slippery,' he said. 'Lots of hairpin bends.'

It was easy to see why this part of the country was so vulnerable to flash floods – towering stacks of teak logs extended for miles on either side of the mountain road that crossed the Ponnya range. The forest had previously absorbed rainfall; without it, the bare mountainside cascaded with water when it rained. As the road rose into the mountains, I kept thinking that we had seen the end of the logging, but each time we turned another corner, there were more miles of felled teak ahead of us. Soon there were clearings in the forest, too, and trucks piled high with felled trees. In the hills of northern Magway, the illicit teak industry was thriving, and before long we were held up by a convoy of logging trucks as they navigated the hairpin bends.

As we made our way deeper into the hills, the road crossed and re-crossed the railway line.

'There are trains running on this mountain,' Kap Khan Mung told me.

This surprised me, because I had been told this part of the railway was abandoned. I challenged him, but he was adamant, telling me sharply that his friend was a train driver. On the subject of the weapons factories, he said he knew nothing, then when I pressed him, he claimed that he had only just moved here. Finally he snapped, saying that nobody here ever talked about the factories. He was sitting in the back of the car beside me, and he became so flustered that he picked up my cap from the seat between us, and thinking it was his, put it on.

What he did want to talk about was the history of the Chin people (like Dustin and many of the people who had been forced to build the junta's railway here, Kap Khan Mung was ethnic Chin), their loyalty to the British, and how they had ultimately been betrayed. The British had annexed the Chin hills after a long battle in the 1880s, but gave the chiefs significant autonomy, which eventually secured their support, and the Chin fought alongside the British in both world wars.

Conscripted into the Indian labour corps, men from the Chin hills were sent to France during the Second World War, where they were supposed to work as porters. But because they were trained hunters, they 'picked up guns and shot the enemy', Kap Khan Mung said, forming a gun with his hands. When King George VI heard about this, he invited ten Chin leaders to Buckingham Palace, where he treated them to tea.

'At the time the Chin people had eaten only corn, it was the first time they ate bread, butter and milk,' Kap Khan Mung said. 'King George promised the Chin people, if there is still England in the world, the Chin people will not face difficulties. The Chin people will not be hungry. If there are difficulties, we will help, the King promised.'

The Chin also fought alongside the British in Burma during the Second World War, but even so, King George didn't keep his promise, Kap Khan Mung said. When the British left, the Chin hoped they would be granted independence, but instead Burmese soldiers arrived.

'They reigned and destroyed for so many years, and now we have to struggle every day for our future,' he told me.

It was late afternoon by the time we turned off the road at a signpost to the tunnel.

'This road is the worst one,' Kap Khan Mung announced, as we bounced along it, pulling off the sunglasses he had been wearing and administering several eyedrops into each eye. 'It is terrible.'

It was terrible: steep, narrow, winding and strewn with boulders. The bushes on either side of the road closed in around us, until we were driving through a tunnel of undergrowth. As I tried to peer through it, a woman carrying a pickaxe loomed beside my window, startling me.

We scraped past the sides of boarded-up huts, along the edge of the road. After a while the undergrowth thinned, and the driver, who had not said a word during the journey, parked the car. There, ahead of us, was the railway track, curving towards a small station, and beyond the station was the entrance to the tunnel, which was flanked, improbably, by Tuscan columns.

On a hill above the station there were two houses, painted white and grey with little wooden porches, which presumably had once housed station staff.

'Who lives there?' I asked.

'The ghosts live there,' Kap Khan Mung replied, and the driver cackled again. 'It is the ghost home!'

We wandered around, looking for someone to speak to about the history of the place, but it was deserted. I suggested that we find the woman with the pickaxe, but by the time we had walked back through the undergrowth she was gone.

We traipsed back to the railway tunnel.

'It takes fifteen minutes to drive through,' Kap Khan Mung said as we all stared at it. 'We should not go inside. It is not safe.'

I walked along the track between the imposing columns to the entrance and peered inside. I had expected to find something here and I realized now, absurdly, that I was disappointed.

Over the days spent trying to get to the tunnel, I had become so caught up in the search, so fixated on reaching it and finding proof that this was part of a military railway, I hadn't considered the possibility that there would be nothing here to see.

Sitting at the edge of the track, I wondered how I had

allowed myself to become so obsessed with finding evidence that the military had built this railway to supply its weapons factories. By fixating on this small point, I had missed a bigger and more disturbing possibility.

Was it possible, I wondered, that the military's railways – all of its railways – were weapons in themselves? Everything I'd heard on my journey so far indicated that they weren't built for economic development, as railways usually were, but instead to increase the military's power, through the state. The use of mass forced labour on the railways had helped the generals to break multiple insurgencies. Building railways also required a large military presence, which subsequently become permanent, helping the military to wield power in the far reaches of Myanmar. In areas that were already under military control, contracts for new railways had enriched officials and their cronies, engendering loyalty. And all over the country, new military bases and factories were connected to the railway network, making it easier (at least, on the lines that still functioned) for soldiers and weapons to be deployed against Myanmar's people.

Two days earlier, Nay Aung and I had stopped at a small station called Sagu. It was abandoned, and built in the same style as the others we had seen, and was in a similar state of disrepair. Across the road from the station there was a military compound, where young soldiers were playing football, their bare chests gleaming in the twilight. Beside the pitch there had been a sign facing the road, and Nay Aung had translated the words on it: 'Only when the Tatmadaw is strong will the nation be strong,' he read.

It was this philosophy that guided everything the military did, transforming even the most basic development tasks into exercises in the abuse of power. The entire railway-building project, like the nationwide expansion of the road network that was taking place at the same time and the frenzied construction of new military bases along these new railways and roads, revealed the single-minded focus of an illegitimate regime that knew its only hope of control was to physically inhabit every corner of the country it occupied. It was a complete subversion of the way governments should function: at the expense of their people, rather than for their benefit.

Just like the nuclear wonks at their computers thousands of miles from Magway, I had been trying to pin down evidence of something specific, when the problem was evident everywhere. Over decades, as the military slowly and relentlessly strengthened itself, including through the construction of infrastructure like this railway, people were dying. They were dying because they were being killed with weapons produced at the factories in these mountains, but they were also being killed in a multitude of mundane and preventable ways. As the generals monopolized the country's resources, they were dying from poverty, or disease, or because money that could have been spent on extending their lives was wasted.

The story that really mattered here, I thought as I sat on the railway tracks, was that Myanmar's military was becoming increasingly powerful and nobody, except small groups of insurgents, had done anything to stop it.

Not only this, but the military's capacity for violence was the very thing that had strengthened it, by engendering fear and enabling it to crush popular resistance. The more powerful the military became, the less likely its authority was to be challenged, either within the country or internationally, regardless of whether its legitimacy was accepted.

As the world heralded a new era of political and economic freedoms in Myanmar, following the election of Aung San Suu

Kyi's party, the generals were taking the opportunity to travel widely and stock up on new weapons. They were visiting Brussels to meet European Union officials and touring defence industries in Austria and Germany.[35]

At home, they were becoming stronger still, taking advantage of newly lifted trade restrictions to build better factories, largely undisturbed, in these mountains and other parts of the country where the details of the abuses they had inflicted on their people were already being forgotten.

Who would realize, if they stumbled across this place, that this collapsed tunnel and the dilapidated railway beyond it had claimed so many lives?

'Come,' Kap Khan Mung shouted, disturbing my thoughts. 'We are leaving.'

I travelled from a small station near the tunnel to Kalay at the railway's northern terminus, on the most dilapidated train I had seen yet. I was heading north to meet Dustin, who lived in Kalay, and who would introduce me to several people who had been forced to build this railway in the 1990s along with hundreds of thousands of others, mirroring the events that had taken place during the same decade in Myanmar's far south.

The service left in the early morning and I had arrived at the station in the dark, to find two small carriages beside the platform that were bounded by open-air balconies for storing cargo. Shining my torch inside one of the carriages, I saw there were dozens of people sleeping on benches that were fixed along the walls. They had spent the night there, wrapped in thick blankets, to avoid travelling to the station from their remote villages in the dark.

I found a space on one of the benches, beside a young boy

wearing a woollen hat, who was sleeping on his brother's knee. Slowly, as dawn broke, the train filled up with more passengers and their cargo. A builder in a hard hat who was carrying a laptop bag sat opposite me. Beside him, a young woman dressed in black sat down, and put on a large straw bonnet that she fixed in place with a floral ribbon. She rubbed her arms and eyed my T-shirt disapprovingly.

'You will be cold,' she said.

A light shone through the darkness as the train's engine backed towards us, connecting with a clunk, followed by a lot of banging, as if it was being fixed into place with a hammer. A guard sold me a ticket through the open window, and introduced me to the policeman on board. Then he tested his whistle, the driver tested his horn and fired up his engine, and finally, we inched out of the station.

Once we picked up some speed it was, indeed, very cold. We were a long way north of the dry zone now and as the wind whipped through the holes in the carriage where windows and doors should have been, and up through the broken floorboards, everyone pulled their clothes tightly around themselves, trying to keep warm. But as the sun rose and golden light flooded the carriage, I was glad of the fresh air. My companions shrugged off their blankets and stretched, soaking up the warmth of the morning sun. The policeman on board lit a cheroot and smoked it on the balcony at the back of the train. A monk went outside to join him, and held onto the edge of the balcony as if he was standing at the prow of a ship, with his robes billowing behind him.

When we stopped at a small, rural station, everyone climbed out. The guard appeared at my window and told me to get off the train too. There was a teashop at the station, whose owner had set out bowls of breakfast for us all on a trestle table: a traditional Chin meal of corn porridge with fried bread. As we all ate together, the woman who had warned me about the cold insisted on buying me a cup of tea.

For the rest of the journey, I stood at the back of the carriage with the policeman, who showed me how to hang off the edge of the balcony when the train was moving. It was exhilarating, holding onto the rusting bars with only a small wooden step to prevent us from falling, as the train rattled over bridges, and we peered down into the clear waters below.

We arrived into Kalay in the afternoon, a place distinguished by its abundance of churches from every Christian denomination imaginable. There were Nazarenes, Methodists, Baptists, Presbyterians, Seventh-Day Adventists, Latter-day Saints, members of the Endtime Message Church and of the Tahan Assembly of God.

'Seventy per cent of people here are Christian,' Dustin told me as we toured the town.

Many Chin people spoke excellent English because of their links to the church. Dustin, however, spoke particularly good English, because he loved country music, and had learned the lyrics to hundreds of songs when he was young.

He and his friends were much more cosmopolitan than the Burmese farmers I had met in central Myanmar. Privately educated at church-run schools with international connections, they wore Western clothing, listened to the Eagles, and travelled overseas. But as an ethnic and religious minority, they had suffered disproportionately under military rule, and their international links were so strong partly because so many Chin had fled the country as refugees.

Now, over dinner at an Indian restaurant in town, Dustin and I were discussing the railway. He spoke as if the events that took place here in the 1990s were unique; like other people I would meet in Kalay, he had no idea that other people in other parts of the country were being forced to build railways at the same time.

Hundreds of thousands of people, he told me, including his cousin, his uncle, and the headmaster at his school, were forced by the military regime to build the railway that I had just travelled on. They had been made to abandon their livelihoods and endure months of backbreaking work, while being abused, beaten and even killed. There was not even a point to their suffering, he said; after the tunnel collapsed, the railway that was supposed to connect their homeland to central Myanmar led nowhere.

Over the next few days, Dustin and I visited members of his family and others he knew who had worked on the railway, listening to stories that were remarkably similar to those I had heard in the south.

We went to see his former headmaster, who lived on a farm in a village outside the town. A stocky, bespectacled man with greying hair, he recalled how he had only just been appointed the village chief in early 1993 when soldiers from a local infantry battalion showed up in a convoy of more than ten cars, in uniform and carrying guns.

Reading from his old diary, he told us how the village heads had been called to a meeting, and how each village was assigned a section of the railway to build. At least one person from every house in every village had to work; any family that couldn't send someone to work had to pay.

They had to provide their own food and tools and they slept at the worksites, under the trees if it was dry, or beneath shelters fashioned from branches. There were no machines: the local people built the railway by 'manpower only', the old man told us with some pride.

'I never believed it could be done,' he said, 'but in the end we did it.'

The military at the same time was increasing its use of civilian porters and human shields in this region, in campaigns against ethnic insurgent groups. As it consolidated control, it built new barracks across the remote, mountainous region, supplied by new roads. There were new hydropower dams and irrigation canals, all built with forced labour. Entire villages were razed in mass-relocation campaigns, prompting allegations for the first time in this part of the world of ethnic cleansing. An estimated 40,000 people fled across the border into India and Bangladesh, and from there they sought asylum across the globe.[36]

Just like in the south, there had been preventable deaths. A man that Dustin's former headmaster knew was crushed by a falling tree. There were landslides, people drowned, others died from starvation, because they fell sick, or because they were beaten or tortured to death. If any village failed to complete their assigned tasks on time, soldiers would beat the village leader.

The local infantry battalion was feared, the former headmaster said, because of its brutality. Its soldiers around this time allegedly detained four Chin community leaders, accusing them of supplying weapons to a local insurgent group, the Kuki National Army. They killed one of the men first, a pastor, breaking his bones, cutting open his mouth to the neck, and then wrapping a plastic bag over his head. They made the other three prisoners touch his mutilated body, and then tortured them, cutting and burning their skin and pouring salt into their wounds. Two of them died this way. The last man, a village headman, they buried alive.[37]

Because of this and other terrifying stories that circulated between the villages, nobody at the worksites complained about the hard labour. They were guarded at all times by soldiers, according to Dustin's former headmaster. Miming a gun being fired, he said, 'We worked because we feared the gun.'

It was testament to his bravery that he challenged one of the soldiers who tried to assign more work to his village.

'After a serious argument, the soldier tried to beat me, and then aimed his gun at my chest, from this porch,' he said, pointing towards the open door. Luckily for him, an official who worked for the regime but was also sympathetic to the villagers managed to calm the soldier down.

Later we visited Dustin's uncle, a jovial, passionate man who wore a ragged vest that exposed his tanned chest, and who was still angry about being forced to work on the railway for free.

'The soldiers never helped us,' he said. 'They were just standing next to us, always shouting at us to work well, or work fast.'

I asked him if the government had provided them with anything.

'Nothing,' he spat. 'This was how they ruled, and we did not dare to get angry, or strike back.'

There was no point to the railway, he added, echoing Dustin's complaint. Few people wanted to travel by train because 'they knew the quality very well – it was built by force, and we were only thinking about how to get the job done quickly'. Anyway, he said, there was no reason for local people to travel to the other end of the line.

I remember my last day in Kalay vividly because it was the last time I believed that the changes taking place in Myanmar since the 2015 election, however imperfect, were moving in the right direction. Nothing I had seen or heard so far on my journey had shaken that belief. The stories I had heard concerned events that had taken place in the past, sometimes decades earlier. I had not wondered while listening to them whether Myanmar was changing for the better, but instead what it meant to try and move on from the past, within the bounds of a constitution written by the military. What did it mean to try and move on, when elected lawmakers were still nervous, and journalists couldn't do their jobs without being harassed, or worse, and there were places in the country where nobody dared to go? How wide was the space to push for reforms, for equitable peace, for genuine development and for civic freedoms? How much was the military willing to give?

I spent the last afternoon before this illusion of progress was shattered with Dustin's uncle in his garden in a Kalay suburb, a lush overgrown place overrun with fruit trees, where pigs and rabbits roamed.

'*Parlez-vous français?*' the old man asked me when we arrived.

'A little,' I replied.

'I lived in Paris for five years,' he said, studying me carefully. 'I used to speak a bit of French. *Mais je l'ai oublié, parce qu'il n'y a personne ici* . . . to practise with,' he finished, in English. He had lived in Germany, too, and had visited Blackpool as one of two Burmese representatives at a Methodist conference.

He was a tall, proud old man, with neatly trimmed grey hair, and he lived here in comfort, in a wooden house painted blue, with a swing seat hanging from the wide front porch.

'There was a big garden here, once,' he said, waving his hands towards the yard. 'I sold off most of the land because it became too difficult to manage.'

We spent hours that afternoon talking and eating fruit from his trees: slices of pomelo, sweet lemons in green skins and beans imported from America. In the evening we drove to his church, a three-storey building painted dark green in a sprawling compound that bordered a bamboo forest. There was an expanse of grass and a yard where children played on bicycles and roller skates. There was a youth chapel, a Bible school, a printing press, a bookshop, a library and even a church-run hospital. Dustin explained as we wandered around the grounds that people here finally felt free to practise their religion, a liberty that had only felt real after the previous year's election. It was a long, happy day in which I felt, for the last time in Myanmar, a real sense of hope about the country's future.

But that night, 9 October 2016, I was packing my bag in preparation to catch an overnight bus to central Myanmar, and then across the mountains to Rakhine State, on the border with Bangladesh, when I received a text from Nay Aung.

'Hi mate,' it said. 'This morning had conflict at Rakhine Division. Please check news online and let me advise you this moment you should not go to Rakhine Division.'

I pulled up the news on my phone: the BBC was reporting that attacks targeting police outposts on Myanmar's border with Bangladesh had left nine Border Guard Police dead. Police said that militant members of the Rohingya minority (the predominantly Muslim ethnic group whose oppression attracted outrage on the international stage in 2017), armed with knives and slingshots, had coordinated the attacks near Maungdaw in the north of the state. Several attackers had also reportedly been killed in the raids. The assailants had looted more than fifty guns, and thousands of bullets.[38] I phoned Nay Aung, who was furious about the attacks.

'They killed the police,' he said. 'They should not do that.'

He implored me not to travel and then threatened to tell Special Branch that I planned to go.

'It's for your security,' he said. I called several contacts in

Yangon and Rakhine, who said they thought it would be safe on the road through the mountains. I tried to reassure Nay Aung. I would spend a couple of days in Mrauk-U, the capital of the ancient Rakhine kingdom that was now a tourist destination, and if the fighting did not escalate, I would continue on to Sittwe, the state capital.

The following evening, back in central Myanmar, I waited for the bus in a guesthouse lobby. It was due to arrive at 8 p.m., but that hour passed, and then another. Sometime before midnight there was a shout and a decrepit vehicle pulled up. It was a wreck, without seatbelts, and fitted instead with tattered cushions and a powerful air-conditioning system that reduced me to shivering within minutes.

After midnight, we reached a barely paved road that ascended into the Rakhine mountains. At each turn, as the bus corkscrewed higher, the vehicle pitched as if it would tip over the edge of the pass. I was worried, because Nay Aung had been worried, about the safety of the road, and my restless sleep, when it came, was filled with dreams of stolen weapons. I was heading towards the epicentre of a storm, and the beginning of Myanmar's descent into yet another long period of catastrophe.

PART TWO

'The general belief in the intrinsic value of roads, railways, and other forms of public works as instruments of native welfare must be dismissed as an illusion; only too often they do more harm than good to those whom they are supposed to benefit.'

J.S. Furnivall, *Colonial Policy and Practice: A Comparative Study of Burma and Netherlands India*[1]

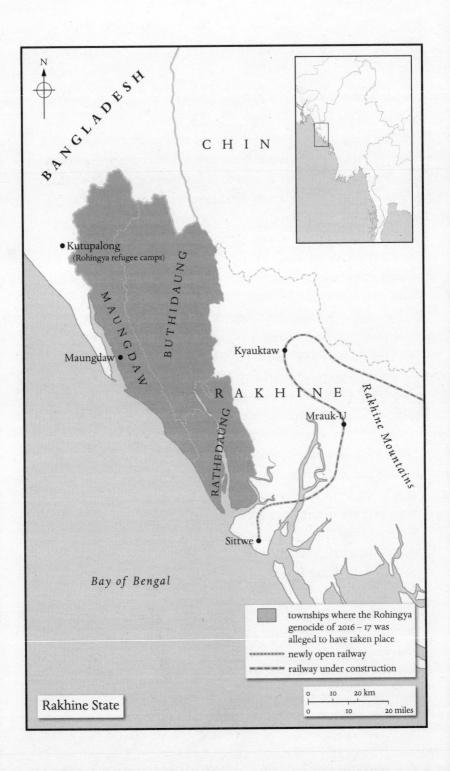

N

BANGLADESH

C H I N

• Kutupalong
(Rohingya refugee camps)

M A U N G D A W

B U T H I D A U N G

Maungdaw •

Kyauktaw •

R A K H I N E

R A T H E D A U N G

Mrauk-U •

Rakhine Mountains

Sittwe •

Bay of Bengal

townships where the Rohingya
genocide of 2016 – 17 was
alleged to have taken place

newly open railway

railway under construction

0   10   20 km

0   10   20 miles

Rakhine State

4.
Rakhine

Than Myint greeted me, unsmiling, in the porch of his house. A small, wiry man, dressed in a short-sleeved shirt and a simple *paso*, he shook my hand, telling me he hadn't slept well the previous night. I had slept badly too. The mattress at my hostel was damp, much like everything else in Mrauk-U during the monsoon. My walk through the town's maze of streets that morning had revealed trees weighed down by layers of moss and buildings swollen with rain.

There were neglected structures everywhere, sinking into the marshy ground and creating the impression, to the casual observer, of faded splendour. Walking among the temples and stupas on the outskirts of Mrauk-U, I had been stunned by their sublime beauty, cast against the Rakhine mountains.

But the derelict condition of the town's cultural heritage was a source of immense anger to Than Myint. To him, it represented the subjugation of the Rakhine people after their once-powerful kingdom was sacked by the Burmese Konbaung dynasty two centuries earlier and handed over soon afterwards to the British – and the mistreatment the people here had endured ever since.

As we sat down at a table in his small yard, the amateur archaeologist spoke to me about the past as if it had happened only recently. He described how in 1784, the Burmese army had trekked over the vast mountain range that once divided the

Burmese Empire from the Rakhine kingdom. The soldiers sacked Mrauk-U and looted the Maha Muni, a twelve-foot cast-bronze image of the Buddha that was the pride of the Rakhine people. As the defeated Rakhine fled, were captured and forced into slavery, or died from disease or starvation, much of the kingdom's cultural and intellectual heritage was lost, including the documents in the royal library, which burned to the ground.

It was this war that first drew this part of the world into another war with another, stronger empire, setting its history on a course that few in the Rakhine court could have foreseen. When Mrauk-U fell, large numbers of its inhabitants, both Buddhists and Muslims, fled into territory that was claimed by foreigners from the West – the British East India Company, which controlled large parts of India's northeast. Rakhine rebels used Company territory to stage attacks on Burmese-held outposts, sparking retaliatory raids across the border. Before long, British Indian soldiers had been drawn into the fight. After Burmese soldiers killed a group of sepoys at a British outpost, in 1824 the Governor General of India declared war on the Burmese king. It was a border dispute between two aggressive and expansionist empires, and what followed was a two-year war.

When the Burmese eventually surrendered, having put up a fierce resistance but in the end finding their muskets and cannonballs no match for British rockets, they were forced to pay a £1 million indemnity, and to hand over several regions that would be incorporated into British India. Two of these became the first pieces of British Burma, which was administered as a province within India: Tanintharyi, the country's southern peninsula, where I had been just a few weeks earlier, and Rakhine.[1]

At independence in 1948, more than 120 years later, the

British would hand political power back not to the Rakhine people, but to Burmese nationalist leaders hundreds of miles away, in Rangoon (now Yangon). Sitting in the ruined landscape of Mrauk-U, surrounded by the scars of these events, I understood why they mattered so much. Historical memory was longer here than it had been on the other side of the mountains, because the Rakhine people still saw themselves as living in an occupied state.

When he was sure I had understood the problem, the archaeologist pointed across the road to a small, polluted lake that was framed by a collection of half-buried stupas, where several children were fishing. His house, like the other buildings in the town, was built among sprawling ruins: ancient temples, stupas and walls that had been incorporated into expanding neighbourhoods, or partially demolished to clear space for hotels, built for tourists who never came. What was needed, Than Myint said, was a 'great excavation plan' that would restore Mrauk-U and the ruined cities in the nearby river valleys to their rightful position in history. But as the vice chair of the Mrauk-U Ancient Cultural Heritage Conservation Organization, Than Myint was one of just a handful of people who were fighting to stop the inappropriate development, demolition and botched restoration work that were now threatening to obscure this history forever.

There was so much work to be done that he hardly knew where to start, he said, studying me seriously from beneath his bushy eyebrows. 'Mrauk-U needs many, many plans.'

Even though the military regime had recently transferred power to new, elected officials, it was impossible to work with the officials in Aung San Suu Kyi's government. Just like everyone else in Myanmar, he said, they had been living for fifty years in what he called 'the basket of the military junta'. Their perspectives had been so limited by this experience that they behaved in much the same way as junta officials had done.

Aung San Suu Kyi's government had inherited the administrative systems designed by the junta, and even though many of the new officials hated the military, their views had nevertheless been shaped by its ideology, particularly when it came to ethnic minorities and their cultural heritage.

'They believe that only Burmese culture is important,' Than Myint told me, sadly.

A Rakhine nationalist party had been the only ethnic minority group in the country to win a majority in a regional legislature in the recent election, but Aung San Suu Kyi had disappointed the Rakhine people by appointing a member of her own party as the state's chief minister.[2] Any hope of change that had existed here in the run-up to the election was already dwindling. Facing what they feared would be further erosion of their culture under the country's new leadership, many ethnic Rakhine were turning to the past, and finding solace in an older identity that was anchored in their once proudly independent kingdom.

Than Myint had always been aware of his people's troubled history, but for most of his life he hadn't thought about it too much. He was a civil servant in the junta, and he kept his head down, knowing that this was the best way to survive while the military remained in power.

But then one day in 2009, he realized this was no longer possible – and it was this moment that I had come to talk to him about. Walking through the town that day, he noticed there were bulldozers parked among the pagodas. Than Myint had always been a conservative, cautious man. But now, for the first time in his career, he started asking questions, and the more he asked, the more he felt compelled to keep asking.

He learned that military vehicles had rolled over the mountains, signalling the start of multiple new infrastructure projects. New battalions were arriving from central Myanmar, and there were unfamiliar soldiers on the roads. There were rumours that a military airport would be built near Mrauk-U. Stories of land confiscations, with administrators and soldiers relocating entire villages, forcing their residents to give up their homes and farmland with little or no compensation, were circulating. This was because the junta wasn't just building an airport; it was also building a great railway that would connect sleepy, tropical Rakhine State across the mountain range that separated it from the Ayeyarwady River valley, to central Myanmar.

Despite being conquered by a Burmese king, annexed by the British government, and then incorporated into independent Myanmar, Rakhine had remained isolated, neglected and largely untethered, from both the British Empire during more than a century of occupation, and from the Burmese state. But now it was being pulled towards the centre of modern Myanmar. Within just a few years, it would come to play a central role in the military's attempt to solidify a unified nationalist ideology in Myanmar's people that was both shaped by and defined in opposition to the British colonial state – and that would require a dramatic national reimagining of Rakhine's complex history.

Junta officials claimed the railway was being built for local people, but Than Myint knew that local people had never wanted a railway, or asked for one. Instead, he saw it as an incursion, and when he got hold of the plans, he was outraged. The railway would cut through some of Mrauk-U's most sacred religious sites, posing what he saw as an existential threat to the ruined city.

'They marked the path for the railway across the Dhan-yawadi Palace grounds,' he told me earnestly, with his elbows propped up on the table. Dhanyawadi was the capital of the first Rakhine kingdom, and home to the Maha Muni shrine, which had once housed the bronze Buddha statue, before Bur-mese soldiers carried it away over the mountains. Today, the plundered temple remains a pilgrimage site for Rakhine Bud-dhists, who view the stolen icon as a symbol of lost Rakhine sovereignty. Building a railway through the palace grounds would have been considered the gravest of insults. Yet officials from Myanma Railways and the junta's archaeological depart-ment had already approved the route.

The realization shocked Than Myint into action. Before he knew it, he found himself making plans with a close friend, a Rakhine historian and a former director in the archaeological department, to lead a protest. At the same time, the junta's prime minister Thein Sein, who would soon become Myan-mar's president, was touring the area regularly, to inaugurate newly built sections of the advancing railway, and a new road that would connect Rakhine over the mountains to the south.[3]

On his visits Thein Sein gave speeches about the importance of development, and of fostering what he called 'Union Spirit'. This was the junta's shorthand for one of its central myths, which was used to justify the state's physical expansion into Rakhine. Union Spirit represented the responsibility, shared by all of Myanmar's indigenous 'national races', including the Rakhine people, to overcome the divisions created during the British occupation and to restore the nation (meaning the ter-ritory delineated by the colonial administration, and claimed by the modern state) to its former unity.

At the time, the junta's railway minister was Aung Min, the general who built the railway through the delta in the wake of

Cyclone Nargis. During one of our later meetings in Yangon, Aung Min would explain to me the philosophy that guided the junta's railway-building drive in ethnic states, including in Rakhine.

'There are 135 ethnicities in Myanmar,' he told me, referring to an official list of indigenous races that the junta published after 1988, and which didn't include the Rohingya. 'As part of nation-building they needed to have a common ideology and a national identity.' To help build this identity, the country's dictator Than Shwe had instructed his cabinet, including Aung Min, to remove the geographical barriers to integration in the country's borderlands, including by building new railways that would connect the ethnic states to the centre.

Than Shwe recognized that British-built railways in central and northern Myanmar had transformed isolated villages into thriving economic corridors supported by large towns, whose populations shared a common identity. The power of these railways to create some degree of homogeneity under a central state authority, which could dispatch its agents into areas that were no longer considered remote, bringing with them new ideas,[4] had inspired Myanmar's leader, who was now trying to impose the military's ideology on Myanmar's diverse people.

'The Senior General wanted to promote a Myanmar identity, just like in America where different races live together but call themselves American,' Aung Min had explained, referring to Than Shwe.

'After building railways across the country, people here will say – we are all Myanmar. So we must build railways, the Senior General said.'

I wondered whether the irony of trying to build a national identity after independence by following the British example of building railways had occurred to the generals. Than Shwe apparently didn't question the idea that the physical expansion of the state, measured in miles of new roads and railways, would somehow create the conditions needed for people to live together peacefully under its guardianship.

But then it was not only the British who used railways to weld disparate groups of people together. As early as the mid-nineteenth century, leaders of countries around the world saw railways as a unifying force.[5] And the junta's railways were not just designed to unify, they were specifically designed to be internal corridors that stopped just short of the country's borders, orienting the state inwards and directing the people in the borderlands towards the centre.

But rather than producing 'cordial relations among the national races', as one state media report optimistically claimed,[6] the railway in Rakhine exacerbated divisions. One exiled media outlet accused the junta of 'launching a psychological offensive' and, in the words of one resident quoted, of systematically destroying everything the Rakhine people valued.[7]

Now, outside his small house in Mrauk-U, Than Myint was drawing a map in my notebook, showing the railway heading north from the Rakhine capital of Sittwe, and then curving back on itself towards the sacred Maha Muni temple. The staff at a small museum nearby had persuaded the contractors to avoid building through the temple itself, he said, but the route still passed through its grounds.

It then bore south, directly through the ruins of Vesali, the capital of the second Rakhine kingdom. At the same time, contractors bulldozed a path through the Mrauk-U archaeological zone, even though large parts of the railway to the west were not yet finished. In Than Myint's view, this revealed, once again, 'their sincere intention to destroy our cultural heritage'.

If this was the regime's intention, there would be nothing too surprising about it. All across Myanmar's ethnic states, the generals were destroying sites of cultural importance and replacing them with infrastructure: hydropower dams were flooding indigenous land, special economic zones were flattening ancient villages, and railways and roads were being built through sacred forests.

'Three railway stations in the middle of our three ancient Rakhine cities,' Than Myint announced, putting his pen down. He had painstakingly written in my notebook the names of the pagodas, walls, platforms and moats that had been ruined. Some, he labelled 'crossed and destroyed', others 'crossed half' or 'mostly destroyed'. Now, he closed the notebook and stared at me.

'The first in Dhanyawadi, the second in Vesali, and the third in Mrauk-U,' he said. 'What do you think that means?'

Before I'd had time to reply, he told me the answer was obvious. By building railway stations in the middle of these ruined cities, the junta hoped that they would be overrun with people.

'That way, we would destroy our own culture, by ourselves,' he said.

I asked him if he would take me to see the railway, and he disappeared around the side of the house to fetch his motorbike. Hitching up his *paso*, he climbed on, telling me to jump on the back. As he revved the engine I gripped his shoulders, and we buzzed together along the town's narrow streets. Before long, we had emerged from the dense mass of buildings onto an open track, and Than Myint's motorbike was alternately jumping over the rocks that littered our path, and sinking into patches of soft ground, releasing immense jets of mud.

'Look at these roads,' he shouted over his shoulder. 'This is why the Rakhine people want independence.'

Soon we were driving along the abandoned railway route, which was elevated above a swamp. Several times we had to get off the motorbike and push it. It had been damp and muggy when we left Than Myint's house, but now the rain was falling hard, and our clothes were soaked. The mud became thicker, and more difficult to drive through; up ahead, two men and a dozen children were trying, without success, to push an over-turned oil truck back onto the path. Beyond them, we overtook a lone monk and a cowherd, who were striding barefoot through the mud. They knew what I would soon find out, that shoes were useless on this road.

Abandoning the motorbike when it finally stalled, we continued on foot to a ditch that marked the edge of a field. Jumping over the ditch, we sank immediately into the swamp. It was wet enough that we could wade through it, past a herd of grazing cows, to a concrete platform and the mildewed frame of a railway station. The concrete walls had cracked, holding up a roof that was no longer there. The window frames were rusting, and inside, the ticket office and concourse were overrun with weeds. Pointing into the distance, Than Myint showed me where the route that had been carved out for the track cut across an old city wall.

As we picked our way through the abandoned station buildings, Than Myint told me about his campaign to stop the railway being built. Having exhausted all other options, he and his friend soon began seriously considering a plan that just a few months earlier would have seemed unthinkable: they would write a petition to the country's dictator, Than Shwe. After sending the letter, they learned from a friend in the military that if the timing had been different, they would have been arrested and imprisoned, charged with fabricating complaints to interrupt a national project. But the generals were distracted, having just held an election that would end decades of junta rule, and rather than imprisoning Than Myint and his historian friend, they agreed to find a new route for the railway.[8] As more civic freedoms were introduced in the years that followed, Than Myint continued lobbying the government, writing to officials, holding meetings, and speaking at conferences. The year before I visited him, the project was suspended, and the junta's archaeological department agreed to remove the stations it had built.

Not only had the junta's railway done nothing to improve relations between the central Burmese state and the Rakhine people, but the fragments of track that now scarred the landscape were instead a physical reminder of the divisions between them. Rather than creating a shared identity, these fragments had become symbols of a coercive relationship.

But while Than Myint might not have agreed with me, I also saw them as symbols of resistance. What remained of the railway represented an incursion that had ultimately failed, and the temples in Mrauk-U might be dilapidated but they were still standing.

Than Myint said the government was still trying to find a new route around the town. The problem was that there was no other route. To the east of the town the Laymyo River flooded the plains each year, and any new railway would need to be partially rebuilt after every monsoon. There were also the ruins of another ancient city, Parein, to consider, which was believed to be about 900 years old; flooding over the subsequent centuries had buried most of the city's walls and monuments, and nobody knew exactly where they were. To the west of Mrauk-U the land was laced with creeks, and a railway would need to be supported along its entire length by bridges. Wherever it was built, Than Myint said, it would mean more flooding; the abandoned embankments already cut across two valleys, channelling water from the Laymyo Valley into the town.

Even if a solution was found in Mrauk-U, the government would never be able to build a railway across the Rakhine mountains. As the deputy commissioner of British Burma concluded in an 1888 report, the mountains were 'so maze-like in character that any line which could be selected, whether following the valleys in their contortions, or zigzagging over the spurs to obtain the necessary incline' would be too expensive to be worth building.[9] A later survey found that any railway would need to shadow the river, which was closely hemmed in on both sides by high ranges of unusually steep hills, and would require dozens of bridges: in three days, the survey party waded across the river fifty-six times to try to find a way through.[10]

Much like the British more than a century earlier, the junta had no access to modern tunnel- and bridge-building technology. Its engineers were hardly able to build functional railways even on flat ground, let alone through mountains whose soil was badly suited to supporting heavy structures.

'Unlike other *yoma*,' the archaeologist said, using a Burmese word for a mountain range, 'in our Rakhine *yoma*, the rocks are soft.'

We walked together across the fields to a nearby pagoda, which, like the abandoned station, was receding into the undergrowth. Inside the temple, the Buddha statues that gazed down from the walls were coated in layers of lurid green moss. Than Myint pointed out the botched restoration work, as we walked along narrow passages. Several officials from the archaeological department were camping in a central courtyard with their families. Young women shrieked with laughter and chased each other through the halls, while others slept on mats, beside the embers of a small fire.

'We don't really know where our people came from,' Than Myint reflected, as we sidestepped the sleeping women. One of the biggest challenges to finding out, he said, was that many of the documents that would have substantiated the distinguished Rakhine chronicles were lost when the royal library burned to the ground. Other accounts of Rakhine history were written by ethnic Burmese historians, which meant they weren't reliable, or they were in English and held in archives and libraries in cities hundreds of miles away, like Yangon, or thousands of miles away, like London.

Than Myint had access to the internet now, but apart from a few web pages by Rakhine bloggers, he hadn't found much content about Rakhine history online. For years, he had been trying to understand this history using what he described as 'clues'. These clues included language: the Rakhine and Burmese languages were very similar, indicating a long shared history, while in Bangladesh and eastern India there were also people who spoke dialects of Rakhine. The Buddhist religion was another clue, connecting Rakhine with Myanmar and Southeast Asia to the east, and with India and Sri Lanka to the west. But this shared religious history had been obscured by successive invasions, he explained, segueing to a subject that I had hoped to avoid, because I knew where it would lead.

'There are 200 million Muslims in India, and their frontier is Rakhine,' he said. 'The Rakhine people want independence. But more importantly than this, and I don't say this in proud emotion, but as fact: the Rakhine people want to resist the spread of Islam.'

As a border of cultural conflict, Rakhine would never be peaceful, he went on. From the Mujahideen that had taken control of the north of the state in the years after Myanmar's independence, to Islamic insurgencies throughout the 1970s and 1980s,[11] Islam had posed a dual threat for as long as Than Myint could remember, both to the Rakhine religion of Theravada Buddhism and to the Rakhine race itself.

His understanding of history didn't have a place for the Muslim traders and migrants who had lived for centuries in Rakhine, or the Muslim army from Bengal that had once helped a Rakhine king to repel the Burmese, or the Muslim officials who played important roles in the Mrauk-U court.[12] Having been educated in the junta's schools and with limited access to independent information, Than Myint, just like the officials he despised in the archaeology department, had grown up in what he called 'the basket of the military junta'. He had absorbed the junta's propaganda, and he understood history in much the same way, believing that Myanmar had always had fixed borders that divided the people who belonged from those who didn't.

Within the country, there were fixed ethnic identities. There were some Muslims who were native to Rakhine, including a small ethnic group called the Kaman. But there were also many outsiders, including Bengali immigrants who had invented an ethnic identity, Rohingya, and were claiming to be an indigenous 'national race' so they could invade and occupy Rakhine land. In his view, this was a threat to Rakhine identity that rivalled only the threat from the Burmese in the east.

The pressure was now intensifying, he explained: there were four or five Muslim villages encircling Mrauk-U. I pointed out that these villages were ghettos and the Rohingya who lived there had been unable to leave without permission for several years.

'Rohingya is not their name,' Than Myint spat. 'They called

themselves Bengali until recent years. There are pro-Pakistan terrorists in Bangladesh, who use these Bengalis as their tools.'

Becoming upset, he told me that he had files containing evidence of the Rohingya's links to terrorism, but he couldn't show them to me because they got mixed up when his house flooded earlier in the year. Like so many documents throughout Myanmar's history they had been no match for the country's tropical climate.

'That is the truth,' he was saying, 'bad or good, acceptable or not acceptable. They take advantage of corruption in the Burmese government to . . .'

He trailed off and I didn't ask him to finish his sentence. We left the temple in silence, both unsettled by our argument, and walked Than Myint's motorbike back across the fields.

Crossing a narrow bridge at the edge of the town, we entered a dense warren of bamboo huts. Beneath sheets of tarpaulin bearing the United Nations refugee agency logo, men sat around, as groups of women breastfed their babies. Their living conditions were a reminder that much of the ethnic Rakhine population was desperately poor. As I waited in the coming days to travel on one of the few parts of the junta's railway that was still open, near the state capital of Sittwe, I would watch as five old women emerged from the paddy fields beyond the track, carrying sacks across their shoulders. They were bent almost double, their spines curved from decades of hard physical work. Without teeth, their mouths had caved in, and the swollen soles of their bare feet were riven with cracks. Two women squatted to defecate beside the track, then they all trudged on.[13]

From the train, I would watch mothers walking out of the mist to the market, clasping babies to their chests and balancing pots filled with vegetables on their heads. We would pass cowherds with hardened faces, skeletal old men, and gangs of topless workers who crushed stones by hand, and who would be paid almost nothing for this gruelling labour by the contractor tasked with widening the road.

The people here voted the ethnic Rakhine party into the state legislature, and when the Arakan Army, a new Rakhine insurgent group, swept through Rakhine seeking to restore its 'fatherland' to its former glory, many would throw their support behind its promise to liberate them from decades of grinding poverty under Burmese rule. The Arakan Army fought on a nationalist platform that included safeguarding the ethnic Rakhine identity and defending and developing the impoverished region. It was the same vision that had inspired Than Myint's cultural campaign, and it would resonate deeply with the ethnic Rakhine who felt that for decades they had been abused by the Burmese state.

The Burmese military and Rakhine nationalists might have been aligned on the question of the Rohingya, but unlike the generals, most people here were struggling to survive. Poverty was driving tens of thousands of young men and women in search of work elsewhere in Myanmar, including at the deadly jade mines in the north, or overseas, further fuelling fears that the Rakhine people were at risk of losing their homeland. It was easy to see how these fears could erupt into violence, both against the Rohingya, who were portrayed even by the government as a threat to the Rakhine people, and against the Burmese. The more their heritage was threatened, the more they would seek to define and defend it.

But while the Arakan Army's fiery rhetoric might have won it support, most people had little to gain from the war that the armed group would soon wage against Myanmar's military, for control of Rakhine State.

As the Arakan Army advanced, fighting was already bringing suffering to communities in the hills. Just over a year after I visited Mrauk-U, Burmese police would open fire on a peaceful protest, killing seven people who were demanding the right to commemorate the anniversary of the fall in 1784 of the Rakhine kingdom.[14] Within two years, the revolution would reach the town, and bullets would rip through the thatch settlements and ricochet from the crumbling temple walls.

It was not just the Rakhine archaeologist who was haunted by the legacies of long-collapsed empires. Earlier that week, as my night bus creaked and groaned from central Myanmar over the tortuous Rakhine pass, the distant past was also bearing down on the parts of the country that I had left behind.

Deep in the mountains, at a string of police checkpoints, immigration officials had marched up and down our bus, shining torches into our faces and collecting our identification documents for inspection. They were looking for people without documents, people who identified as Rohingya. Half asleep in the early hours of the morning, with my head propped against the window, I had glimpsed military vehicles overtaking us on the narrow road, distinctive green trucks, with caged sides and canvas roofs, and inside them, the pale faces of soldiers gazing out into the darkness.

Like us, they were heading west from central Myanmar, and like us, they had a long way to go. By the time the sun rose, we were still deep in the mountains. The journey had clarified for me the scale of the geographical barrier to central government control over Rakhine. Running from north to south for hundreds of miles, the high, rugged Rakhine mountains stretch from Manipur in northeast India to the southwestern tip of the

Ayeyarwady delta, forming a formidable boundary that isolates the state from the rest of Myanmar.

It was late morning before we stopped for breakfast in Ann, a town at the far side of the mountains, and the headquarters of the military's Western Command. As I sat outside a roadside restaurant, warming my face in the sun, another truck packed with soldiers rolled past, heading in a cloud of dust towards the conflict in the north.

For the first time on my journey through the mountains, I had just enough phone signal to check the news. I read accounts of how, armed only with home-made weapons, members of a new Rohingya insurgent group, the Arakan Rohingya Salvation Army, had hacked nine border policemen to death. Security forces had sealed off the north of the state, which is home to a large Rohingya population. Despite the lockdown, reports were already emerging of a ruthless military operation, including arbitrary killings and sexual violence. Villages were burning, and tens of thousands of people were desperately packing up everything they could carry and fleeing across the porous river border to Bangladesh.[15]

It was a major escalation in a long-running conflict that would have profound consequences, exacerbating communal tensions and narrowing the space for moderate voices across the country. The government would soon claim that those killed were jihadists, citing information gathered during interrogations. It would say that allegations of systemic rape were false and that Muslim terrorists had set fire to their own homes.

In the eyes of the outside world, the moment that military trucks began rolling over the mountains towards Myanmar's western border with Bangladesh in October 2016 was also the moment that the country's peaceful transition from despotism to democracy began to fall apart, and the beginning of Aung

San Suu Kyi's personal fall from grace. For me, it was the beginning of a search for answers to the question of why the military would carry out such brutal operations against a minority group at the same time as setting the country on a path to political and economic reform. It was a search that would take years, and would eventually lead me thousands of miles from this forested mountain range back to Britain, the place that I called home.

Even now, as I scrolled through my Twitter feed outside the restaurant in Ann, it was clear that far from being consigned to distant memory, the politics of Myanmar's colonial past were taking on a new and vicious life. Condensed into just a handful of characters, the argument now playing out on Twitter and other social media sites was over whether the Rohingya were interlopers or native to Myanmar. In other words, whether they had been living in Myanmar before the first Anglo-Burmese war began in 1824, the first of three wars that would see Britain occupy the country until its independence in 1948.

Nationalists argued that the Rohingya were illegal immigrants, who could not prove they had lived, as a racial group, in the country before the British occupation. But, went the counter-argument, this was not only impossible but absurd. Before the British occupation, the Burmese kingdom had indistinct and porous borders that included parts of modern-day India. The people who lived in it, including the Rohingya, did not see themselves as having fixed racial, or ethnic, identities, let alone the documentation to prove it.

To me, looking in on this debate as an outsider, it felt as if something fundamental was changing in the way that people across the country were thinking about themselves and their history. But perhaps it was also that for the first time as a modern nation, millions of people across Myanmar were having a public conversation not just about the Rohingya, but about the colonial past, and what it meant to be a Burmese citizen today.

As my companions at the roadside restaurant tucked into a lunch of fried rice, accompanied by bottles of beer or glasses of whisky, I found myself reflecting on my own journey, and the story I was piecing together. I had set out to investigate the recent history of a military dictatorship, which seemed to have little, if anything, to do with my life back in Britain. But now, scrolling through post after incendiary post about how the British encouraged Muslims from Bengal to settle in Rakhine, and how communal divisions had deepened during the Second World War, and about the bloody years that followed, as Muslim leaders at independence called for the north of the state to become part of East Pakistan, I realized that I needed to look further back in time, if I wanted to understand what was happening today. It occurred to me how little I really knew about British rule in Myanmar, which lasted for more than 120 years – almost twice as long as the country had been independent.

During the two years I had lived in Yangon, I had been charmed, more than anything, by the relics of the colonial state, including its architecture, which was badly neglected but had mostly survived the decades of military rule. I lived on the top floor of one of the tallest buildings in my township in downtown Yangon, and in the evenings after a long day at work, I would climb onto my roof to look over the decaying city. To the east was Pansodan Street, a boulevard leading to the river that was lined with British-built administrative buildings, where clerks still processed stacks of paper documents, much as they had in the days when the city's banks and trading houses were run by British merchants a century earlier. I loved the imposing Port Authority building, with its Corinthian columns and arches, which dominated the skyline by the docks; and the Strand Hotel on the waterfront, where sunburned Western men dressed in linen suits puffed on cigars, ordered cocktails from crisply dressed Burmese waiters, and pretended that the empire had never come to an end.

I had spent days exploring the abandoned, overgrown villas in the former British administrative quarter, including the Pegu Club, where, looking out from the dilapidated wooden balconies, it was easy to imagine young colonial administrators and their wives dancing on the lawns. Nearby, I had often eaten dinner at the colonial-era Governor's Residence, a luxury hotel, where tourists paid hundreds of dollars a night to experience what the hotel's website called the 'elegance of a long-gone era', sipping gin and tonics on the fan-cooled verandas and sleeping on white linen, in teak four-poster beds.[16]

It wasn't just the tourism industry that fetishized British colonial rule. The British ambassador's house in Yangon was a sprawling colonial-era mansion in the centre of town, fitted with teak flooring and set among lush gardens. There was an exclusive British club in the grounds, which stocked imported British food and beer. The embassy hosted parties, including events marketed as celebrating ties between Britain and Myanmar, where guests were served scones and cucumber sandwiches, and where I had listened to one ambassador talk about the shared history of our two countries as if it was a mutually beneficial partnership, rather than a military occupation.

In Yangon, my friends and I often talked about politics, but our discussions lacked historical context. When we did discuss Myanmar's history, it was usually in terms of before and after the political transition, comparing life when the country was isolated from the world with what it was like now. More often, we talked about our social lives, our holiday plans, and the trivial difficulties of expat life – we were expats, never immigrants – which ranged from recalcitrant taxi drivers, to the curfews that interrupted our evening plans, the intolerable heat, and the lack of good-quality meat.

We were far richer and more privileged than almost everyone in Myanmar, except the generals and their cronies, yet most of us didn't think too much about the reasons for this, even as we moved through the same physical spaces where our ancestors had amassed their wealth and power. We were distracted by the excitement of being abroad and by our extravagant lifestyles, which also shielded us from the bleak realities of life for most people in the country where we lived.

It was only now, having spent weeks on the road, that I began to think more deeply about the legacies of British rule. As our bus driver ushered us into a yard behind the restaurant, where we congregated around troughs of murky water to wash, it occurred to me that I could piece together the history of the British Empire in Myanmar in the same way that I was charting the expansion of the military regime: by following the colonial government's tracks, and investigating why and how it built railways.

At the time, I assumed the information would be relatively easy to find. After all, the British Empire was famous for producing information – too much information even for the archives to handle.[17] But when I ran a few cursory searches online, I was surprised by how little came back. At first, I assumed that I wasn't looking hard enough, or in the right places. Presumably the information existed, but in books, or paywalled periodicals, or archives that hadn't been digitized, rather than on free and more accessible websites. Britain is a cornucopia of obscure books, and it's also a nation of railway enthusiasts. Entire rooms at bookshops in towns all over the country are dedicated to books about railway-building, and I was sure that the next time I went home, I would find a few relevant titles.

Months later, when I sat down in the Asian and African Studies Room at the British Library and began to look through the catalogues, I realized there wasn't a single history of Myanmar's railways there.

I wrote to British and European railway enthusiasts, academics, historians and archivists, but none of them could recommend a single title. One man, a retired German railway engineer called Dieter Hettler, now in his nineties, replied to tell me he was writing a history of Myanmar's railways, and that as far as he knew, it was the first that had ever been written.

We became friends and he later shared a draft of his book entitled 'Railways of Burma/Myanmar', which was a technical history, with chapters on the types of locomotives and carriages used on the lines, and specifications of tracks, bridges, tunnels and signalling equipment. But there were only hints in these pages at why the railways were built, their impact and their legacy.

So, once again, I found myself piecing the story together, only this time from colonial-era documents and unpublished manuscripts held in archives, including surveys, reports from expeditions to map new railway routes, ministry manuals, codes of conduct, articles in contemporary newspapers, and official correspondence, much of it written in curling script on faded paper, or contained in enormous, leather-bound books.

One of the most prolific writers on railways in British Burma was an English businessman called John Ogilvy Hay, who moved to Rakhine from Calcutta in 1853, the same year the first colonial railway opened in British India.[18]

When he arrived in Akyab, as the Rakhine capital Sittwe was then known, he found a landscape remarkably similar to the one that was unfolding around me, as my bus left Ann along a road that unwound from the mountains.

Rakhine is a narrow strip of land that arcs south from the Bangladesh border along the Bay of Bengal, intersected by networks of rivers that meander through its alluvial plains and splinter into tidal creeks.

The monsoon was coming to an end, and the paddy fields that sprawled below us were lurid green, spotted with thatch huts, figures in conical hats and water buffalo. It was a peaceful scene that belied the bloody wars that have been waged here over the centuries by outsiders. Driving through the villages that afternoon, there was nothing to suggest that this quiet place, with its faded wooden houses, was quickly becoming the epicentre of a major international crisis. It appeared old and forgotten, an outpost that saw little activity beyond the rice-planting seasons, the harvests, and the fishing boats that plied the quiet waterways leading out to the sea.

When Hay arrived in Rakhine, which was then known as Arakan, it was a sparsely populated colonial backwater. Then, as now, transport was mostly limited to jungle paths, waterways and the sea. The small British community in Sittwe, the largest settlement, was only connected to the rest of British Burma and the empire beyond it by a government steamer that docked at its port just once every six weeks.

In the three decades since the British had annexed Rakhine in the 1820s, the centre of the town had been laid out, drained, and planted with fruit trees. The population of the province had tripled and its rice trade was steadily expanding. But what lay beyond the town was still unknown to Hay and the other British settlers. District officers could only travel inland by boat, and few had strayed more than a few miles from the port. The mountains beyond, which separated Rakhine from the Burmese kingdom, were British possessions on paper alone.

But Hay was optimistic, believing he could profit from what he saw as vast new opportunities. The East India Company had just invaded Burma for a second time, and its governor-general Lord Dalhousie – who is remembered as the architect of the Indian railway system – had seized the country's entire coastline, including the fertile rice fields in the delta and all three Burmese ports, and established a new capital at Rangoon.[19] It was an aggressive war that was described by one British Liberal MP at the time as less of a war than a massacre. New weapons meant the Company's soldiers were able to kill entire Burmese armies 'with scarcely the loss of a man on our side' – setting a precedent for British rule in Burma for decades to come.[20]

Yet there was little interest in Britain about what was happening in Burma, despite the fact that some 20,000 British troops now occupied a territory there as large as England. This was partly because most of the soldiers who fought in Burma were Indian, and it was Indian taxpayers who paid for both the invasion and the subsequent occupation;[21] but it was also because the Company was fighting so many other overseas wars. With Dalhousie at the helm, it had perfected the art of making money through conquest, annexing a quarter of a million square miles in India in less than a decade,[22] opening up new markets where British merchants could sell their textiles and ironware, fending off unemployment and unrest in industrial towns at home.

This was an age when powerful men in colonial outposts

could make decisions that affected the fate of millions of people with almost no oversight from Whitehall, and with little scrutiny from the British press or public. Soon after Hay moved to Sittwe from Calcutta, the East India Company was dissolved by an act passed by the British parliament, marking the start of direct British rule on the Indian subcontinent, including in Burma. The Company and its private army had ruled over more than 200 million people with an unusual degree of freedom and impunity, and its dissolution led to greater oversight from London.[23] But there remained a feeling among the British in India, and particularly among British businessmen, that anything was possible, if only the right connections could be made.

As Hay began to build a new life in Sittwe, and Rangoon was rebuilt in the image of Calcutta, the great railway age in Asia was also just beginning, facilitating a dramatic expansion of British imperial power into territory that would have been impossible to occupy with warships alone.

The first public railway in British India, a 21-mile suburban line in Bombay, had just opened to great fanfare. Capitalists in London were transforming India with new railways, and the British press was filled with reports of engineering marvels that cut across the vast peaks of rock forming the Indian Ghats and running for hundreds of miles across wild mountains and through untouched forest.

Within fifty years, some 24,000 miles of track would be laid, shrinking the empire in India and drawing its wonders closer.[24] It was an age when, for British men, space and time could be condensed, power consolidated and fortunes made, simply by venturing out into an unmapped landscape with a measuring wheel, a compass and an aneroid barometer, and then laying down miles of ballast and track.

Like thousands of other British amateur railway enthusiasts who were now clamouring to transform a patch they had claimed as their own into a place of international significance, Hay had a vision, which he would energetically propound for three decades, in a relentless campaign of letters, pamphlets, articles and map-making. He wanted to build a great railway that would join Rakhine with Eastern Bengal – and then across the Rakhine mountains to British Burma, and further east to China.

'GIVE, GIVE, GIVE, US RAILWAYS,' he wrote in the *Arakan News*, the local newspaper that became the mouthpiece for much of his crusade. 'Our harp has been strung to this one tune, and nothing shall silence or overpower it but the Railway whistle, sounding over the length and the breadth of the land.'

Central to Hay's argument was that only a small part of Rakhine was being cultivated, and this was because its population was so small. Not only was it small, he wrote, but the ethnic Rakhine were lazy and refused to work, even for their own profit (drawing on the pseudo-Darwinist prejudices that shaped British views on race at the time). On the other hand, the Muslims in Chittagong, in East Bengal, who already migrated for several months each year to Rakhine to sow the rice and reap and ship the harvest, were industrious. Capital investment was needed to clear large tracts of unoccupied land for new plantations, and most Burmese had no savings, because they traded in goods rather than money. Muslim families from Bengal were already filling the gap, moving to Rakhine to become moneylenders.[25] If a railway was built connecting the two provinces, Hay argued, immigrants from Chittagong would 'pour down' it, transforming what he saw as an unproductive wasteland into profitable parcels, growing everything from tea and coffee, to cotton, tobacco and indigo, and the isolated town of Sittwe would become a great shipping port.

It was a classic colonial formula that had already reshaped the globe: occupied land was only profitable if it could be worked, and if indigenous labour was unsuitable, then new workers had to be brought in. In Burma, most of these immigrants were from India. While Hay was calling for his new railway to be built, a dramatic change in Burma's demography was underway that would have devastating consequences in the centuries to come.

But Hay's vision was even more ambitious than this: arguing that Rakhine would never benefit from being part of Burma, which was also thinly populated, he proposed joining it instead, under a new administration, with the British territory of Chittagong, whose population density was almost twenty times greater. There were other reasons to redraw the borders, Hay argued, including the chain of mountains that formed a natural boundary between Rakhine and the rest of British Burma, the 'differences between the Arakanese and Burmese races', and the animosity between the two, which meant that in his view they could never amalgamate.

Hay's vision was deeply rooted in his identity as a British man, at the height of the empire. Back home, there was little to distinguish him from anyone else. But here, thousands of miles from home, in a place he had no connection to and hardly knew, he saw himself as a king, backed by the world's strongest military and in a position, as long as he could make a good enough case for it, to redraw borders and move populations – to carve up entire worlds for profit.

The obstacles that stood in his way were not the complex, established systems that had shaped this part of the world over thousands of years. Instead, Hay was concerned about whether investors could be convinced to pay for a survey; whether the British government would guarantee the new line; whether it was possible to make a case for its profitability; and then to pull the right strings with the people who mattered, who were invariably not in Rakhine, but in Calcutta and London. Hay considered these obstacles surmountable because he believed he had a whole province and its people at his disposal. He proposed handing over 'half [of] Arakan' to incentivize companies to build the railway, land that he saw as wilderness, occupied 'only [by] wild tribes'.

In his writing, he never questioned the idea that constant and vigorous expansion driven by capital, industry, and the 'civilizing' influence of the British over both land and people, was a force for good. The idea that handing over large portions of land to British railway contractors, or to immigrants from Chittagong, might cause tensions with the people who had farmed it for centuries or generate resentment towards the colonial system, didn't appear to occur to him. Hay records just one meeting with what he called 'the leading Natives' of the town, who all conveniently agreed with him that the land was much too empty, and a railway had to be built.

In the end, Hay's railway wasn't built, because British officials had no real interest in developing Rakhine, which was peaceful and already making a profit from its rice trade. Officials ignored or discouraged him, telling Hay there were other districts in India that needed railways, or other infrastructure. There was a brief period of renewed interest at the end of the century, when the Indian government considered building an imperial highway to China, and enthusiasm for the idea continued among railway enthusiasts until after the Second World War. Four routes were surveyed, covering a huge expanse of territory from the Himalayan foothills to the tidal rivers of the

Rakhine delta. But then, as now, the region's hostile landscape shaped its destiny. All the routes were considered too difficult, or too expensive, and it remained a colonial frontier – or in Hay's words: 'a waste howling wilderness of which nothing can be made'.[26]

Like so many other railways being planned around the same time in Burma, Hay's railway existed only in the collective colonial imagination. From a 30-mile line across the Kra Isthmus that would have connected the Bay of Bengal with the Eastern Seas, providing an alternative to the long, dangerous shipping route by the Strait of Malacca,[27] to the multiple new routes mapped by British envoys and private adventurers who wanted to open up overland trade with the markets of western China,[28] the imperial archive relating to British Burma is crowded with correspondence, articles, tracts, surveys and reports about railways that don't exist.

But Hay's writing was important because the ideas that underpinned it would take root in Rakhine and across the country, altering the course of its history. Hay was one of the first people to propose building a railway in Burma, at a time when the British only occupied the coastline, and the Burmese monarchy and its heartland remained intact. In the years that followed, it was men like Hay with dreams of railways whose collective writing would shape how the British understood Burma, driving the invasion and annexation of the Burmese kingdom, the deposition of its king, the dismantling of its economic, religious and social systems, and the dispossession of the Burmese people, leaving a vacuum that would be filled after independence by the country's armed forces.[29]

Railways would become the means by which many people in this remote outpost of empire would first come into contact with the British state, and railways would facilitate the spread of new ideas, including theories of racial hierarchy that the British used to justify colonial rule.

Now, as the generals used the same racist ideology to generate support for mass violence against the Rohingya, across the country obscure historical documents, including colonial records, were being dusted off, typed up, forensically examined, revised and weaponized. As Burmese and Rakhine nationalists found common ground in their quest to prove there had been no Rohingya in Rakhine before the British occupation, everything was being analysed, including writing about British plans to build a railway to Bengal.

Several decades after Hay gave up lobbying colonial officials, a British company built a short railway connecting Maungdaw and Buthidaung, the same two townships in the north of Rakhine that were now being flooded with government troops.

This railway was very different from Hay's grand imperial highway: the 18-mile line connected boat services between two rivers, providing an inland water route for rice to reach the mills in Sittwe. The idea was that it would be used by seasonal labourers from Chittagong, so they didn't have to carry their produce on foot, along miles of jungle paths. But it was a failure: the company building it ran out of money and the governments of India and Burma had to step in. When the railway opened, it was hardly used, because the workers didn't want to pay the fare, preferring to walk. After six years of losses the company was liquidated, and the line dismantled.[30]

Yet its short, unhappy history would be held up by nationalists in the years after I visited Rakhine as proof of insidious British plans to populate Rakhine with 'Bengalis'.

One blogpost, entitled 'Historical evidence of a Chittagonian Bengalis transporter train' would claim 'there were no Bengalis in Rakhine' until the railway was built, allegedly facilitating immigration and large-scale settlement (even though it did nothing of the sort). 'The hidden agenda of so-called "Rohingya" is very dangerous to our NATION Myanmar and our ethnicity,' the post warned. 'It has been created by INVADER Chittagonian Bengalis . . . in order to genocide to the Buddhist Rakhine people in Buthidaung and Maungdaw.'[31]

A popular Rakhine journalist who was in the north of the state reporting on the conflict would find time to visit the abandoned British-built railway, discussion of which had become a nationalist dog whistle. In a subsequent article he described how two railway tunnels that had been carved through the mountains were still there, as were the rusting piers of a bridge, and girders bearing the name of an English company.[32]

The geographical boundary between Burma and Chittagong, where this railway was built, is known in Myanmar as *anouk-taga*, or the 'Western gate'.[33] It was through this gate, in the Burmese imagination, that the East India Company invaded the Burmese kingdom in 1824, beginning more than a century of humiliating British rule. It was through this gate, too, that Indian colonial subjects are imagined to have entered the country, despite the fact that the war was mostly fought in Rangoon, and that most Indian immigrants arrived by boat to the capital of British Burma, rather than crossing the border from Bengal.

Now, almost two centuries later, Myanmar's military was claiming to be closing this same gate to illegal immigration from Bangladesh, sealing the gaps in its flimsy national myth. It would emerge, in the months and years after I left Rakhine, that after driving the Rohingya from the north of the state, the military would dramatically reshape the landscape in the townships that border Bangladesh.

Soldiers were destroying Rohingya villages, and they, along with Aung San Suu Kyi's democratically elected government, would later build new roads and settlements over the villages they had razed, tying the isolated north more closely to the rest of the state.[34]

Not only was the military driving out the Rohingya, but having made them stateless, the military and the civilian government would try to erase the physical traces of their existence from northern Rakhine. Once the Rohingya had been removed, there would be attempts to populate the north of the state with ethnic Rakhine Buddhists from the south, and the few refugees who returned would be rehoused in segregated settlements.[35]

The Rohingya were the victims of the military's attempt to create a homogeneous nation, or in the words of junta leader Than Shwe, a 'We are Myanmar' identity. The assimilation, expulsion or extermination of minority groups has been a crucial ingredient in creating territorial nation states throughout history. And the operation itself was shaped both by the Burmese experience as an imperial power, and as a colonized nation. By erasing the group that had become a scapegoat for all the problems associated with the British occupation, the idea was that the country could return to a glorious past untouched by British rule – and its 'national races' would be able to live in harmony under the guardianship of a Burmese power, once again.

In the pale morning light, the rusting railcar at Sittwe Station appeared shipwrecked, as if it had washed up on this faded stretch of coast. Raucous crows shook the palms that surrounded the empty platform, then swooped away to circle a landfill site at its eastern end.

'You know, I never take the train,' Aung, my contact, said to me, as we watched. 'Mostly, Rakhine people don't take the train.'

We were at the southern tip of the Rakhine capital, where the Kaladan River meets the Bay of Bengal. Beyond the railway station was an artificial peninsula that had been developed into a paved park with palm trees and manicured flowerbeds, where the city's young Rakhine residents gathered in the evenings to drink and relax. There was a lighthouse just offshore, and a naval base to the east. And to the northwest, just a few miles along the coast, were internment camps where most of the city's Rohingya Muslim residents had been held since deadly sectarian violence tore through Rakhine State four years earlier.[36]

The ethnic Rakhine who were displaced by the violence in Sittwe remained free, and many of them had returned to their homes. But the Rohingya were now confined to settlements that were hastily assembled beside the railway track, which now marked the western boundary of their prison. This section of track was one of the only parts of the junta's railway in Rakhine that had ever opened, and it had been closed for much of its short existence.[37] Its main function was now to shuttle the city's imprisoned Rohingya residents back and forth through the camps.

Aung was a tall, handsome and softly spoken Rakhine man with a receding hairline and a fondness for designer polo shirts. He was also a broker, and one of his lines of work was to arrange permits for foreign journalists and aid workers to visit the camps. Restrictions on access meant that foreigners had to work with a government-approved translator if they wanted to even meet any of the city's Rohingya residents, and the rule was strictly enforced. At my hotel a sign above the welcome desk had specified which areas of Sittwe were restricted, including 'Bengali quarters/villages', meaning villages where the

Rohingya were confined. Aung had picked up my papers several days earlier, while I was still in Mrauk-U, securing approval
from immigration officials just hours before the entire department left Sittwe for the north of the state, which had been
designated a counter-terrorism operation zone, following the
attacks by Rohingya insurgents.

'They are going there to check for illegal immigrants,' he had
told me ominously.

As we waited on the platform to travel into the camps, the
only thing that hinted at the trouble in the north was a small
cluster of police barricades outside the station, painted red and
white and strung with barbed wire. But Aung was anxious, just
as everyone here seemed anxious, about what might happen
next.

'Sittwe is normal for now,' he explained. 'But in Maungdaw
soldiers and police have died, and what happens in Maungdaw affects what happens here.'

A janitor dressed in a navy boiler suit turned up to sweep the
platform, raising a cloud of dust. But he couldn't sell us tickets,
and neither could he tell us when the train might leave. The
ticket office, a small hole in the wall covered by a grate, was
shut. Through the grate, a man was sleeping on a bench with
his knees raised, and I asked Aung if we should wake him.

But he ignored my question and I wondered, as he turned
his back on the sleeping guard and strolled back along the deserted platform, whether he hoped the train wouldn't run at all.
Despite having spent plenty of time in the camps, Aung had
never travelled through them by train before, and conditions
were different now, after the attacks and as the crackdown
unfolded in the north.

Aung was unusually sympathetic to the Rohingya. He had
grown up in the city's Muslim quarter, which was now a ghetto

surrounded by barbed wire, whose few remaining inhabitants couldn't leave without permission. While he profited from their incarceration, earning $100 a day for permits, transport and unspecified fees, he also facilitated meetings that helped to keep them connected to the outside world.

His friendship with a young Rohingya man who I will call Anwar enabled this flow of information. But Aung's sympathy for the Rohingya only went so far. Like Sittwe's other Rakhine residents, on some level he believed the government propaganda that portrayed them as a threat.

It was not just physical barriers that now divided the Rohingya and Rakhine communities. The end of Than Shwe's dream of building a railway across Rakhine State had marked the beginning of a new stage in the military's nation-building project. The world had changed dramatically since the days of the British Empire, and nations could no longer be so easily built simply by laying down miles of track. The power of physical borders and the infrastructure within them was being eroded, as communities were increasingly created and controlled online.

The 2012 riots in Rakhine State coincided with the dismantling in Myanmar of online censorship infrastructure. Pre-publication censorship was abolished and new media outlets started publishing online – and distributing their content on Facebook.[38] As communal violence erupted, most of these new publications didn't interview the insular and isolated Rohingya community, many of whom didn't speak Burmese. Instead, they quoted Rakhine victims and officials from the military's proxy political party, which was then in power. Generals-turned-officials with new Facebook accounts wrote long, inflammatory posts, which the new journalists cited too.[39]

Millions of people who had never been to Rakhine and who

knew little, if anything, about the state's history, were learning about the Rohingya for the first time, and were being told they were illegal immigrants who were dangerous and violent. Most people had never heard the word 'Rohingya' before: it didn't feature in school textbooks about the country's 'national races', or in junta-era media.[40] On the internet, where Burmese-language content was still scarce, many of the posts that mentioned the Rohingya indicated the name had been invented by Bengalis.

At the same time, a smear campaign targeted foreign media,[41] playing on a long history of xenophobia rooted in the colonial occupation, and an endless stream of content was shared on Facebook about atrocities by militant Islamist groups al-Qaeda and the Islamic State, which at the time was taking over large parts of Syria and Iraq. This, combined with posts containing maps showing the spread of Islam in Asia, and alleged plans by Islamic extremists to invade Myanmar, meant the 'Western gate' was increasingly seen as under attack.[42] It didn't matter, of course, that much of what people were reading wasn't true; it only mattered that they believed it was true.

The military's use of the internet to promote a national identity by spreading fear of outsiders was just as crude as the railways it had tried to build. Yet, by the time I travelled through the country, most ordinary people believed that the Rohingya were aggressors and deserving of violence. It wasn't just Than Myint, the archaeologist in Mrauk-U, who feared them. Several people had earnestly repeated to me chunks of the propaganda that was spreading so widely online.

In Myanmar's south, a Buddhist monk had told me that most of the world's terrorists were Muslim, and blamed the violence in Rakhine on the Rohingya. In Magway, the military heartland, a young man had told me he was afraid of Muslims because they beheaded cows and chickens; and the night before I travelled to Rakhine the owner of my guesthouse warned me not to go.

'The Indians have come again,' she said, citing posts by prominent Burmese monks on Facebook, and inadvertently revealing how the Rohingya had become a proxy for Indian immigration under colonial rule, which many people believed had represented a genuine threat to the Burmese way of life. I asked her what she had read.

'Their plan is very bad, to kill the Burmese people. They want to slit our Burmese necks,' she said.

Back at Sittwe Railway Station, the conductor had arrived, and was beginning the long process of removing a wooden wedge from behind the front wheels of the rusting train. Aung seemed reassured when a group of armed police turned up and ushered us into the railcar, where we sat in an eight-seat compartment behind the driver's cabin, which was normally reserved for Buddhists, railway staff and security forces.

There was an identical compartment at the other end of the carriage, and between the two was a larger area, reserved for Muslims. The train had become a symbol of the institutional-ized racial segregation in Rakhine, which human-rights groups were comparing to apartheid.

'Mostly the train riders are Muslim people,' the conductor explained. 'A few are Rakhine, and they are separated. The staff arrange it for them, to help the people.'

Later, when the conductor pushed through the carriage, col-lecting the fare, he didn't speak to the Rohingya passengers, but used sign language instead. When I asked him why, he explained that they did not speak the same language.

'They understand orders – go here, go there, sit down, this way,' he said, and laughed.

Now, he said he was in Sittwe on a three-month placement from Yangon, and that no permanent staff were assigned to this route, because nobody wanted the job. He hadn't wanted to come here either, he added, but he had no choice. His smile faded when I asked if he had seen any unrest, on the train or in the camps.

'No,' he snapped. 'Nothing happened.'

Had anything changed since the attacks in the north? I pressed him.

'The situation is normal,' he replied. 'Nothing has changed.'

Before we left the station, the driver, a small, serious man in a crisp white shirt, beckoned me into his cabin, so that I could look out of the door at the front of the train. The door was pinned open, revealing the track ahead of us, and as we jolted away from the platform, I watched the track disappear beneath my feet. Snaking through a thicket, we emerged into an expanse of flat, parched countryside on the city's outskirts. To the west of the track, fields scattered with palm groves extended to the sea; to the east ran a barbed-wire fence.

Ahead of us was a level crossing, where a guard waved us through with a green flag. Just beyond him we came to a checkpoint staffed by police, with assault rifles slung across their shoulders. Aung passed my papers through the window to a policeman, who examined and stamped them, and then the train edged into the camps.

Soon there were people walking beside the track, which like the railway I had travelled on in the delta was the best road around. The women were dressed in bright skirts with matching blouses and colourful headscarves, and the men wore white *taqiyah*, rounded caps, white jackets, or shirts and *paso*.

A cluster of huts came into view, woven from thatch with roofs that had been patched up with sheets of green-and-blue tarpaulin, and then a small station, bathed in sunlight. Several dozen men, women and children crowded around the train, helping one another into the carriage. They were shadowed by police officers who climbed in behind them, each clutching a rifle to his chest.

'For security,' Aung said, when he saw me looking at the guns.

Aung's friend Anwar was not with them, but I knew what he looked like from his Facebook profile, and I saw him from the open door at the front of the train before we reached him. He was standing beside the track, dressed in a black shirt with a white collar and cuffs, and black suit trousers, and he was staring intently at the train.

'I don't dress like this normally,' he said with a grin, as he swung himself into the carriage, pointing to his shirt and his black suit trousers, which made him look like a young professional on his way to the office. 'But for this trip, I thought I should dress smart.'

We walked together to the train's Muslim compartment, leaving Aung flanked by police.

'Things have totally changed since the problems happened in the north,' Anwar told me as we sat down. In the four years since the camps were built, conditions had been gradually improving. There was a steady flow of international aid, and deals had been struck between wealthy Muslim and Rakhine traders – Anwar said 'Muslim' at first, rather than 'Rohingya' – who sold supplies that made life inside a little more bearable.

But since the attacks, food had been scarce, and even fishing at a creek inside the camps had been banned. There were new checkpoints, and groups of more than three people were being broken up, sometimes violently. Four farmers eating together in a hut in the fields had been taken to a monastery and beaten.

'We are all afraid, even if nothing happens,' Anwar said, glancing at Aung. 'We hear about them killing people and raping women and setting fire to homes in Maungdaw. That's why people are worried, because they have family there. As for me, I worry the problem will transfer here and they will do bad things to us.'

He pointed to the makeshift camps in the distance. On the periphery nearest the railway were rows of outhouses with battered doors. Beyond them, sheets of tarpaulin formed the outskirts of a settlement that had been his home now for four years.

'Can you imagine?' he went on. 'Before 2012, we all lived together.'

Beyond the train an expanse of barren land separated the railway from the labyrinth of bamboo huts, thatched with palm-leaf, that had become Anwar's prison. Outside the crowded longhouses, women were cooking on small fires, or washing their children with buckets of water. Older children dashed along the alleyways, leaping over emaciated dogs.

Beyond the camps, barbed-wire fences separated the Rohingya from a sprawling military base, which in turn formed an impenetrable barrier between the camps and Sittwe, the city they had once called home. Aung and I had driven through the base the previous day, along its wide, tree-lined boulevards, where emaciated Rohingya men and women toiled in the sun, repairing parts of the road that connected the barracks to the camps, while burned-out oil drums lay smouldering at their feet.

'This place was free before and now people are living here like animals,' Anwar said. 'The only food for our meals is rice, oil and salt, and there is no work, except carrying heavy loads for the army. For our children, the future is dark.'

Beneath Anwar's easy charm there was an intense anger,

fuelled both by the violence his people were suffering, and his own inability to improve their fate.

Above all, like many young Rohingya refugees I would later speak to in Bangladesh, Anwar felt let down by Aung San Suu Kyi. Like them, he had planned to vote for her before the military-backed Thein Sein government stripped the Rohingya of their voting rights just before the 2015 election.

'I thought that if I had the right to vote I would vote for her, and in my dreams I already voted for her,' he told me, as we gazed out at the camps. 'She said so many good things in her speeches, and I thought she would identify a durable solution for our Rohingya people. After she won the election, she accepted so much money from foreign governments, and what did she do with it? Supporting her father's army, buying more weapons, killing her people.'

His profound disappointment in Aung San Suu Kyi's failure to help the Rohingya would soon be shared across the world, as more than 700,000 Rohingya men, women and children fled into Bangladesh to escape another brutal military operation the following year. Outside the country, a United Nations Fact-Finding Mission would find that generals in Myanmar's military should be investigated and prosecuted for genocide.[43]

But inside Myanmar, millions would rally behind the military, including most of Aung San Suu Kyi's party. They had been primed since 2012 to interpret the events that were now unfolding in the north as proof that the country was under attack, and few would believe the stories of atrocities against the Rohingya that would be broadcast around the world. Unused to handling media of any kind, let alone during a crisis of this magnitude, Aung San Suu Kyi's new government would clumsily deny the abuses had taken place, or parrot the military's argument against foreign interference.

Caught between two increasingly polarized narratives, Aung San Suu Kyi herself would fail to speak out for the Rohingya, and would be swiftly and viciously denounced by the Western leaders and activists who had admired her for so long. For decades, when she was under house arrest and unable to speak to the media, they had celebrated her as a moral icon. Now, when she was leading a government and publicly defending its actions, they condemned her silence – which wasn't really silence at all, only a failure to live up to their expectations. Organisations and institutions from Amnesty International to the City of Oxford and the US Holocaust Memorial Museum rescinded the awards they had given her.[44] Celebrities including musicians Bono and Bob Geldof accused her of complicity in abuses against the Rohingya.[45] Archbishop Desmond Tutu warned his fellow Nobel Peace Prize laureate that if the 'political price of your ascension to the highest office in Myanmar is your silence, the price is surely too steep'.[46]

What was missing from the public narrative of Aung San Suu Kyi as fallen human-rights icon was a deeper look at why the military was driving the Rohingya from Rakhine. I would repeatedly be asked by friends back home why this was happening – there must be more to the story, they kept saying, than what they had heard on the news.

That day, on the train with Anwar, a young man who had been stripped of the most basic liberties and who feared every day for his life and the lives of his friends and family, I wasn't entirely sure either. It was only when I travelled further into Myanmar's hinterland, and back into the country's past, that I began to understand more about what had happened in the years between the British invasion through the 'Western gate' and the military's attempts to seal it shut – and how these events were now casting a long shadow over the people who lived on this small crescent of land on the Indian Ocean coast.

On the train, Anwar was talking fast. 'The fucking Myanmar government calls us terrorists, but they are a terrorist government. We are citizens of Myanmar, we are not immigrants. It's not just me. I am many. I am the Rohingya youth. I am the elderly who are worthless. I am the victims who are suffering in this humanitarian crisis. I am the 1.5 million who are denied citizenship and freedom and movement, who are fleeing religious persecution. I was born here and I want to stay here, so why is my fucking government accusing me of being an illegal immigrant from Bangladesh?'

He paused, then taking a breath, he shot me another smile and pulled out a cigarette. 'I'll need to smoke if I'm going to talk so much,' he said.

A blast from the horn signalled that we were already pulling into the final station, at the edge of a Buddhist village; the railway beyond it was damaged and a broken bridge meant trains could go no further. There was no platform, so we jumped down onto a patch of grass. The other passengers lifted one another down from the train, before dispersing into the fields. The sun was already high in the deepening blue sky, and we ducked into a small building for shade while we waited for the train to take us back into the camps. A policeman sat with us and stared at us, with his gun slung across his lap. Beneath his gaze, we fell into silence.

After a while, Anwar mentioned he was thirsty.

'There must be a shop nearby,' I said without thinking. He looked uncomfortable, and then reminded me that he wasn't allowed to go into the village beyond the station. Aung volunteered to go instead, and when he returned, Anwar asked me to take photos of the two of them, in front of the train. At first they stood awkwardly beside one another: Anwar in his suit trousers and brown leather sandals, Aung in a red Giordano polo shirt and Rakhine velvet slippers. Then Anwar threw his arm over Aung's shoulder; they were about the same height. They posed beside the carriages, pretending to climb the steps, and then stood together in front of the engine, while I documented this moment of easy, unguarded affection.

I later sent the photographs to Anwar, including an image of him standing on the track with his hands stuck nonchalantly in his pockets. He was laughing at something with Aung, whose face was half-turned from the camera. Anwar used the image as his Facebook profile picture, accompanied by the caption: 'Smiling . . .' But he cut Aung out of the picture. Online, where divisions were now spiralling out of control, it was impossible to admit to a friendship that just a few years earlier might have been unremarkable.

Anwar later posted the cropped photo again, with a new caption.

'The smile on my face doesn't mean my life is perfect,' he wrote. Like so many optimistic posts I have since read on Facebook by Rohingya men and women, his words revealed an extraordinary resilience in the face of unimaginable hardship. 'It means i appreciate what i have and what Allah has blessed me.'

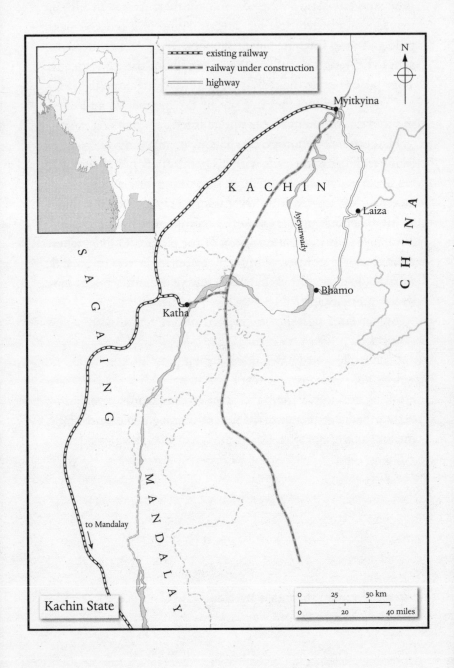

N

existing railway
railway under construction
highway

Myitkyina

K A C H I N

Laiza

Ayeyarwady

Bhamo

S
A
G
A
I
N
G

Katha

C H I N A

M
A
N
D
A
L
A
Y

to Mandalay

0   25   50 km

0   20   40 miles

Kachin State

5.

Kachin

It took me almost three days to travel to Myitkyina, the capital of Kachin State in Myanmar's far north. I caught a bus back across the Rakhine mountains, then a train through the central dry zone, where gangs of children roamed the wide sandy valleys where rivers should have been, gazing up at our train as it clanked overhead. There were cornfields, but mostly it was arid land, broken only by clusters of thin palms and men driving herds of cows across the plains.

Further north we edged through jungle so dense that it engulfed the railway. Branches smacked against the open windows, as we forged a path that closed quickly again behind us. I spent a night at a station in the jungle, on a bed fashioned from hardboard planks, before boarding a train to the north, where a pair of heavily tattooed guards let me sit between them, with my legs hanging from an open doorway.

The rice harvest was underway, and I watched workers in the fields shuttle bundles of dried paddy into piles and feed them into decrepit machines, which spat out the waste in soaring arcs. Between stations, traders jumped onto the train, gripping sacks of leaves and rice, then leaped off again and slipped away into the fields.

Beyond the plains I watched dark mountains emerge in the eastern distance, shrouded by clouds that hung across them like frozen smoke. Soon, we were passing through tunnels of jungle, broken only occasionally by views of expansive beauty, and then stopping at tiny, sun-streaked stations in villages made entirely of wood and shaded by ancient banyan trees. Slowly, gently, as the shadows grew longer, we eased into Myanmar's majestic north.

I was travelling to the northernmost point on the country's railway network, on lines that were built by the British, in search of answers about a long line on my map that was shaded yellow, indicating that a new railway was being built. This railway would connect the Kachin State capital for 300 miles into northern Shan State in eastern Myanmar, and it would pass through territory along the Chinese border that was contested by the Kachin Independence Organization, one of Myanmar's oldest ethnic armed groups.

But when I reached the Kachin capital of Myitkyina, station staff told me that work on this railway hadn't even started, except on a small section of track further south, towards a city called Bhamo. Instead, conflict had broken out, and even the older British railway that I had just travelled on had become a battleground, just as it had been repeatedly throughout Myanmar's history. The legacy of this British railway, which opened in 1898 – connecting the Burmese heartland with the independent Kachin tribes in the far north for the first time – was still raw.

My map of the network was open on a desk and as I looked at the black line representing the older railway to the north, along which colonial power had moved, I remembered that in my backpack I still had the brass medal that the antique-shop owner had given me in Yangon. It was issued in 1977, to mark the centenary of the country's first railway. The British-built network was not somehow separate from the military's railways, it was the very foundation on which they were built. The colonial railway to the north, which I had just travelled on, was itself a text that would reveal how its history was being remembered now, or in other words, how the past was shaping the present.

As I left the station in the late afternoon, the daylight was already waning, the shops were closing and the streets were emptying, as cars parked up for the night. Checkpoints were being assembled on the city's outskirts – the unofficial curfew would begin when the last of the light was gone. More than anywhere else I visited in Myanmar, this northern state in the Himalayan foothills felt like a territory under siege. The Kachin had been independent before the British occupation, and they had been fighting for their freedom from the Burmese state ever since.

But since the political reforms began and the generals stepped back from direct power, some of the Kachin elite believed there was an opportunity to change the system from the inside. Among them was a stateswoman called Maran Ja Seng Hkawn, who had recently been elected to the Kachin parliament. She had also signed several business deals with the government, including a contract to run train services to the north, becoming Myanmar's first and only private railway operator.[1]

I found this fascinating, particularly because Ja Seng Hkawn's father, Maran Brang Seng, had led the Kachin Independence Organization for twenty years. I wanted to know why a woman with such deep connections to the Kachin insurgency had wanted to take over a strategic railway that was used to deploy Burmese troops to the north – and why Myanmar's military had agreed to hand over control.

It took me several days to track Ja Seng Hkawn down, with

the help of several contacts in Myitkyina, but eventually we were put in touch, and she invited me one morning to her office in the centre of town. She was late for our meeting. When she finally arrived, she apologized, explaining that she hadn't finished work until after midnight the previous day. There was so much to do these days, she told me, pulling up two benches for us to sit on. She was small, around the same height as me, and much more glamorous: her lips were painted pink, and jewellery sparkled on her fingers and in her hair.

As she poured us each a cup of green tea and asked one of the women in the office to prepare us two bowls of noodle salad, she began to reminisce about her past. I soon realized she was setting out her credentials, and making sure that I understood exactly what she and her family had sacrificed for the Kachin cause.

As a child, she told me, she remembered meeting her parents just twice, after they left when she was several months old to join the Kachin Independence Organization. By the time Ja Seng Hkawn finished school, her father had risen through the ranks to become the armed group's leader.[2] She left Myitkyina to join her parents in the jungle, and for years she worked for the Kachin resistance.

'It was a very tight time,' she told me. 'But by the grace of God, mentally I was very strong, so I was not afraid of anyone.'

Just like in Rakhine, history weighed so heavily here that decades of it had to be explained before any conversation with an outsider could even begin. In Kachin, the story that was told and retold was of the unfinished struggle for autonomy. In Ja Seng Hkawn's telling, it all started with a broken promise, on the eve of the country's independence from Britain.

Divisions at the time ran deep: the British railway to the north had welded two previously independent territories together, but the British had barely tried to unify them. They had ruled Kachin, like other upland areas, indirectly, through local chiefs known as *duwa*, while the Burmese had endured a military occupation that was perhaps more overtly despotic than anywhere else in the empire, with its institutions dismantled, its hereditary elite exiled, imprisoned or killed, and an entirely new and foreign administration imposed at gunpoint by Indian soldiers.[3]

Ethnic differences had hardened under colonial rule. By the time Burma became independent, the Kachin saw themselves as a separate race, who not only inhabited their own territory, but spoke different languages to the Burmese. Most Kachin had converted to Christianity, which meant they practised a different religion. They also saw themselves as a martial race, with a long and proud history of independence. Having recently proved their military credentials while fighting beside the British, against the Burmese, in the Second World War, they had no intention of giving up their freedom.[4]

The country's charismatic Burmese leader, General Aung San, who negotiated independence from the British, understood this, Ja Seng Hkawn told me. He promised the Kachin and other upland groups that if they stood beside him as a unified nation, they would receive full administrative autonomy and the right to secede in return.[5]

'Aung San gave a very strong message to the people that they were guaranteed never to be enslaved again,' she said.

But even before the country's new constitution had been finalized, tragedy stuck. In July 1947, six months before his dream of independence was realized, Aung San was assassinated.

'The constitution, when it came out, was all upside down, and very different to what the ethnic leaders were hoping for,'

Ja Seng Hkawn said. 'When they saw this, one after another they turned against the Burmese leaders.'

Uprisings broke out across the country, including in Kachin in 1961, but after the Burmese general Ne Win staged a coup the following year, government forces slowly and brutally won back territory, ending insurgencies in the delta and the central heartland, and in the major cities that were connected by the British-built railways, including Myitkyina.[6]

By the time Ja Seng Hkawn finished school two decades later, Ne Win was still in power, and the railway to Myitkyina had become a symbol of the Burmese occupation – and a key battleground in the Kachin fight for independence. As the only overland route to the north, it fixed Kachin State to a country that its people had never wanted be part of. It was controlled, as it had always been, by an occupying power, only it now shuttled Burmese rather than British troops to the barracks that fortified the line.

Earlier that week, I had visited a retired train driver who had spent much of his career on the front line, dodging bullets fired by Kachin guerrillas from the jungle beside the tracks. Deepak, or Zaw Win as he was known to his Burmese colleagues, lived in a house set among the fields on the outskirts of Myitkyina. Banana leaves and golden flowers adorned the gate, and his courtyard was strung with coloured flags inscribed with Devanagari, the Hindi alphabet.

A cheerful, stocky man, whose chest and arms were decorated with tattoos that were barely concealed by his string vest, he told me that he was descended, on both sides of his family, from train drivers who had moved from India to work in British Burma and who, at independence, had decided to stay behind.

He recalled how his grandfathers had driven trains for the

colonial regime, and his father had driven trains for Myanmar's military regime, and how they had all risked their lives, day after day, to transport soldiers to the hostile north. When Deepak joined the railway department in the mid-1970s, he said, Kachin soldiers had attacked the railway so many times that he lost count.

'There was fighting both day and night,' he told me, rubbing a hand over his scrubby, short hair. 'They always shot at the front of the train, and they had bombs as well – landmines.'

Deepak said he was often afraid, and sometimes felt like giving up his job, but even so he kept driving. His father was shot dead by Kachin insurgents while driving a train on the same railway when Deepak was just six years old, and he felt a responsibility to continue his father's work.

He led me into the house where he showed me photographs, framed on the walls and in albums, of his father: shirtless and gazing at the camera, wearing a railway department cap and holding a rifle, leaning from a carriage window, walking across a railway bridge.

There were photographs, too, of the aftermath of attacks: broken bridges, smashed-up engines, and scarred bodies. As he described those terrifying years, the men and women who had been passing through the house stopped to listen. These were cherished memories in a family whose identity had become inseparable from the railway that its men had lived and died on for so many years.

The attacks happened so frequently, Deepak said, that the railway was always heavily guarded, and a flatbed car loaded with heavy steel beams was attached to the locomotive to detonate landmines. Kachin fighters would cut and slew the tracks, or simply blow them up, and wait for the next train to derail. Then they would hammer the carriages with bullets, killing Myanmar soldiers, but often also civilian passengers and railway staff.

For civilians who had no other way to travel, it must have been frightening, knowing that they could be attacked at any moment, particularly when their trains broke down in the jungle, just as my train had broken down on the way to the north. The soldiers never fought back, Deepak said, because 'they were hiding among the public' – effectively using civilians as human shields.

Over the years, he became an expert at keeping the train moving under fire. He took immense pride in his profession and his knowledge of the engines, and how he and the other railway staff made do with very little.

But by the 1980s, after decades of living and fighting in the jungle, and with no prospect of winning the war, Kachin leaders knew that something had to change. They controlled parts of the mountainous borderlands, but they lived in almost total isolation, largely forgotten by the rest of the country and the outside world.

Ja Seng Hkawn believed their only hope of achieving their political goals was to get the message out, and when she visited China in the mid-1980s on a cultural exchange, she introduced herself to a group of European tourists, and told them about the Kachin plight.

'They had no knowledge of Myanmar or Kachin,' she told me, 'but I saw a sparkling light in one of the men's eyes, which meant he was interested.'

He wrote his contact details on a small piece of paper, and promised he would try to help.

Back in Kachin, she told me, she shared the contact details with her father, who was still the leader of the Kachin Independence Organization, and who decided to travel to West

Germany, to meet the man who had given Ja Seng Hkawn his details. Her father didn't have a passport, and so he walked across the mountains to Thailand, in a journey that took him six months, and bought a fake passport in Bangkok, before flying to Bonn.

'The tourist helped my father to give information to the German leaders,' she told me. 'This was God preparing a meeting with the right person. God used me – one very young girl.'

She claimed that the German government, which she said had been providing financial and military support to the military regime, cut the funding after her father presented evidence that it was being used against ethnic people. Once he was back in Myanmar, he then began trying to unify ethnic and pro-democracy groups, as well as travelling to other countries to spread the word about their cause. Having given up hope of independence, he now saw the conflict as the first step in a struggle for federalism, and a ceasefire agreement with the military was eventually drawn up. The idea was that it would contribute to Kachin autonomy within a federal system. But in late 1993, just months before it was signed, Brang Seng suffered a stroke, and he died the following year.

History would soon repeat itself. Just like Aung San's broken promise, the ceasefire agreement didn't turn out to be anything like the Kachin people had hoped.

'In every single sentence,' Ja Seng Hkawn said bitterly, 'the military grabbed the upper hand. We could not protect our land, or our people, and we suffered many things.'

The ceasefire broke down in June 2011 and attacks on the railway to Myitkyina started up again just a few weeks later. In the country's newly liberated media, a war of words soon escalated. State media called the Kachin terrorists and accused them of attacking non-military targets, while spokespeople for the Kachin Independence Organization told journalists they were simply trying to prevent the military from reinforcing and resupplying its troops.[7]

Within just a few years, more than fifty attacks on the railway had been reported,[8] as thousands were killed in fighting across the state, and more than 100,000 people were displaced[9], and it was in this fraught environment that Ja Seng Hkawn applied for a tender to operate the trains.

While some of her contemporaries saw an enemy that could only be removed by force, she saw an opportunity to build a more peaceful and prosperous future. As one of just a handful of powerful women in a political landscape dominated by men, Ja Seng Hkawn, like her more famous Burmese counterpart Aung San Suu Kyi, wanted to continue her father's work. Like Aung San Suu Kyi, she was also a pragmatist, who believed it was possible to cooperate with Myanmar's military, despite the misgivings of many people who surrounded her.

Ja Seng Hkawn knew exactly what the Kachin people had sacrificed, and how much had already been lost, but she had also witnessed, year after year, the devastating impact of the civil war. As the leader of the Kachin Women's Union, she knew that women had suffered more than most, and she had spoken out about the undocumented rape and sexual abuse that shadowed the fighting.[10] In simple terms, more fighting meant more abuse. It also meant more deaths, more displacement, more profiteering, more drugs, more environmental destruction, and more racial hatred. On the other hand, cooperation was risky, and by taking over a strategic asset that the Kachin Independence Organization had spent decades targeting, she was compromising their position as well as her own.

Topping up my tea, Ja Seng Hkawn didn't answer my question about whether she had taken over the railway specifically to broker

Built in the 1990s, by the time I visited Dawei Railway Station, it was already decrepit.

A train leaves Yangon Central Railway Station at dusk.

An abandoned railway station building in central Myanmar. Across the country, stations built by Than Shwe's junta are now deserted and overgrown.

My fixer, Aung, waits for the train to leave a rural railway station in Rakhine State.

Teashops at Naba Station on the northern railway to Kachin State.

Moe Tar Gyi station platform on the abandoned railway from Katha to Bhamo.

Travelling south from Kachin State towards Mandalay.

Two Buddhist monks travel on the railway from Mandalay to northern Shan State.

The spectacular colonial-era Gokteik viaduct is a vital link between northern Shan and the central plains. Now more than a century old, it is in danger of collapsing.

While fighting multiple insurgencies in the 1970s, Myanmar's military feared the viaduct would be blown up, cutting off the overland route to China. So, they built another railway bridge shadowing its passage across the Gokteik gorge.

Interviewing a railway official at the abandoned station yards in Namtu.

A condition of travelling on the abandoned railway from Namtu to the Bawdwin mine was that I hired my own train; here, the driver climbs into his cabin.

A young food vendor stands on the tracks, blocking the railway to Loikaw during a Marian festival in Kayah State.

The rice wine stall at the Marian festival where I spent a day sitting with my guide, Clement, and his friends and listening to their stories.

Standing on the deserted highway outside Myanmar's parliamentary complex in Naypyidaw, the new capital city built by Than Shwe's regime.

A soldier stands guard at the Defence Services Museum in Naypyidaw.

Nine photographs courtesy of Libby Burke Wilde.
All other photographs provided by the author.

peace. She simply said she wanted to create opportunities for the Kachin to run their own industries. For too long, most people here had few choices: they could fight in the jungle, or extract and sell their resources while destroying their own land. She wanted to 'revolutionize the system', she told me, and she took over the railway simply because there weren't many tenders on offer.

But while the attacks had stopped since her services started running, even though fighting continued elsewhere in the state, nothing here had fundamentally changed. The head of the railway police at Myitkyina Station would later tell me that security forces remained on high alert, and two landmine clearance trains swept the track every night. They were right to remain vigilant – four years later, in 2021, when the military staged another coup, Kachin fighters would once again take up their positions in the jungle beside the line.

But the story of resistance to this railway did not, in fact, begin with Aung San's broken promise to the Kachin people. Back in London, years later, as I read through colonial records and the diaries of British soldiers, I began to understand how central the British railway to the far north had been, both to establishing colonial control over the country, and to forming the divisions that had defined the lives of the people who had lived here ever since.

The story began in the cold season of 1888, when a British survey party accompanied by 170 armed soldiers was sent out into the jungle that I had travelled through, to map a route for a new railway into the northern mountains.[11]

Like me, these men were strangers, travelling into a distant and unknown land. Like me, they were reliant on the goodwill of the local people they were with, and their armed escorts.

Like me, they would have been concerned by reports of fighting in the surrounding jungle, but with no way of knowing how much of a threat it posed to their party, as they travelled north.

They travelled by cart along dirt tracks, camping outside the villages and washing in the cold mountain streams. When the tracks petered out, they continued on foot, employing local porters to carry their luggage and to clear bamboo and undergrowth, as they trekked over the steep forest-covered hills.

In this unfamiliar landscape they were at a military disadvantage. The engineers were told to prepare for attacks and to avoid entering any villages alone, or straying far from their camps. There were other dangers too: when the monsoon came, more than a third of the survey party fell sick with malaria, fever and dysentery, and most of them turned back, leaving just a handful of men to map the remaining valleys, keeping close to the Ayeyarwady River – which originates in the Himalayan glaciers of northern Kachin – and camping on its banks.

Nonetheless, the expedition was a success, and the party returned with the first accurate map of the region, as well as valuable intelligence that would soon be used to bring both the people of the north and their land under British control.

Three years earlier, in November 1885, British troops had invaded Mandalay, waging their third and final war against the Burmese kingdom. Armed with the world's first fully automatic machine guns, they won the war in just eleven days, deposing the Burmese king and sending him into exile.[12]

The war against the Burmese king had been unjustifiable, but the British had tried to justify it anyway, claiming they were removing a tyrant from the throne. Having convinced themselves that they were liberators, they expected to be welcomed by the Burmese people. Instead, they found themselves, in the words of Charles Crosthwaite, the man who would soon become the British Chief Commissioner, in 'an enemy's country',[13] as a fierce, decentralized resistance erupted across the entire Burmese kingdom.

This was an ideological war waged by Burmese patriots, at a time when nationalist consciousness was taking hold across the colonized world, and it was fought in a landscape that Crosthwaite described as 'one vast military obstacle'. Northern Burma's expanse of malarial swamps and jungle-clad mountains, which the British had hardly visited, let alone mapped, provided the ideal cover for resistance fighters to hide and regroup.[14]

Vastly outnumbered and faced with spontaneous uprisings everywhere, the British responded by flooding the territory with over 40,000 Indian Army soldiers and military police, more than four times the number that fought and won the war against the Burmese king. There were mass summary executions and later, mass arrests, trials and hangings.[15] But this alone was not enough. The British needed to deploy troops quickly to suppress rebellions, which was impossible on the country's jungle paths.

Soon after the Third Anglo-Burmese War ended, engineering parties were sent out under armed guard from Rangoon to survey a railway through the newly annexed territory towards the sacked Burmese capital of Mandalay. Its construction was approved without any serious discussion about its economic viability. Some 24,000 labourers were rounded up and a battalion was formed to protect them as they worked. The railway was built specifically to carry artillery, and its stations were designed to withstand attacks. It opened in sections so that soldiers could be shuttled to the advancing front line in the war against insurgents that followed annexation, gradually expanding British authority from the cities to the villages between them[16] – a tactic that Myanmar's military would later try to use against ethnic insurgencies.

British troops meanwhile, in Crosthwaite's words, 'thoroughly explored and . . . cleared' the surrounding forests and 'vigorously disarmed' Burmese leaders. These were euphemisms that, like much colonial writing at the time, obscured and sanitized British violence (the entire campaign was known as the 'pacification' of Burma). At the same time, entire villages of people who 'appeared to be living harmless lives' but were suspected of providing support to the resistance were forcibly relocated to new sites, under British control. Tens of thousands of people were moved, and their former homes were burned to the ground, in the same strategy that would later form a core part of the junta's counter-insurgency campaigns in Myanmar's borderlands.

The effect, wrote Crosthwaite, 'was magical'. In the country's heartland, he went on, uprising after uprising collapsed, 'as a tiger shot in the head falls in his tracks'.

Back in Britain, there wasn't much interest in what was happening, even at the time. Nobody in a position of authority had seriously wanted to annex the Burmese kingdom except the Secretary of State for India, Lord Randolph Churchill. He had been swayed by a powerful commercial lobby that included British merchants and explorers who had spent years bombarding ministers and the Foreign Office with letters calling for a new railway to be built through Burma to China, opening up the Chinese interior to British trade. Arguing that it would be 'a most remunerative investment', Churchill had convinced the Indian viceroy, Lord Dufferin, to invade.[17]

Dufferin went to war without a mandate, at a time when the British parliament was prorogued, and was heavily criticized for it afterwards. One Liberal lawmaker called it 'an act of high-handed violence for which there is no adequate justification' and presciently warned of a prolonged period of anarchy. Others called it unjust and unjustifiable, a 'kind of freebooting expedition'. But when a Liberal government took office in Britain soon afterwards, they didn't reverse the policy. Britain at the time was partitioning the tribal kingdoms of Africa, and carving up the islands of the Pacific; within a decade the British Empire would cover around a quarter of the world's land mass, and Burma was quickly forgotten.[18]

Once the railway to Mandalay was finished in 1889, and even before the surrounding towns had been forced into an uneasy peace, Crosthwaite turned his attention to the far north, where there were large tracts of territory not yet policed or administered by the British, and vulnerable to attack by tribes.

There were no roads, and even the Ayeyarwady River became so narrow in places that it was impassable by any kind of boat for several months of the year.[19] Plans were quickly drawn up to build a railway, even though the British still knew very little about the people who lived in this part of the country, except that a man named Aung Myat, who was the hereditary ruler, or *sawbwa*, of a place called Wuntho on the planned railway route, was hostile to the British and was likely to be harbouring Burmese rebel leaders from the south.[20]

Considering his court to be 'unpleasantly close to the British frontier', Aung Myat had moved it across the hills, and was 'very suspicious and distrustful of the real purpose of such a strong party marching through his country', the British engineer who led the railway survey later wrote.[21] Aung Myat was right to be worried; this was a reconnaissance, and the railway authorities attached to the Public Works Department were not civilians, but military personnel.[22]

Within a year, with work on the railway underway and

construction workers advancing towards his territory, Aung Myat was forced to make the same impossible choice that people in Myanmar's north have been faced with ever since. Do you collaborate with an occupying power, as Ja Seng Hkawn was doing, and enjoy the rewards – a downtown office, lucrative business contracts, and an opportunity to change the system from the inside? Or do you fight, even if your chances of winning are impossibly slim, and risk exile, injury or even death?

Aung Myat chose to fight. Gathering hundreds of men, he staged a fierce rebellion, attacking the new military outposts, destroying the British infrastructure, and setting fire to two railway construction camps. As their houses burned, the staff panicked and fled, as did the workers on a 150-mile stretch of track further south. It brought the entire project to a halt. As rumours spread that several members of the engineering staff had been wounded and were missing, the survey parties that had been finalizing the route through Wuntho were ordered to return to military posts until stronger escorts could be spared.[23]

Aung Myat and his men had realized the same thing that people all over British India already knew: that colonial railways were weapons of war. Even before India's first railway was built, the British Governor General was arguing that a line connecting Delhi to Calcutta would strengthen the military's hold on the country, enabling troops to be moved quickly between the two cities.[24] During the Indian uprising of 1857, just four years after the first colonial railway opened in British India, Indians who understood that their way of life was under attack destroyed worksites, ripped up half-finished lines, and murdered railway engineers. By the end of the uprising, colonial officials were convinced that railways were the key to establishing and maintaining control over their growing Indian empire.[25]

When Aung Myat attacked the railway infrastructure in Wuntho, it was taken extremely seriously. Reinforcements of British Indian troops, including Gurkhas as well as military police, were quickly sent to the frontier. Some 2,500 armed men drove Aung Myat and his troops from the plains and cleared the surrounding country, before attacking his hilltop stockades and killing and wounding hundreds of his men, until, according to an official report, they were 'thoroughly beaten and cowed'.[26] Thousands more fled, including Aung Myat, who went into hiding among the Kachin in the north. After his palace was razed to demonstrate to the people that his rule was over, his former subjects were disarmed.[27]

But the British didn't just have better weapons and transport infrastructure, they also had the telegraphs and post offices that enabled them to control information and its dissemination in English around the world. Many British newspapers were run by or associated with businessmen who had vested interests in the empire, and they helped both to encourage and justify British expansion.[28] As British soldiers killed Aung Myat's men, readers of the *Evening Telegraph* in Dundee learned that he was 'a troublesome native chief' who had been 'taking unwarrantable liberties with the Queen's subjects on British territory' even though his land had not yet been annexed. In Madras, the *Weekly Mail* described the death of forty-nine of his men in a single battle as 'excellent', while in London the *Evening Standard* reported that in another clash, fifty-three Wuntho men were left dead on the field. 'The little war,' the article explained, 'has thus had a brilliant commencement.'[29]

There are very few surviving Burmese primary sources that

document the resistance after the Third Anglo-Burmese War, including in the north.[30] Most of the public sources that do survive were written by British officials, soldiers, journalists and travel writers, who were all to some degree part of the establishment, and bound by what the writer George Orwell called the 'pukka sahib pose' – a code of conduct that corrupted and censored the British in Burma. 'In England,' wrote Orwell, 'it is hard even to imagine such an atmosphere.' In British Burma, where every white man was 'a cog in the wheels of despotism', every kind of freedom was permitted, except the freedom of thought and speech.[31]

In British writing, the same view appears again and again: that the railway was built in the interest of people in Burma, even if they didn't yet realize it. Those who lost their lives fighting against the invasion of their homeland were described as marauders or wild tribes, and the violence against them was simply the price that a barbarous and backward people had to pay for progress.

When the 'little war' in Wuntho was over, the British administration sent in teams of engineers and workers to extend the railway and the telegraph. The temporary military posts that Aung Myat had razed were soon replaced by barracks, police stations, courts and prisons: the permanent infrastructure of colonial occupation.[32] Despite occasional attacks on British infrastructure including the railway,[33] the message was clear. Wuntho, with its thousands of square miles of territory inhabited by some 150,000 people,[34] had been absorbed into the British Empire.

But the work was not yet done. Further north, the planned railway route was inhabited by Kachin tribes who the British had never visited, let alone, in the words of the Chief Commissioner, 'brought into order and subjection'.

In the north, they didn't even try to justify the invasion, simply telling the Kachin chiefs and other tribal leaders, who had never been ruled by the Burmese king, to pay tribute and obey orders, or face the consequences.

Mechanized, professional British units stormed and captured villages that were defended mostly by swords and spears, killing indiscriminately and setting fire to the houses and rice stores, clearing a path for the railway to advance north.[35] By the end of 1898, a decade after the first railway survey party ventured into the jungle, the British position in the north was transformed. Now, as well as their superior weapons, they controlled infrastructure that enabled them to cover far more ground than local resistance groups, making any serious challenge to their authority impossible.

As I researched and read these accounts, I became increasingly frustrated by the gaps in this history. Piecing the story together felt like trying to recreate the history of the junta's railways using only pro-military sources, and I knew that no matter how hard I tried to read between the lines, I would inevitably absorb at least part of the British imperial world view.

With many of the men and women who fought to defend their homeland dead, imprisoned, in exile, or illiterate, and unable to access the telegraphs, post offices and printing presses that enabled British accounts to dominate the historical record, there were so many stories that had never been recorded, and were now lost – not only about the resistance, but even about the people who built the railway, and the conditions they worked in. There are only hints in official reports about how dangerous the work was: the railway was built by hand, at a time when steam excavators were cutting out much of the back-breaking work on new railways in Britain. Many of the workers were subsistence farmers, who had never worked on a railway before.[36] They were paid very little, and just like the civilians who built the junta's railways, they appear to have been considered dispensable. The jungles they built through were more 'malarious and deadly' than any other part of the country, and at least half the construction party was reported to be sick at any one time.[37] How many, like the neighbours of the people I had met in Myanmar's south, were killed by cerebral malaria or other diseases? How many were killed by falling trees, as they cleared a path through the jungle, or were buried when the earthwork collapsed?

Just like in modern Myanmar, where the military's control over information meant that many of its abuses were never documented, let alone collectively discussed and remembered, so it was in British Burma. Once British control had been established, the violence that attended the railway's construction was largely forgotten, except by the people who had experienced it.

What survives instead, more than anything else, is contemporary writing about the railway itself. It was technically challenging, particularly in the far north where it was built through a narrow gorge with steep spurs and deep ravines, and after it opened there were frequent floods and landslides that required parts of the line to be repeatedly rebuilt.[38] But the British administration celebrated its success in establishing control over the region and its people. When the railway opened, the Indian viceroy, Lord Elgin, made a high-profile journey by special train from the capital at Rangoon, over more than 700 miles, to Myitkyina.

The British made a point of opening their colonial railways with much fanfare, just as Myanmar's military later would, inviting local dignitaries to festivities and fireworks, and large numbers of local people were assembled to welcome Lord Elgin on the platform.

Flanked by a guard of honour of 100 Gurkhas and military police, he gave a speech, congratulating the people of the north on becoming connected for the first time with 'the great world, progress and civilization'. Now that they were ruled by the British government, he said, they had obtained 'not only peace and security of life and property from the attacks of depredators' but also 'a full measure of prosperity and contentment' and 'all the benefits and blessings' that flowed from British rule.[39]

The Myitsone-Mandalar Special Express was identical to any other train service in Myanmar, except there were fans in the ordinary-class carriages, and young men dressed in uniform, who handed around laminated menus before we left the station. A marketing brochure that Ja Seng Hkawn had given me claimed the lights would work and the toilets would be clean, which they were, relatively, at least when my journey began.

But the carriages on her private service were much the same as on public railways, with the same grimy ceiling fans, and dusty seats, and stickers featuring Burmese celebrities plastered over the green walls. There were also, to my disappointment, Burmese police officers wearing the same badly fitting grey shirts, who planted themselves beside me.

The day was dull and hot, but I was looking forward to being on the move again. I was heading south from Myitkyina to Katha, where George Orwell spent two years as an officer in the Indian Imperial Police force, and where he set his novel, *Burmese Days*. I would then travel east towards Bhamo near the Chinese border, another town where the Kachin Independence Organization had been fighting Myanmar's military.

A decade earlier, the junta had started building a railway between Katha and Bhamo. It was a branch line, which would have connected the planned 300-mile railway through contested territory along the Chinese border to the mainline network, and it was the only part of the project that was ever built.

Even this short section had been abandoned when the Kachin ceasefire broke down in 2011, and fighting started up again, but I was hoping to find someone in Katha who would drive me along the route. I wanted to find out why this railway was built, and how the Kachin who lived along the route felt about it, particularly given the long history of resistance to the British-built railway I was now travelling on – the only other line in the far north.

As we rolled out of Myitkyina, I saw in the daylight what I had missed when arriving by train into the city at night. Beyond the thatched palm settlements that encircled the station, densely at first and then becoming sparser, we passed sprawling barracks and training fields. There were signs of militarization everywhere. At small stations, groups of soldiers sat around with rifles slung across their knees, and on the roads, green army trucks shuttled women and children between the fortified buildings. Reflecting the mood, a group of young boys in a backstreet aimed wooden guns at the passing train.

At lunchtime I walked to the dining car and ordered a cup of tea. Small groups of men were huddled around the tables smoking cigarettes and sharing bottles of whisky and beer. They were dressed in the unofficial uniform of Kachin traders: dark woollen hats, jackets, and golden jewellery set with jade. Kachin was, after all, the largest source of jade in the world.

At the far end of the carriage, a man wearing a fake Armani T-shirt and jade earrings raised his glass.

'Hello,' he shouted. He stood up, staggered towards me and

slammed his mug of beer and the remains of a greasy omelette onto my table. 'USA?' he asked, leaning over me.

I shook my head. 'England,' I said.

He appeared to be very drunk, but his questions were pointed. 'Where are you going? Which hotel?' he asked me, adding, 'Only one?'

I had often been asked this question by policemen, and it meant, 'Are you travelling alone?' I didn't answer him, pretending not to understand.

'One-man show?' he shouted, pushing his face so close to mine that I was bathed in his sour breath. 'No husband? No boyfriend?'

As I wondered how to escape him, a tall, slender old man with a kind face appeared and tapped my interrogator on the shoulder. He stumbled away, and the old man said something too quietly to hear over the din of drunken conversation.

'Ja Seng Hkawn,' he whispered, this time into my ear, and then he smiled, and walked away. Knowing that this was a place where security forces offered no protection, she must have asked him to look out for me.

'He paid for your tea,' the waiter told me when he came back, showing me the cash. Later I looked up and down the train for the man to thank him, but he had gone.

We pulled into a town called Naba in the late afternoon, where there was a branch line to Katha, but I had missed the only train that day. The towns were close, so I took a local taxi: a trailer lashed to the back of a motorbike. It was a thrilling ride, along winding paths that cut through the jungle. The canopy blocked the low afternoon light, throwing the road into shadow, and as I inhaled the heavy, sweet scent of the trees, men and women on motorbikes streamed past us from the nearby mines, their limbs streaked blue-grey with mud. My driver stopped occasionally to pick up one of the men and women who were trudging barefoot along the edge of the road, and the trailer gradually filled up as we careered deeper into the jungle.

I thought that we were travelling towards a sleepy town formed from wooden houses on stilts that was set into a bend in the river, so it was a surprise when the jungle fell away, and the dirt path widened into a two-lane concrete highway. As Katha's sprawling suburbs unfolded, we passed half-built trading centres and imposing multi-storey villas, secured by electric gates. It was clear that the town had recently become rich, and at first I couldn't figure out why. But then I realized that we were near the Chinese border. So much money was being pumped into China's southwestern provinces that it was spilling over into Myanmar, largely through the black market, and transforming the once-impoverished villages and towns here beyond recognition.

The sun was setting as we pulled up outside what my outdated guidebook claimed was Katha's only guesthouse. It was a dilapidated, damp hostel on the waterfront, whose sleeping cubicles were divided by sheets of hardboard. But its receptionist, an earnest, bespectacled young man, spoke some English, so I stuck around. He didn't know much about the new railway, he told me. But he did have a friend who was a tour guide, and who agreed to drive me the next day to the abandoned stations on the outskirts of town. Feeling only a little guilty that I wasn't staying at his hostel, I said goodnight, and checked into a shiny new Chinese-owned motel nearby, which had impeccably clean sheets and charged half the price for a room.

The next morning, my guide turned up early. He was dressed like a chauffeur, in a pink silk *paso* and a white shirt fastened with a diamond stud. Introducing himself as Minn, he placed his velvet shoulder bag neatly on the front seat of his car, and suggested I sit in the back.

He was excited about our trip, and having done some research the night before, he drove me first to the old British train station in the centre of town, where we tried to interview the stationmaster. A surly man with a paunch, he avoided my eyes, telling me when I pressed him for information that the new railway had closed because there weren't enough passengers. That was it, he said, tapping his fingers on his desk. He had nothing else to say.

'He didn't want to talk,' Minn said, conspiratorially, when we were back in the car. 'He told us there were no passengers, but in fact most people were afraid to use the train.'

Minn told me not to worry. He knew another place where we might find answers about the railway's history, and soon we were pulling up outside a single-storey office on the other side of town.

'My name is Han Win,' said a wiry, sunburned man, standing up from behind his desk, as we walked in. He was the 'high clerk' for the new railway to Bhamo, he said, and this was the project office.

Delighted that someone was showing an interest in his work, he produced a thick folder of notes and slapped them onto the desk. Drawn to the sound of our voices, several men emerged from a back room, and by the time Han Win had finished reading us a list of statistics about the railway, they had pulled up plastic chairs, and gathered around us to listen.

'At first, we were very happy,' Han Win said in English, pausing to enjoy the suspense he was creating. He smiled at the other men, who smiled back.

'At first, no problem,' one of them chimed in.

During the ceasefire years, the junta wanted to develop the region, he said, including building a new railway that would connect the mainline network through Katha, to Bhamo, which at the time was peaceful. The generals awarded construction contracts to ten companies, Han Win said, writing the names down for me on a piece of paper. But none of the companies had much, if any, experience building railways, and almost immediately, they ran into problems.

Katha is built on a narrow ridge and connected to Bhamo by an expanse of floodplains that are interlaced by networks of streams, or as one British railway engineer wrote in 1888, an 'enormous swamp'.[40] But this did not deter the generals. Even though the railway made slow progress, state newspapers were soon reporting that its very existence in this part of the country proved the Kachin conflict was finally over.

'Bhamo–Katha Railroad Project, a Fruitful Result of Stability and Peace', read the headline of one article, which quoted a local resident saying, 'Local people . . . never dreamt about such a railroad here,' and 'We thank the government very much for restoration of peace and stability and for the railroad.'[41]

There are two roads that lead through Myanmar to the Kachin Independence Organization's headquarters of Laiza, on the Chinese border. The northern road passes through Myitkyina and the southern road passes through Bhamo. When the junta started building the railway, it would almost certainly have appeared to the Kachin military strategists who had spent decades blowing up the railway to Myitkyina that the military was closing in on Laiza, through Bhamo – and it wouldn't have helped that the military's regional commander was personally opening stations and inspecting progress on the line.[42]

It wasn't just the railway; economic activity had accompanied militarization everywhere in the state, from the jade, amber and gold mines to logging sites, and new hydropower projects in the mountains that would flood large areas of indigenous land.

As people elsewhere in Myanmar cautiously welcomed an era of new freedoms, Kachin leaders once again demanded, and were again refused, a place in a federal union and the internal autonomy that Aung San had promised them. When the military tried to pressure the Kachin Independence Organization to become a militia under its command, and Myanmar troops broke the ceasefire terms, and attacked Kachin positions near a Chinese-backed hydropower dam east of Bhamo, conflict erupted again across the state.[43]

In mid-2011, Myanmar military units moved quickly into Bhamo, and began arresting, torturing, and killing Kachin civilians in the surrounding villages.[44]

Han Win spread a map across his desk showing the railway route meandering east from Katha alongside the river. Now, he pointed to a village called Mansi, just south of Bhamo, which was circled in red, and where there had been a temporary railway office.

'Terrorists attacked the office,' Han Win told us. The staff panicked and fled, and the companies abandoned the project as Kachin troops planted landmines in the station buildings and on the tracks. Unlike in Wuntho, where work on the British railway started up again soon after Aung Myat's rebellion, the landmines brought construction to a permanent halt. There has never been any systematic landmine clearance in Myanmar, because landmines are still used both by the military and by non-state armed groups. Instead, the military built a cheap dirt road parallel to the route, and used it to drive tanks to Bhamo.

Since the railway closed, flooding had dislodged the earthwork, and landslides had blocked the track, Han Win told us. If

Aung San Suu Kyi's government wanted to finish building it, he said, it would have to start all over again. But it was unlikely to do this, both because of the landmines and because the new government was cutting costs. So why were these men still here? It was almost, I thought, as if the generals might just walk into this office again one day, to finish the work they had started.

Han Win and his colleagues weren't the only ones who were still working. Later that morning, as Minn and I walked through what we thought was an abandoned station at the edge of town, we were startled by a man who emerged from the derelict ticket office.

'I just want to know if my station will open again,' he told us, morosely, when we asked him what he was doing there. He was the stationmaster, and he had lived here with his extended family ever since the railway closed. Years had passed, and still nobody had told him whether to stay or go. Neither had he asked – after all, he was still being paid, and his family was living in a government house for free.

'He is ready to do his duty,' Minn said, as the man listed the requirements of a job that he was no longer required to do. Minn was dressed so smartly that he looked as if he might be an official, and I realized the stationmaster was justifying his existence here, just in case we had the power to send him away.

'At any time,' Minn translated, as the stationmaster offered to show us his documents, 'he's ready to perform all his duties.'

He was the last who had stayed behind. By the time we reached the third station on the railway, I realized that the entire region we were driving through to the east of Katha was deserted, in stark contrast to the busy road I had travelled on the previous day to reach the town. The road was becoming increasingly rutted, and Minn was slowing down more often to navigate gaping holes. The railway beside us was covered with earth, indicating that the surrounding valley had recently flooded, and I began to wonder idly, and then a little less idly, whether any of the landmines on the tracks had been dislodged.

Minn and I had fallen into silence, and when we came to a village I found myself hoping that it would be busy, and my growing sense of unease would lift. But as we drove on, it quickly became clear that this village was deserted too. Several miles later, Minn stopped to talk to a woman who was standing on the side of the road, holding out a collection bowl. She was raising money for a new pagoda at a nearby monastery, she said. 'There are Myanmar soldiers staying there,' Minn translated, as she spoke.

At the next station, we parked the car and walked along a narrow path, through a tunnel of undergrowth. Inside the station, as we walked through the empty rooms, we came across two mats and two blankets rolled up against a wall, beside a large bamboo sieve and a ceremonial knife.

I was about to pick up a phone charger from the floor that was attached to a portable solar panel, when two teenage boys walked out of the bushes. They were each carrying a machete, but they didn't seem threatening; one of them was also carrying a ball, and I noticed there were scuff marks on an open wall beside the building, where they had been playing.

They were living here while they dried their sesame harvest, they told us, because there was a shelter above the platform that protected it from the rain. Their village had no electricity, one of them added, as if that also explained why they were here.

It occurred to me that camping out at an abandoned station was something that two young men might do in a war, and then I realized, at last, why there had been nobody on the roads.

I had assumed that the villages around Katha were peaceful, because we were on the Myanmar side of the Kachin border. Now I realized that the Myanmar troops staying at the monastery must have been there on active service. I had imagined that the front line in the conflict would be obvious, but when both armies were always on the move, setting up and then dismantling temporary bases, the borders of the war were always shifting.

Back in the car, the road soon became noticeably worse, but there was one more station that had once been open, and Minn suggested that we visit it before turning back. The jungle had been closing in on either side of the road, and now we entered a gully where the trees that surrounded the car were coated in a film of red earth. As our tyres displaced the loose clay on the road, the clay rippled, as if we were driving through water. The wind picked up, and soon our car was enveloped in a cloud of swirling dust.

When the road opened out again, Minn pulled up on a verge beside a small shophouse. Scrambling up a bank beside the road, I peered down at the abandoned railway, where two men were walking along the edge of the track. Seeing me, they stopped, and one of them formed a gun with his hands.

The owner of the shophouse was a Kachin woman, who ushered us into in a small, partially covered restaurant at the back, pressing sunset-yellow cans of Royal Lipo energy drink into our hands. Sitting down, I looked around the room. Pinned to the wall in one corner was a tattered Liverpool FC poster, featuring the words 'You'll never walk alone'. Slumped in a chair beneath the poster was an old man, whose arms were mottled by faded tattoos. His eyes had been fixed on me since I walked in, and when I met his gaze, he flashed me a crooked smile that revealed a small set of stained red teeth. Minn sat awkwardly beside me, as a young man sauntered in, beamed at us, and threw himself onto a chair. 'What are you doing here?' he asked.

As Minn quietly explained, and I reflected on how absurd his explanation must sound, I noticed that this was the same young man who I had just seen on the railway track.

'We are researching the abandoned railway,' Minn was saying, politely. 'This woman is British, and she has been researching railways all over Myanmar.'

The two men exchanged glances, evidently unconvinced. It didn't make sense that anyone would come all this way, travelling for miles along a deserted road, to a place that had been desolated by war, just to look at a railway. Nobody came here unless they had to, and definitely not foreign women accompanied by well-dressed Burmese men. The younger man appeared more amused than suspicious, but he kept glancing at the old man, whose gaze never left us.

'Any questions?' Minn asked me. He wanted me to take the lead, to prove to them that I was a researcher as he'd claimed, and to justify our presence here. I asked the same questions I had been asking all over the country. Had any land been confiscated for the railway? Was there any forced labour? Why had the project been abandoned?

Every time the young man started to answer, the older man spoke over him. No land had been taken, he said. All the land was owned by the government. There was no forced labour, nor any labour issues at all. The companies brought in their own workers from the south. In the brief time the railway was open, it mostly transported freight, he said, charcoal, timber and food. It was abandoned now because it had flooded, and there was no money for repairs.

'Also, they were fighting each other,' the young man said,

becoming the first to mention the war. 'The government military attacked the Kachin army, so the Kachin people were afraid to travel by train.'

The old man was now drumming his fingers on the table. When I asked whether Myanmar soldiers had used the railway, and even before Minn had translated the question, the old man interrupted.

'No soldiers used the trains,' he said.

Had there been fighting on the line? I asked.

'No,' he replied. He was trying to shut the conversation down quickly, but the young man evidently wanted to talk about what had happened here. After a long silence, he gathered the courage to speak again.

'Three years ago there was fighting on the railway, and the railway closed,' he said. 'It cannot open again until there is peace.'

When he heard this, the old man unfolded his wiry limbs, stood up, and marched out of the restaurant, with an energy that surprised me. The young man relaxed, and began to speak to Minn more openly than he had before, describing how soldiers had used the railway to carry supplies. But as he spoke, the women in the doorway disappeared, and a Kachin soldier dressed in a bomber jacket and khaki pants burst into the room.

A squat, muscular man with broad, high cheekbones, he swaggered towards us, and Minn began whispering to me fervently in English.

'They have informers,' Minn said, meaning the Kachin Independence Organization. 'I am wearing Burmese clothes. They think we are government spies . . .'

He trailed off, as the soldier flung his khaki bag onto the table next to us. Up close, I could see that his face was scarred and weather-beaten, making him appear older than he was. He can't have been much older than me, in his late twenties at most, but he was agitated and drunk, which made him frightening. I could smell the alcohol on his breath, as he leaned towards me and stuck out a stubby hand, displaying rough, cracked skin around the knuckles of his misshapen fingers, one of which was missing.

I reached out to meet his hand, which he clasped, giving me a handshake so firm that I almost shouted out in pain. Withdrawing his hand, he pulled a battered smartphone from his pocket and took our photograph, and then he turned his back on us, and strode out of the room.

Standing up, I watched him walk outside, stumbling and muttering to himself, as he photographed Minn's number-plate. He staggered backwards and then, as if suddenly remembering where he was and what he was doing, he turned and marched back into the restaurant. Sitting down, he pulled a ledger from his shoulder bag, and called over the owner, who rushed to his side. They spoke for a while in Jinghpaw, the Kachin language. Not understanding what they were saying, Minn began to panic.

'The Kachin army doesn't like strangers,' he told me, in English. 'Here, they have full authority. They can even kill us.'

Hearing Minn speak English, a language that he didn't understand, the soldier turned on him.

'Who are you? What are you doing here? Show me your identification,' he said, in Burmese. As far as he was concerned, we were both foreigners.

Minn fell silent, and pulled his identification card from his bag.

'Are you government officers?' the soldier asked us. I produced my passport, hoping it would help to convince him that we weren't. His jaw twitching, he seized our documents, and began copying the information painstakingly into his ledger.

We were just 100 miles from Wuntho, where Aung Myat had staged his rebellion, and more than a century had passed, and yet through it all, men like this Kachin soldier had held their ground.

It wasn't just the people who lived on the periphery: the war was everywhere in Kachin, and it affected everyone, whether they lived in the jungle or in the cities, causing divisions between those who benefited from the union with Myanmar, and from the conflict itself, and those who were disproportionately harmed by it.

But while the Kachin appeared to be a long way from winning the war, they hadn't lost either. Just as in Rakhine, this abandoned railway was instead a symbol of the junta's failure to expand, or even establish, state control. Myanmar's generals had tried to weld communities together by force, replicating techniques used by the British colonial state. The mistake they had made was that this strategy requires the state to be significantly stronger than the groups it wants to assimilate.

Back in the 1890s, the British had a significant advantage in weapons, infrastructure and communications over the people they conquered. In modern Myanmar, the military's advantage over the population they subjugated was much slimmer. By the time the regime had amassed enough resources after the collapse of Ne Win's socialist regime to try to defeat multiple insurgencies at once, China had become a market economy, and the Kachin and other armed groups who were based on the border could simply export jade, timber, drugs and other goods, and import the weapons and related materials they needed to keep the resistance alive.

The British railways had enabled colonial troops to be

deployed much faster than resistance forces, which then only had access to jungle tracks and waterways. But in modern Myanmar, insurgents could travel quickly using the roads. And the Kachin no longer lived in isolation as they had during colonial rule – or even when Ja Seng Hkawn was young. As Christians, many of them spoke English, and they had strong connections to the West, particularly to America, which had not only provided support to the Kachin people but had imposed harsh economic sanctions on the junta.

But stalemate was nothing like victory, and with no end to the fighting in sight it was hard to imagine a future in which the violence didn't simply grind on, while fear and mistrust deepened.

In the teashop, the Kachin soldier was still hunched over his book, chewing his cheek. Minn spoke to him, explaining, trying to appease him, pointing at me, and at himself, and then explaining again.

There were more questions – who were we, what were we doing there – and it was only when the younger man intervened that the tension broke.

He explained, loudly, in Burmese, to Minn and me that we needed permission from the Kachin Independence Organization if we wanted to visit the area, and he explained to the soldier that we would return to our car, and drive back the way we came. As the soldier considered whether to let us go, Minn and I jumped up, and rushed out of the restaurant, without looking back.

KACHIN

• Muse

CHINA

Namtu
Bawdwin Mines ◻

Lashio

MANDALAY

Hsipaw   SHAN

existing railway
highway

Mandalay

Northern Shan State

0   25   50 km
0   20   40 miles

N

6.

Northern Shan

Our driver revved the diesel engine, releasing clouds of black smoke. He revved it again, and again, as if he was firing up a generator, until our tiny green locomotive creaked out of the railway yard and edged along a haphazard line of wooden sleepers, which stretched into the mist, towards the hills beyond the town.

We had walked that morning along the tracks, picking our way towards Namtu Station, between fences that were topped with barbed wire, and then past rows of abandoned wooden carriages that converged on the approach to a sprawling loco-motive shed. Inside the shed, dozens of coal-streaked engines, carriages, and heaps of old machinery were all coated in a thick layer of dust.

There were guards milling around, as there always are in Myanmar long after an industrial site has been abandoned, and at the far end of the shed a cluster of mechanics was crouched around a car-train, a type of rail bus made from the body and wheels of an old Hino truck. Stepping over filthy dust sheets, we wiped cobwebs from the engines to reveal the names of their now-defunct British manufacturers: W.G. Bagnall, Kerr Stuart, GEC.

This station and its yards had been restricted from the public ever since the railway, which served the mine at nearby Bawd-win, had closed several years earlier. The entire region had been closed to foreigners since the 1960s, and it had taken me months to secure a permit to visit.

Permits were only given out at all because the mining railway was famous among European railway enthusiasts, who had convinced the generals to let them pay thousands of dollars to commission steam trains, to take them on supervised tours of the mine.[1] One of the conditions of visiting Bawdwin was that I would hire my own train, and luckily a diesel-powered trolley had turned out to be a fraction of the price of a steam engine. Another condition was that I would travel with a chaperone.

'We are going up that mountain,' Ronnie said, with a grin, pointing towards a peak in the distance. The smell of diesel grew stronger, and our view was soon obscured by clouds of toxic smoke, as we began the slow climb between steep embankments, into the hills.

A septuagenarian who had lost one of his legs when he was a child and now walked with a crutch, Ronnie was also a local table-tennis champion, and the lead singer of the eponymous Ronnie Club Band, a twenty-two-member ensemble that specialized in Rod Stewart and John Denver covers. With his fake Gucci satchel, he was nothing like the government stooge I had dreaded being assigned. Intensely energetic, he looked much younger than his seventy years, which was partly because he dyed his hair jet black.

We had been rattling for some time between steep embankments, when the track opened out and corkscrewed around the river, and Ronnie shouted to the driver to stop. This 540-degree spiral, he told me, was a highlight of the journey. Having claimed to be a railway enthusiast, and now fearing I would be exposed as a fraud, I did my best to appear enthusiastic, as Ronnie spent half an hour showing me all the best vantage points to photograph the track. Back on the train, the engine struggled as the route became so tortuous that it felt at times as if our cart would topple into the valley below. Although it was small, it was highly unstable, and it rocked ominously, throwing us from one side of our shared bench to the other.

I gripped the wooden frame beside me, where a window had once been, while Ronnie gleefully described the landslides that over the years had taken down chunks of the hillside, along with portions of the track. It had been repaired so many times, he said, that it was a miracle trains could still run.

Then, suddenly, we had reached the top, and our driver was bowing towards the pagodas that were now visible on the distant hills, with his hands pressed tightly together in gratitude for our safe arrival.

On level ground, we passed along a low ridge, where nothing grew except soft ferns and long grasses, which Ronnie said proved how metalliferous the land was. Then, beyond a grove of trees, the mining village of Bawdwin came into view. Spread out across the valley, it clung to the sheer hillside so tightly that it seemed to have been carved from the land itself.

Our driver stopped the train, and we jumped out and continued on foot, and soon we were weaving a path between the low, wooden houses. Their frames had been patched up with corrugated-iron sheets, and up close I could see that everything here was choked with weeds. There was no noise, except for the trickle of a nearby stream, and the crunch of our feet on the small stones that littered the path.

'It's a sleeping city,' Ronnie said, as I marvelled at its existence.

Two years earlier a road had been built, enabling the people who lived here to come and go by motorbike, and the previous year a landline had been installed, which was fixed up to a network of wires and bamboo poles. But except for the road and the landline, and a few old television sets, little had changed at Bawdwin since the mine was nationalized half a century earlier. The people here lived in the same houses, sent their children to the same school, and died in the same hospital. Food still arrived once a week, and water was still sourced from the mountains using the same old pumping station, which was now so badly rusted it barely worked.

The company that operated the mine paid its former workers a retainer, Ronnie said, the equivalent of £2 a day, but the skilled workers and young people had left the town, and those who stayed behind were struggling to survive.

Like them, Ronnie had dedicated his life to this mine, as had his Sri Lankan father, after he was sent here by steamer when he was just twenty years old, from Cape Town, where he had worked for the British as a mining engineer. It was painful for Ronnie to see the mine closed, and he had been coming to terms ever since with how and why, over the course of his life, its fortunes had changed so dramatically.

These were the same questions that had drawn me to this derelict place. I wanted to know why, having tried and failed to build their own industrial railways, including in the south, where I had walked along abandoned tracks that once connected the mainline network to cement factories and rubber plantations, the junta had closed this working line. The mine at Bawdwin might be deserted now, but it was one of the world's largest undeveloped zinc, lead, silver and copper deposits, and it had once embodied British ambitions for this part of the world as a thriving centre of extractive activity, suppling global markets with valuable minerals.[2]

When Ronnie's father arrived into the port in Rangoon, he took a train to the very edge of British India, where, deep in the jungle near the Chinese border, the mine at Bawdwin was thriving. The British had built a new railway across the northern Shan States, a semi-independent territory administered by Shan princes. Prospectors, speculators and engineers had flocked to the region, and in particular to Bawdwin, where the Chinese had once mined silver.[3]

Two smelters were built, connected to a narrow-gauge railway through the mountains – the same railway that Ronnie and I had just travelled on. As new mineral deposits were discovered, operations were scaled up. By the time Ronnie's father arrived in the early 1920s, the company that operated the mine, Burma Corporation, was one of the largest industrial mining companies in the world, and was churning out vast quantities of minerals that were shipped across the British Empire. Its mining complex at Bawdwin featured everything that was needed to entice workers from across the English-speaking world. There was a European club, a horse-racing track and tennis courts, rugby and football teams, a company store, a hospital and schools, all catering to more than 20,000 employees.[4]

Most of the workforce, like Ronnie's father, were immigrants. They had already trained and worked under British supervision elsewhere in the empire, were much more employable, and often worked for less than the Burmese. They came here from all over the empire, but mostly from India, as well as from Nepal and neighbouring China. The Shan and other indigenous groups were employed to do subsidiary tasks, like forestry, while the Burmese, who had no experience working in a modern, industrial economy, were sidelined, and never given a chance to learn.[5] Profits were paramount, and the British government didn't intervene; after all, Burma was a province in British India, whose citizens all had equal legal status.

The mine at Bawdwin was doing exactly what the colonial state in Burma was designed to do: creating and freeing wealth as efficiently as possible – just not for the Burmese.[6] It typified an economic model that was being replicated all over the country, transforming the economic structure of a colony that until the Third Anglo-Burmese War had been based on the export of rice, and creating the foundations of Myanmar's economy today.

After the war, armed construction parties were sent out into the mountains to build new railways that would form new economic arteries, and extending from these arteries, hundreds of miles of cheap railways were laid by companies everywhere in British Burma, connecting the central network to new mills, mines, quarries and factories.[7]

Tramways carried logs through the teak forests in the country's heartland and in the north. Narrow-gauge railways shifted limestone to new cement works, and light railways were laid beside onshore oilfields, alongside pipelines carrying crude. Locomotives were used everywhere, from new tin and tungsten mines, to new rubber and sugar estates. From the far corners of the country, vast quantities of timber and minerals were ferried by train along with a rich array of other resources to the crowded dockyards at Rangoon.

Just a handful of businesses monopolized this trade, almost all of them British. Profits flowed to investors in the City of London, the financial heart of the empire, and to its banks, exchanges, brokers and shipping companies. At the same time, the railways made it easier for immigrants like Ronnie's father to move to the industrial centres, contributing to the exclusion of the Burmese from the economy. Meanwhile, traditional industries were crushed by competition, as British manufactured goods, particularly textiles, were dispatched to the far corners of the country by train.[8]

Few investments were more profitable than the railways themselves, and soon after Britain annexed Burma in 1886, Lord Rothschild, a powerful City banker who was a close friend of Randolph Churchill,[9] took over the entire railway network on a long-term contract. Burma had few roads, and in parts of the country without navigable waterways the Burma Railway Company had a virtual monopoly on trade.[10]

The administration in Rangoon leaned so heavily on British companies that by the 1920s its governor was claiming that Burma owed 'the main part of its development to the great firms' that had invested in the province.[11] But it wasn't so much development as a constellation of extractive enclaves that, like Bawdwin, were tied more closely to London, through British telegraphs, railways and ports, than to the surrounding villages and towns.

By the time Ronnie's father arrived by ship into Rangoon, in the early 1920s, the city had become the largest immigrant port in the world, and among the dispossessed Burmese, desperation was turning to anger.

Mass rallies were already being held in the cities as an independence movement gathered strength. Drawing together everyone from farmers who had lost their land, to monks and university students, the movement was unified by the rallying call 'Race, Language, Religion' or, specifically, the Burmese race and language, and Buddhism, the Burmese religion, all of which were being denigrated under British rule.[12] By the time Japanese troops marched into the jungle of southern Burma in December 1941, an army of young, impassioned Burmese soldiers, the original iteration of Myanmar's armed forces, was marching beside them. Burmese independence leaders, includ-ing Aung San Suu Kyi's father General Aung San, had sought help to overthrow the British, and they believed Japan's prom-ise to liberate them.

The colony in Burma, at the eastern frontier of British India, had never been a priority for the British Empire, and its defence had always been neglected in favour of India's northwest. Now, it was exposed and extremely vulnerable. As the first Japanese bombs fell on Rangoon, killing as many as 2,000 civilians, the city's British and Indian residents fled towards the border.[13] The Burmese had nowhere to go.

Ronnie's father was still working at Bawdwin when the mine was seized by Japanese forces. They rounded up the employees who had been unable to get away, or who chose to stay behind, and forced them to continue working. He was still there in 1945 when the British bombed the mine, destroying the buildings and stores.

'The Japanese occupied everything, so the British bombed their own mine,' Ronnie told me.

He was showing me around a small hospital, built into the hillside, where the wounded had been treated. It was once the best hospital in the country, he said. Now, the wooden walls and wrought-iron beds were so decrepit it was impossible to tell if they were ever cleaned.

An elderly man was sitting outside in the sunshine, and he told us that his grandparents had been treated here, after the village was bombed. His grandfather was injured, and his grandmother was so badly burned that she died.

'Many people in my family died because of bombs,' he said, quietly.

It wasn't just Bawdwin that the British bombed. As they retreated towards northeast India, in the longest retreat in

British military history, they tried to destroy everything they left behind – which mostly meant the railways and the towns and extractive enclaves that had sprung up around the network.

Two years later, in 1944, the British drove the invading Japanese back along the railways, through central Burma into Southeast Asia.[14] This time they were supported by the young Burmese soldiers, who by then had realized Japan had no intention of 'liberating' their country, and switched sides. By the end of the war, two-thirds of the railway network had been destroyed. Some 27,000 soldiers fighting for the British and 144,000 Japanese soldiers had been killed, and through conflict, forced labour, famine and disease, an estimated one million Burmese civilians had died.[15] The Burmese wanted independence, but they never asked for their country to become a theatre of modern warfare, and while they sacrificed more than anyone else for Britain's victory in Burma, it was not their war.

Millions of Burmese children, including young boys who would later become generals in Than Shwe's junta, were bystanders. Than Shwe himself grew up in a railway town called Kyaukse. He was eight years old when British troops defending his hometown killed some 500 Japanese soldiers who had advanced along the railway from Rangoon. Shortly afterwards, the Japanese shelled Mandalay Railway Station 30 miles to the north, which sparked a fire that turned a city of wooden buildings to ash.

He was nine when the British bombed Kyaukse's railway yards, destroying the station and warehouses, and eleven when the Allies recaptured the town, leaving hundreds more people dead. These were formative years, and Than Shwe would have remembered them when he was overseeing logistics, including troop movements, in the War Office under Ne Win, movements that at the time were still almost all by train. He would have understood that the lack of infrastructure in the borderlands was holding the military back.[16]

When the war ended, the British tried to patch up the damage to the railways and other industries,[17] but their attention was now focused elsewhere.

In 1947 the British prime minister Clement Atlee signed an independence agreement with Aung San Suu Kyi's father, General Aung San, the founder of the Burmese armed forces. Giving Burmese independence leaders de facto control over a territory that was much larger than the old Burmese kingdom, the British left, taking much of the skilled workforce with them. But just six months before the transfer of power was complete, Aung San was assassinated, and the newly independent government descended into factionalism.[18]

The country the British had left behind was deeply divided along ethnic and political lines, flooded with weapons, and fully versed in the language of modern violence that was the legacy of the Second World War. Within a year of independence, seven serious armed insurgencies had broken out, overrunning much of the countryside.[19]

Their focus was on disrupting communications, with the railways as a main objective – just as they had been for the British and the Japanese in the war. At first, this meant dynamiting bridges, burning stations, and holding up trains. But soon, whole lengths of track were being torn up and carried away into the jungle. Before long, more than a third of the railway network, or some 600 miles of track, was in the hands of insurgents.

Rangoon was cut off from the network, accessible only by air or sea, and government services ran only in daylight hours, on short, isolated sections of track. With trade paralysed, food prices soared. Attacks were so frequent that services were accompanied by improvised armoured trains, made bullet-proof by steel plating and sandbagging, with loop holes for firing through, and timber wagons loaded with scrap to detonate landmines at each end.

When the writer Norman Lewis travelled through the country in the early 1950s, he found that only one of its railways was still operating, the main line connecting Rangoon with Mandalay. Trains would typically travel no more than 50 miles before coming to a place where the line had been dynamited, or a bridge blown up. Large parts of the track had been removed, and travellers often complained of being haunted by ghosts, because there were so many unburied corpses in the jungle beside the line.[20]

The newly independent state was struggling. Within a decade, Ne Win, the head of the armed forces, staged a coup. He soon began to win back control over contested territory, helped by the counter-insurgency strategy known as *phyet lay phyet*, or 'four cuts', that Myanmar's military has used against ethnic minorities ever since.[21] It drew on tactics including mass forced relocations that had been developed by the British under Chief Commissioner Charles Crosthwaite. These tactics had been used again by the British in the 1930s to crush rural uprisings,[22] and later by Ne Win himself, in the year before independence, when he jointly commanded a major counter-insurgency operation with British troops.[23]

Some of the staff from the British-owned Burma Corporation had stayed on at Bawdwin, running the mine through a joint venture with the Burmese government. For Ronnie, who was also a child at the time, these years were a golden age.

'In those days Bawdwin was just like a small England,' he

told me now, as we walked through the village. 'Every year at Christmas the company celebrated with sports and games like track and field, and there was lunch and toys for all the children.' The British men wore moustaches, and the women wore beautiful dresses, he said. 'Ooo, it was lovely.'

But soon Ne Win ushered in radical political, economic and social changes under a programme known as the Burmese Way to Socialism, withdrawing Burma almost completely from global affairs. Indian and Chinese immigrants were forced out, industry was nationalized, and internal trade became the legal monopoly of the Ministry of Trade, through shops known as People's Stores.[24] By the mid-1960s, Ronnie's enchanted childhood world was disappearing.

The mine was nationalized, and the British workers who had once organized football matches and given out toys packed up and left. After that, Ronnie told me, there were no more shipments from England, or from anywhere else. The workers, who were now overseen by soldiers, were told to make do with the materials they already had.

There were still parties at first, including on Independence Day (4 January), and the cinema hall stayed open, although it stopped showing foreign films. At first the soldiers were kind to the people, but then they began to abuse their power.

'General Ne Win started to bully the public,' Ronnie said.

Before long he had learned to despise the country's leader and the soldiers who answered to him.

'Soon, we were living under the gun,' he said. 'There were no rules, no order, nothing – only the military government.'

Shut off from the world, the mine became increasingly isolated and unproductive, as fighting between a dizzying array of armed groups raged through the surrounding hills.

Ne Win visited the mine only once, in the 1970s, by which

time his paranoia was so great that soldiers ordered everyone in the town to stay inside. Nobody was allowed near the football pitch, where Ne Win and his entourage arrived by helicopter, flanked by armed guards.

'Even the hospital patients weren't allowed to look out of the windows,' Ronnie recalled. 'There were insurgents everywhere, and Ne Win was scared.'

Production at the mine had fallen precipitously, and the regime eventually sought help from a group of German geologists and engineers, but it wasn't enough.[25] The entire economy was on the verge of collapse, sustained only by occasional foreign-aid payments and a vast black market.

Ne Win's attempt at self-reliance had failed. Like every other newly decolonized country that had experimented with economic autarchy, Myanmar would soon be drawn back into the global economy, a system that was developed and still controlled by the old colonial powers.

As the public institutions that still existed were swept away by nationwide protests that paralysed the country for much of 1988, the military once again stepped into the vacuum. This time it would dramatically restructure the Burmese state, the economy, and its own engagement with the outside world.

Ronnie was now marching off again, towards a collection of cavernous sheds that extended into the hills beyond the village, and which housed a complex of mining machinery that had once formed the heart of this community.

A man wearing a pale-grey Zhongshan suit came out to meet us, and then ushered us inside. Stepping over dust sheets, I gazed up at the iron scaffolding, the vast cogs, the walls hung with giant spanners, the pulleys that looked like trapeze rings, and the levers that operated chutes designed to transport men deep beneath the earth. There were generators, ropes and golden plaques bearing the names and addresses of British manufacturers, like the English Electric Company of London, which was sold in 1968.

It was a monument to a Britain I could not reconcile with the country I had grown up in – a place whose people revelled in the power of industry, of coal, smoke and steam, of great mill engines and powerful railway locomotives.

'This,' Ronnie was saying, 'is the winder for the Marmion shaft, which goes 1,400 feet underground and is connected by a 3-mile tunnel to Tiger Camp.' Hot, wet dust rose from the tunnel and swirled around us, as light streamed in through the windows.

'That red shed,' Ronnie went on, leading me back outside into the sunshine, 'is the control room. It's made of zinc – from England. More than 100 years old, and still in good condition. Some of these machines are from Birmingham, England. Some are from Stafford, England.'

I wondered what he imagined these places were like, but he had moved on, and was pointing to a sign fixed to a rickety lift that read, in English: *top deck 9 men bottom deck 12 men*.

'Which level do you want to go to?' he joked.

In the village square, there was a large wooden shed containing a raised platform that Ronnie said was once a music hall.

'This used to be a stage, where British mineworkers and their families performed to the Bawdwin public,' he told me, taking out a small comb and plastering his hair across his head. There was a cinema hall, too, which once had a working projector.

'In England,' he asked, 'do your people still live like this?'

I wondered how to explain to Ronnie how far we had moved on. In Britain, it felt like centuries had passed since the end of the empire. Here, at Bawdwin, it felt like the British had only just left, and the gap between the two worlds was widening all the time. Our wealth, technology, education, and the peace we had established in Europe since the end of the Second World War had enabled us to modernize ever faster as the decades passed, whereas thousand of miles away at Bawdwin little seemed to have changed.

I started to tell Ronnie this, explaining that I had never been to a music hall, and that in Britain we usually watched live music now at bars, or festivals. But then I realized that perhaps not so much had changed in Britain, after all: we still watched live music and went to the cinema, and we still extracted what we needed from our former colonies, buying up resources cheaply and selling them for huge profits.

Yes, Myanmar was haunted by the empire, with its ideas about race and the armed conflicts it had set in motion, and its rapacious, extractive logic. But wasn't Britain also haunted by its colonial past? And wasn't it, instead, a sign of how much had changed in Myanmar that this place was now abandoned, and life had moved elsewhere?

I trailed off, but Ronnie had lost interest, and was now pretending to strum a guitar.

'I used to come and entertain with my band here,' he said.

As we sat down for lunch at the only restaurant in Bawdwin, a man wearing khaki trousers and a woollen hat walked in and bought a large bottle of gin. As he was paying, a second man walked in, dressed in a smart black jacket. He looked around, but didn't buy anything. When he left, Ronnie followed him outside. I asked Sai where Ronnie had gone, but he ignored the question, and suggested instead that we start eating. By the time we had finished, Ronnie's plate of *tamin kyaw*, a simple meal of fried rice, was cold.

Sai was our driver. Hiring him and his car had been another condition of visiting the mine, because I wasn't allowed to travel to Namtu alone. I had warmed to him immediately, just as I had warmed to Ronnie. A young Shan man, Sai was energetic and passionate, with a round face, and gaps between his teeth. He spoke five languages and had lived for seven years in Malaysia, working with refugees. Perhaps because he had spent so long outside the country, he spoke much more freely about politics than Ronnie did.

As we waited for Ronnie to come back, we inspected the tiny wooden restaurant that doubled as a shop. From floor to ceiling the shelves were crammed with dusty tins and packaged goods: cans of energy drink, condensed milk, oil and dried noodles. There was a cabinet filled with discoloured bottles of whisky that cost the equivalent of £1 a litre. There were bottles of beer whose labels were disintegrating, and home-brewed rice wine in recycled soda bottles that had no labels at all.

'When I drink this,' Sai told me, holding up one of the bottles, 'my chest gets hot, and I see moons and stars.'

There was Ovaltine, and Dulac milk powder, and sachets of instant tea- and coffee-mix, and cigarettes – WIN cigarettes cost just 30p a packet; Red Ruby and Premium Gold, both made by the military, were double that, but you could buy individual cigarettes. There were cigars made in a small factory near the Chinese border, and I was about to buy several packets to take home to Yangon, when Ronnie came back in, looking anxious.

He asked the shop owner to switch on the old television set in the corner of the room, and we all sat down to watch. A report was breaking on the state broadcaster: the newsreader was saying that coordinated attacks by four insurgent groups had already killed at least eight people across the state. Instinctively, I reached for my phone. State media was not always a reliable source of information and I wanted to check what was really happening.

It was only when I remembered there was no phone signal here that I felt a wave of panic. It wasn't so much because of the fighting, but because I relied on the internet, and above all on my Twitter feed, to verify information; and because without a phone signal, there was no way to contact anyone in case we needed help.

Ronnie was talking to us over the broadcaster. Having lived here all his life, he had his own, more established methods of finding out what was happening, and had been speaking to some local men, who had just arrived in the village with news. A policeman had been shot early that morning (20 November 2016) at the customs yard in Muse, the largest city on the Chinese border, sparking intense fighting. As freight trucks burned, the traders and officials had fled, but not before several civilians were killed.[26]

Fighting had also broken out in Namtu township, where we were staying, Ronnie went on, and on the surrounding mountain roads. He pushed the cold rice around his plate with a fork. (I would later find out that Ronnie's wife lived in Muse, and he must have been extremely worried.) Groups of insurgents were stopping cars and extorting their drivers, he said, and he had heard that some of the roads were blocked. He stopped talking when the man in khaki trousers walked back into the shop.

'The Palaung are here,' he said quietly when the man left again, referring to one of the ethnic armed groups that was responsible for the attacks. 'The insurgents are everywhere.'

Sai, who had said nothing since hearing the news, now told

us that he had family and friends in Muse. Like me, Sai relied on social media for information, but in his case, this meant Facebook, where there were dozens of private groups dedicated to sharing news about the conflict that was sweeping through the region.

Since mobile networks had been rolled out across the country two years earlier, Myanmar had become a nation of citizen reporters, and Sai knew there would already be photographs of the bodies, geolocated and possibly even identified and tagged, as well as detailed information about every outburst of gunfire, every explosion, every new checkpoint being set up on the roads.

Impatient to find out what was happening, and to check that his family and friends were safe, he paid our lunch bill, and rushed outside.

As we walked back through the deserted village, Sai told us how frustrated he was that nothing had really changed since Aung San Suu Kyi's government had taken office earlier that year, in April 2016. It hadn't extended the new freedoms introduced by the previous government, and while some people were making more money from new industries, most of it went to the men with guns, as it always had, while civilians felt no more protected than before.

If anything, Sai said, the fighting was worse.

'The National League for Democracy made a big noise, but now where are they?' he asked, referring to Aung San Suu Kyi's political party. Thinking about this, I was reminded of my conversation with Min, at the start of my journey in Myanmar's far south. He had been hopeful that Aung San Suu Kyi would be able to end the civil conflict, but his hope was tempered with realism, and now I realized what an impossible task her civilian party of democracy activists had set themselves, of ending a war fought by men who didn't recognize their authority.

We hiked up the hill to the railway, where the trolley we had arrived in that morning was waiting. With visible relief, Sai signalled to the driver, who revved the diesel engine. The problems were still the same, Sai went on, as the train chugged slowly back into the hills, and he couldn't see how they would change.

It wasn't just the railway to Bhamo that was occupied by insurgents: Myanmar's entire northeast had been torn into fragments that were controlled by a patchwork of armed groups, whose borders were demarcated by troops, or checkpoints, or landmines. The groups were organized along ethnic lines and they ran their territories like states, with their own governments, laws and policies.[27] Each had its own language, flag, national dress, traditions, and its own version of history. As Burmese nationalism became more aggressive, so did these ethnic nationalisms, until it became hard for anyone to imagine a country that wasn't divided into 'national races' and Myanmar's borderlands had become a microcosm of our world.

The question was, who did this tribalism benefit? These groups weren't only freedom fighters, as they were sometimes imagined to be in the West – this was also a gritty, capitalist war. To control the porous land borders with China and Thailand was to control tens of billions of US dollars or more every year, in both licit and illicit trade, and new alliances or factions were formed whenever there was a new opportunity to make a profit.

Like Myanmar's generals, the leaders of the ethnic armed groups in Shan State were all, to some degree, strongmen, who had become rich because their weapons enabled them to control access to global markets. Like the generals, they used ethnic nationalism to legitimize themselves, and to create loyalty among the people they sought to rule.

'People here are afraid of both sides,' Sai was saying. Ethnic armed groups imposed arbitrary taxes on everything from property to buying fuel, and they illegally conscripted young men and women from among their own ethnic groups. I asked him what happened if you didn't comply with their demands.

'You have to,' he said bitterly, over the noise of the engine. 'If they want to shoot you, you can't do anything, they can just kill you.'

Now, for the armed groups, an opportunity of a lifetime was emerging. Aung San Suu Kyi was in discussions to build a new economic corridor through the region, as part of China's Belt and Road Initiative, including special economic zones, new highways and a high-speed railway. Sai was worried that the attack on the customs yard in the border town of Muse was a sign of things to come, as armed groups fought to occupy the most strategic land, and civilians were once again caught up in the fighting.

Soon we came to an isolated settlement deep in the valley known as Tiger Camp, which was connected by a 3-mile tunnel to the mines, and was encircled by lush green hills. Palm trees towered over an assembly of wooden and sheet-iron sheds that formed the heart of the camp, and as our driver slowed down to pass them, Ronnie asked him to stop. He wanted to share news of the fighting with the few people who lived here, who were otherwise cut off from the outside world.

While we waited, Sai and I trudged across the dusty ground towards an underground railway that had once carried silver ore here through the tunnel that ran beneath the mountain. We walked in silence because this was a silent place. Inside the tunnel, which was filled with dragonflies, the power was still on. There were safety signs in English pinned to the walls, and as I read them, I felt as if a British engineer might emerge from one of the underground workshops at any moment. 'Men are rarely killed outright by electric shock', advised one such sign. 'They can be saved by immediate first aid. SEND FOR but NEVER WAIT FOR A DOCTOR.'

But the only person we met was a middle-aged woman, who was manning a security hut, back above ground. She told us she had been born here, and had lived here all her life. When she was young, she had been surrounded by family; her grandfather was a mineworker, and he had nine children, and dozens of grandchildren. Now, there was hardly anyone left. A few women were employed as guards, and to cut back the undergrowth when it grew too high, but that was all.

As we spoke, I noticed that her jacket bore the name and logo of the company that operated the mine. It was a subsidiary of Myanmar's largest conglomerate, Asia World Group, whose founder was alleged to have once run the most heavily armed narcotics trafficking organization in Southeast Asia.[28] In the months leading up to the political transition, the junta had sold off hundreds of valuable state assets, including Bawdwin, to its cronies. Asia World had closed the mine soon afterwards.

I was fascinated by the company, whose history and operations provided a glimpse into Myanmar's political economy in the decades of junta rule. Its evolution during the political transition into something resembling a legitimate enterprise was mirrored by other, smaller companies, and I had come to see Asia World's fortunes as a barometer for the entire military-linked economy.

The company's founder Lo Hsing Han was from Kokang, a majority Han Chinese region on the Chinese border, which until 1989 was controlled by the Communist Party of Burma. When the party collapsed, and its territory fell into the hands of mutineers, Lo helped Myanmar's generals to negotiate with various factions, striking deals that saw ethnic leaders on the borders given control over their own 'special regions'. The ceasefire terms were never made public, but opium exports soon doubled, and cash flowed into Myanmar's formal economy.[29]

Lo set up the Asia World conglomerate, with multiple overseas subsidiaries that were allegedly fronts for money-laundering operations. Within a few years, an investigation sparked by an Australian television exposé revealed that more than half of Singapore's investments in Myanmar, worth around £1 billion, involved partnerships with Lo.[30]

Western countries soon imposed sweeping economic sanctions, in response to the junta's crackdown on the pro-democracy movement, which were designed to cut off the generals and their cronies from the global financial system. But there was nothing to stop them doing business in China, or Thailand, including with companies that also did business in the West. Large conglomerates with regional connections like Asia World thrived, whereas small, independent businesses collapsed.

By the time the junta ushered in political and economic reforms in 2011, just a handful of companies controlled a vast network of strategic businesses. Asia World owned the largest port in Yangon and toll roads that connected the country's centre to its borders. It invested in oil and gas pipelines, and a new deep-sea port on the Indian Ocean that formed a central part of China's Belt and Road Initiative. It ran jade-mining businesses, invested in multi-billion-dollar hydropower projects, ran an insurance company, and managed a huge portfolio of real estate.

It wasn't hard to see the parallels between 1990s Myanmar and the economy under colonial rule. But there was one important difference: the men who controlled it were now Burmese citizens.

Back at Tiger Camp, I asked Sai why Asia World had taken over the mine, only to shut it down.

'All the military's factories were handed to companies,' was his simple reply.[31] The truth was that Asia World was unable to make it profitable, and Western sanctions had made it difficult for the company to access foreign capital and expertise.

Sai was pessimistic about the mine's future as long as it was controlled by Asia World.

'A foreign company came here – they wanted to invest, but they didn't want to work with Asia World,' he said. 'The workers are getting fed up with this Asia World, because they want to start working again.'

The company was now run by Lo's son, Steven Law, a reclusive businessman with at least two dozen aliases.[32] Before I left Yangon, I had interviewed him in a small office at Myanmar's largest port. A slim, serious man, he was charming and evasive, and I felt for most of our conversation as if he was the one interviewing me. But he did tell me, very clearly, how strongly he felt that he was doing something positive for his people; that he was one of a handful of businessmen creating jobs, opportunities and skills in industries where previously there had been none.

Soon afterwards, the US Treasury lifted sanctions on the port, allowing international trade to flow freely into Myanmar, and the profits of this trade to enrich the family of a man who American officials had once called the 'Godfather of Heroin'. When I phoned Steven Law's assistant to get a comment as the news broke, I inadvertently broke the news to him. Law celebrated that night, his assistant later told me, with bottles of champagne.

Shortly after I visited Bawdwin, an Australian company would sign an option to buy a majority stake in the mine. 'I still can't quite fathom how this deposit is here, unmined, in 2017,' its CEO was quoted as saying.[33]

When Ronnie returned, we climbed into the trolley and rattled back through the hills to Namtu Station. There, Ronnie and Sai walked me back to my guesthouse. As the sun set, I took a bucket shower, scooping out freezing water with a small bowl from a concrete tank and pouring it over my head. It took a while to wash the shampoo through my hair, and it was dark before I pulled on my clothes, when there was a knock on the door.

'Hello?' It was Ronnie. 'May I have your passport?'

Opening the door, I asked him why he needed it.

'It's military intelligence,' he said. 'They want to see it.'

They had been waiting for us outside the guesthouse all day, and had been questioning Ronnie ever since we got back.

'I told them that you'd come here for a visit, that's all,' he said, pausing and adding, hopefully, 'Is that right?'

I reassured him that he was right. He told me that the intelligence officers had wanted to know why I was in Namtu, when foreigners were forbidden from staying in the town. They weren't interested in my permission letter from the civilian-run tourism ministry, because here the military's word was law.

They wanted me to leave as soon as possible, which meant we would leave at dawn. The only thing more frightening than military intelligence was the prospect of travelling on the roads here after dark.

When the intelligence officers had gone, Ronnie walked me

to dinner along almost empty streets. It was only 7 p.m., but most of the town's residents were already barricaded into their homes. The squat brick houses built into the hillside were designed to withstand the war, and their outer walls were fortified with shards of broken glass and coils of barbed wire.

Near the central square, we ducked into a dimly lit teashop, where men in leather jackets and woollen hats were huddled around the low, wooden tables. One of the men, who knew Ronnie, called us over to his table, where he was regaling the others with dramatic reenactments of the day's fighting. There was gunfire, 'Pow, pow, pow,' he shouted, leaping from his seat, and there were explosions, 'EeeeeeeePEW.' There was, in fact, plenty of action: when the first shots were fired, the customs yard had cleared out, as soldiers locked down the highway to China. Bridges were blown up, insurgent groups kidnapped civilians on the roads, and thousands of people fled to the towns, including Namtu, where the displacement camps in the monasteries and churches were already full.

After the stories came the photos, and this was the part that gripped everyone. Phones were passed around, showing posts on Facebook about abductions, and live videos of gun battles, and crude 'before' and 'after' photos of their victims. In contrast, there was nothing on my newsfeed about the violence that was gripping the north. As an outsider, I had no way to access the profiles, groups and networks that people here were tapping into, which had names in languages I didn't speak, and were run by people I didn't know. Even though we were all physically in the same place, we inhabited different online worlds.

It occurred to me as I watched the photos and videos being shared that the proliferation of closed online communities would make it much harder now for the generals to build a national identity, in a country that had never been unified. They had spent decades trying to control information, through censorship laws that were more extreme than almost anywhere else in the world, and they had rolled out internet access to create a more effective platform for their propaganda, which had partly worked. But now that everyone had access to social media, there was simply too much information in too many decentralized silos for the military ever to control. Separatist and dissident ideas, histories and propaganda could reach millions of people who lived within Myanmar's borders without even being detected by the generals, not only because the platforms were run hundreds or thousands of miles away, in China, Russia or the United States, but because officials couldn't infiltrate private groups that they didn't know existed.

That night, I dreamed of the fighting, and early the next morning I sat outside a teashop near my guesthouse and watched the people of Namtu emerge. The women set up market stalls, while the men gathered in small groups, to smoke and share information about the night's casualties. When Ronnie arrived, he told us all what he knew. Overnight, insurgents had blown up a bridge in the town. Every road leading out of Namtu was now closed, except one. Ronnie knew this, because a township officer had called him that morning, to make sure I was leaving.

Sai drove us out of the town, past clusters of stony-faced soldiers. Battle-hardened troops were being deployed across the state, and my evacuation was designed both to protect me from the violence and to hide it from me. I was being sent to safety, which meant I was being sent to one of the few places in northern Shan on the tourist route, a town called Hsipaw, which is a base camp for treks into the surrounding hills. The hills were not really safe for hikers: two German tourists had recently been wounded by shrapnel in a landmine blast while walking in the area, and a few years later another tourist would be killed near Hsipaw after stepping on a mine.[34]

But unlike Namtu, the town had guesthouses licensed to host foreigners. Hsipaw was also the nearest station to Namtu on the old mainline railway from central Myanmar towards the Chinese border. Sai lived with his grandmother at the railway's terminus, a bustling city called Lashio, and we had agreed to meet there in a day or two. I would go by train and he would drive, along roads that I wasn't allowed to travel on, and would never see.

Sai had told me that the railway was safe, but I couldn't shake off a feeling of unease as I waited at the station the next afternoon for the train that would take me north.

The air was thick with the smell of woodsmoke, the light was already low, and the evening mist obscured the trees that surrounded the platform. My travelling companions were wrapped up in thick coats, and when the train arrived, they boarded silently, passing up sacks of tea and chillies and spices that they would sell in the north.

As the train creaked out of the station, a policeman sat down beside me.

'Only one?' he asked.

'Yes,' I replied.

'You must sit in upper class,' he said, reaching for my backpack.

'Why?' I asked him.

'Ordinary class, no,' he said. 'No safety, only one.'

When I argued with him, he strode off to fetch reinforcements, and soon I was being hauled into the relative comfort of upper class. My police guards had transformed the carriage into something resembling a living room, pulling down the thick metal window shutters, hanging their coats on hooks on the walls, swivelling the chairs around to face one another, setting up a small speaker to play music, and passing around a flask of hot green tea.

Despite their hospitality, my police detail worried me, because the insurgent groups that had coordinated the recent attacks had said they were specifically targeting security forces. As the train plunged into the darkness of the jungle, I wondered gloomily if we would all go down that night in a volley of bullets.

But my spirits improved as the jungle thinned and the light held for an hour or two longer, revealing farmers harvesting their rice, and hamlets dotted between the railway and the river. Children raced the train at the tiny rural stations, and just before the sun set I glimpsed a group of teenagers bathing in the river, beside an open fire.

When it was dark, a tall man came into the carriage, and sat beside me. He introduced himself as an official in the state forestry department, but unusually for a Myanmar official, he was dressed in a sweater and blue jeans.

'Are you alone?' he asked.

'Yes,' I replied tersely, wondering why everyone always needed to ask.

'Are you not afraid?' he asked.

'Should I be?' I challenged him.

He looked at me thoughtfully and changed tack. 'What is your job?' he asked.

'I'm a writer,' I said. I didn't feel like telling him that I was a journalist.

'For which department?' he asked me. 'United Nations department? Red Cross department?'

I told him that I didn't have a department, and he gave me a long, quizzical look, as if he was trying to figure out whether I really was a writer without a department, and if so, what that might mean. It was a while before he spoke again, and when he did, it was to ask another question.

'What is your country?'

'England,' I replied.

'Which town?' he asked. 'Tottenham? Chelsea? Arsenal?'

This was what the British were to him: representatives of international organizations, and world-class footballers.

'London,' I told him.

'London is very clean, like Singapore,' he replied.

As the hours passed and we inched through the jungle towards Lashio, there were, of course, no incidents; nobody shot at the train, nobody was injured or killed. It was after midnight when we reached the station, but Sai was waiting for me there, and he drove me through the city's quiet streets to his grandmother's house.

Three small boys met us at the gate, and they showed me to my room, while Sai's sisters, who were wearing matching fleece pyjamas, made me a bowl of noodles. I slept beneath two thick blankets, waking at dawn to the sound of children chanting, and a view from my window of the sun rising over gold-capped mountains.

'A few years ago, this was all jungle,' Sai's friend Yin said, smacking his lips together and spitting another mouthful of sloppy red liquid out of the window.

In the short time we had been driving, he had coated the side of Sai's car with betel juice. We were on the outskirts of Lashio, near the highway that led north from the city through the mountains to the Chinese border, and we were driving through what the two men called a 'new town'.

But it wasn't yet a town, or really anything like a town. Beyond a roadblock that was manned by soldiers, the wide concrete road that connected this new settlement to the highway was deserted. Scattered across the hills on either side of the road were clusters of unoccupied, half-built houses. Plots of overgrown land demarcated with white sticks indicated where more houses, or a school, or administrative buildings might one day be built. But there were none of the other things that you might expect to find in a town, like shops, or restaurants, or a hospital. More importantly, there weren't any people.

We had come to this place on the outskirts of the city in search of answers about the most expensive infrastructure project in Myanmar's history: a $20 billion high-speed railway that would connect China's landlocked interior, through a belt of towns in central Myanmar, with the Indian Ocean. If the railway was built, it would be the only railway connecting Myanmar beyond its borders.

A military truck rumbled past, and then disappeared into a cloud of dust. Yin bit into a fresh betel quid, releasing its intense floral scent, and told Sai to pull up on the side of the road.

Yin had made a lot of money flipping land in these deserted hills. Like many people in Lashio he spoke Chinese, which gave him an edge as a broker, even though foreigners were not legally allowed to buy land here.

Climbing out of the car, he strode towards one of the half-built houses, and knocked on the door, which opened to reveal a middle-aged man and his wife, who was dressed in flannel pyjamas.

Over cups of green tea in their sparsely furnished living room, they told us they had moved here five years ago. The junta had just announced that a major railway station on a new high-speed railway to China would be built here, along with a new town, sparking a scramble for land. 'The new railway station and town were hot news,' Sai translated. Our host was a welder, and he had come here hoping to find work.

The excitement only increased, the welder said, when Myanmar's president Thein Sein turned up with a Chinese delegation to inspect the site of the new railway station. Engineers had already surveyed the route from the border, with battalions from Lashio providing security.[35]

But the route being mapped wasn't new, and neither were plans to build a railway in this part of the country. For nearly 200 years, almost since the railway itself was invented, there had been proposals and attempts by everyone from British explorers and journalists to China's first president, Sun Yat-sen, to build a railway opening up China's landlocked western provinces, through Myanmar, to the Indian Ocean.[36]

'In the British colonial time, the old railway used to cross here,' the welder said, pointing beyond his yard. 'The Chinese company wanted to follow this old, old railway.'

The old railway to the border was first surveyed back in the 1890s, soon after the British annexed the Burmese kingdom. The dream of building a railway to the Chinese interior was a major incentive for the British invasion of Burma, both to access China's fabled riches and to counter French influence in the region. But when work actually started from the sacked Burmese capital of Mandalay into the mountains, it was difficult, slow, dangerous, and much more expensive than the government or the contractors had anticipated.[37]

They had, in fact, been warned: when the Burmese King Mindon sent a delegation to Britain to negotiate with Queen Victoria before the invasion, hoping she would guarantee Burma's sovereignty, his representatives had explained to British merchants that building a railway to China would be impossible, not because the king opposed it, but because the mountains that surrounded his kingdom were impenetrable, even to British railway engineers.[38]

At the time, nobody had listened, but after six years of work, before the railway even reached Lashio, *The Times* quoted the Indian viceroy denouncing the project as a waste of resources, and the plan to extend it into China as an episode of 'midsummer madness'. He also claimed the entire trade at the frontier could be transported in two dugout canoes, or in other words, that the wealth of western China was a myth.[39] When the line reached Lashio, the idea was quietly dropped.

It was revived again almost forty years later, again for reasons that had nothing to do with the people who lived along the route, as Burma was once again drawn into China's orbit. It was 1941, and after Japan blockaded China's eastern seaports, Britain agreed to build a railway to resupply Chinese troops from the port at Rangoon.

But once again, the proposals were made by outsiders who knew nothing about the terrain. 'Never,' wrote the railway's chief engineer, in a subsequent report, 'was a construction of such magnitude attempted under such difficult and adverse conditions.'[40]

The hills beyond Lashio are covered with red clay so thick that the roads could only be used for six months of the year, and in the monsoon they were infested with malaria vector mosquitoes, making work impossible. In the dry season, the jungle was cleared and large areas of marshland were drained to build camps for the workers. New roads and bridges were built into the gorges, to bring in construction materials, but by the time the roads were ready, the Japanese were already advancing through Burma, and materials and workers were both in short supply.

Construction teams had only managed to build one station building on the outskirts of Lashio, when the Japanese bombed the city. The first salvo fell around the station in the city centre, and the second in its stores yard and workshops, killing a large number of the railway staff, and forcing the survivors to evacuate.

Back in China, the director general of railway construction claimed that after the war, Yunnan would become so developed that large quantities of goods would be exported along the Burmese railways to the port at Rangoon. But it wasn't until the 1980s, after the Cultural Revolution, that Chinese officials began thinking again about finding an outlet for trade from the country's landlocked western provinces.[41] Beijing began courting the junta, which at the time was also tentatively engaging with its neighbours after decades of isolation.

The junta's response to being ostracized by the West had been to rail against what it saw as new forms of imperialism and attempts by foreign powers to enslave and humiliate Myanmar. Billboards appeared across the country, featuring slogans in English that called on Myanmar's people to 'oppose foreign nations interfering in internal affairs of the state', and to 'crush all internal and external destructive elements as the common enemy'.[42] But at the same time, the generals knew they needed foreign help.

State media reports from the 1990s reveal a flurry of delegations, dinners and deals. As Western countries condemned the regime's use of forced labour on infrastructure projects, including railways, Chinese state-owned companies supplied the equipment the junta needed to build them.[43]

Just like British investments in colonial Burma, these deals were designed, above all, to create profits for Chinese investors, banks and manufacturers. Companies sold complete sets of equipment to the junta and provided technicians to assemble them. Little by little, Myanmar became dependent on Chinese suppliers, while Chinese banks provided financing with interest-free, and then low-interest loans, which became larger as the years went by.

As China propped up the regime and shielded it from international censure, Beijing also had more ambitious plans. Understanding that China's economic miracle could only be sustained by expansion into new markets, and concerned by finite domestic supplies of minerals, as well its reliance on the vulnerable Malacca Strait for its energy supplies, it increasingly began looking west, including across Myanmar, towards the Indian Ocean.

By the mid-2000s, China was building a railway across the mountains of Yunnan towards the Myanmar border. Soon the junta had announced that the high-speed railway would be extended through the country, setting off the rush for land in the hills outside Lashio.

But what the people who bought land here didn't know was that behind the scenes, Myanmar's relationship with China had been fraying for some time. Dealing with China had been necessary for survival, but the generals were increasingly worried by the country's diplomatic and military dependence on its powerful neighbour.[44] Being better connected to China would bring benefits, of course, and living standards were already rising thanks to new infrastructure in the borderlands and imports of cheap manufactured goods.

But the delegations of Chinese engineers that were turning up to survey the railway ominously echoed the parties of British imperialists who had once marched into these borderlands, with their compasses, perambulators and maps. There were fears that the railway was a debt trap, which might eventually see China take control of the project. At a time when the generals were trying to reorient the country inwards, in what the former railway minister Aung Min had described as the 'heartland' project, the railway was seen as a centrifugal force that would draw the borderlands towards Beijing.

Cities like Lashio were already home to large Chinese populations, and a new railway would mean more settlement, and more competition. Since its independence, Myanmar had been locked into an exploitative relationship with international markets, exchanging raw materials and labour at a fraction of their value elsewhere for imported goods. If the railway was built, the fundamentals of this relationship were unlikely to change.

The country would become more reliant not only on China, but on a global economy that was still ultimately controlled by the West. Whether profits were channelled out of the country through the ports at Yangon, as they had been during the British occupation, or by train across the border to China, it was just another route back to the same economic dependencies that Myanmar's generals had spent so long trying to untangle.

The railway minister Aung Min tried to assuage some of these fears, telling media that Chinese companies would 'only do the things we cannot'. He made the point publicly for the first time that Myanmar lacked the expertise to build a high-speed railway, although the truth was that it could barely build a low-speed railway, and Aung Min was fed up trying to do it alone. Thinking back to all the articles I had read in state media that warned against reliance on foreign nations, I realized how hard this must have been to admit. Aung Min said the railway would enable Myanmar to 'learn the technology so that we can build an express railroad ourselves in the future', and he insisted the government was doing everything it could to make sure it wasn't cheated.[45]

But there was a more serious problem: the technical but highly contentious question of gauge: the width of the railway track. China's railways are wider than Myanmar's, and to avoid passengers and freight having to switch trains at the border, China wanted to build a standard-gauge railway. But the railways in Myanmar are metre-gauge, and the generals were extremely uncomfortable about the idea of China building a high-speed railway that didn't connect to Myanmar's network.[46]

'If we hear that a railway will be built across Myanmar, we see it as a route for the Chinese army to reach the Indian Ocean,' one historian and former soldier later said to me. 'You can imagine what the Chinese army, or their navy, might want to do.'

On the outskirts of Lashio, nobody had heard anything about the railway since Myanmar's then-president, Thein Sein, visited four years earlier. The government officials who bought up land before the project was announced had long since cashed in, flipping it for ten or even twenty times the price, and there were some people who now believed the whole thing was a scam.

'They say it is a fake new town, because the government didn't do anything,' the welder said.

Even so, he and his wife were optimistic. If they waited long enough, they said, the railway and the new town would be built, and they could sell the land they'd bought at an inflated price, and perhaps even make a profit. They had a friend in the government who had advised them not to sell, and most other people who owned land here were holding on to it too.

They'd been closely following news of the railway in Yunnan, which was making steady progress towards the border, and which continued to give them hope. An article in

Chinese state media had recently claimed that the extension of the Chinese rail system into Myanmar was 'just a matter of time'[47] – the route had been mapped, the station sites identified, and the surveys were already complete. All that needed to happen now was for the two governments to renew their agreement.

As the strategic priorities of global powers shifted around them, deals were struck and money exchanged, generations of people here had spent their lives on the brink of being connected to the wider world. They had never been the decision-makers, and even the local officials I spoke to didn't know when, or whether, a railway would be built.

At Lashio Station, the stationmaster had removed his orange-tinted glasses, and told me that he didn't have a copy of the government's plans for the new railway. He was getting his news from state media, just like everyone else.

'We also don't know about that,' he replied, when I asked him if the project had been cancelled or just suspended. 'You should ask the president.'

Leaving the welder behind, we drove on towards a settlement of identical small brick houses. It was not only civil servants who had bought up plots of land here, Myanmar veterans had also been resettled on the outskirts of the city.

'This area is for army people,' Sai translated, as we passed a large sign at the entrance. 'You cannot buy, sell or rent these houses.'

He knew one of the soldiers, and we stopped the car outside a house that looked just like all the other houses. I had expected to meet someone formidable, but the retired sergeant who opened the door was nothing like the man I had assumed we would meet.

Dressed in green army trousers and a cheap polo shirt,

Sein Kha was smaller than I was, less than five feet two inches. His arms, hands and feet were covered with faded green tattoos, and his boyish face lit up when he smiled, to reveal a single tooth.

He ushered us into his living room, whose plasterboard walls were stained with betel juice. Other than a sleeping mat, some kitchen utensils, and several images of Jesus pinned to the walls, he appeared to have no possessions.

We sat together on a sheet of filthy tarpaulin that covered the floor, forming a circle around an ashtray that was overflowing with cigarette butts.

'God gave this house to me,' Sein Kha told us, as Sai translated. 'Thanks be to God.'

He was Wa, an ethnic-minority group, and as flies buzzed overhead, I asked him why he had joined Myanmar's military, rather than the United Wa State Army, which was Myanmar's most powerful non-state armed group.

He explained that when he was young, his house was bombed, killing both his parents. The local church took him in, then gave him a new home with a Burmese couple, who paid for his schooling. When they suggested that Sein Kha join Myanmar's army, he was so grateful to them that he agreed. He served until five years ago, when a soldier from the Myanmar National Democratic Alliance Army, another insurgent group, shot his arm off. He lifted the twisted stump from his shoulder to show us, and massaged it with his one remaining hand.

His isolated, impoverished existence here clarified for me that it was not just civilians who had suffered during the decades of military rule. Now that Ne Win's socialist dream had long since been forgotten, the divide in Myanmar was not just between soldiers and civilians, but also between those who had money and therefore power, and those who did not.

Like the welders, Sein Kha spent his days waiting for news of the railway, so that he could sell this house, and live a little more comfortably. Until then, he would stay here, hoping month after month that his meagre pension would be paid on time, because he needed to keep paying the groups of insurgent soldiers who turned up here, demanding protection money.

I often thought of Sein Kha in the years afterwards, whenever there was news about the railway to China. An agreement with a Chinese contractor was signed, lapsed, and then signed again, and China kept building its own railway across the inhospitable landscape of western Yunnan, towards the Myanmar border.

But the Burmese King Mindon's men had been right when they warned British merchants how difficult it would be to build a railway through these mountains. China had replaced Britain as the world's leading railway power, and China alone had the resources to build this railway, but even so, work was progressing at an extraordinarily slow pace. By 2017, it emerged that construction teams working around the clock had made just 156 metres of progress in twenty-six months, on just one of forty planned tunnels along the route.

'This tunnel has tortured me for nine years and is still nowhere near finished,' a foreman was quoted as saying in an article that called the project the 'railway from hell'.[48]

It described how construction workers and engineers laboured under extreme conditions and encountered 'monstrous obstacles' while digging through this single mountain, including complex geological formations, fault lines and previously undiscovered underground rivers, which created a constant risk of flooding and mudslides.

It was almost impossible to ventilate the passage, and the average temperature of the rock rose to 42 degrees Celsius when the excavators were operating, so the contractor had to bring in up to five tons of ice a day to keep its drilling teams cool.

After a complex drainage system able to deal with up to 78,000 cubic metres of water per day and permanent ventilation had been installed, the tunnel opened in 2019. It had taken eleven years to build and was described as 'the world's most difficult' by Chinese media.[49]

Now, in 2023, while work has been completed on the longest section of tunnels, the railway is still a long way from opening. The mountains surrounding Myanmar remain a fortress, the geographical expression of the military's enduring refusal to let outsiders breach the country's walls, which are now slowly but relentlessly being eroded.

PART THREE

'We may be heading not for general breakdown but for an epoch as horribly stable as the slave empires of antiquity.'

George Orwell, 'You and the Atom Bomb', 1945[1]

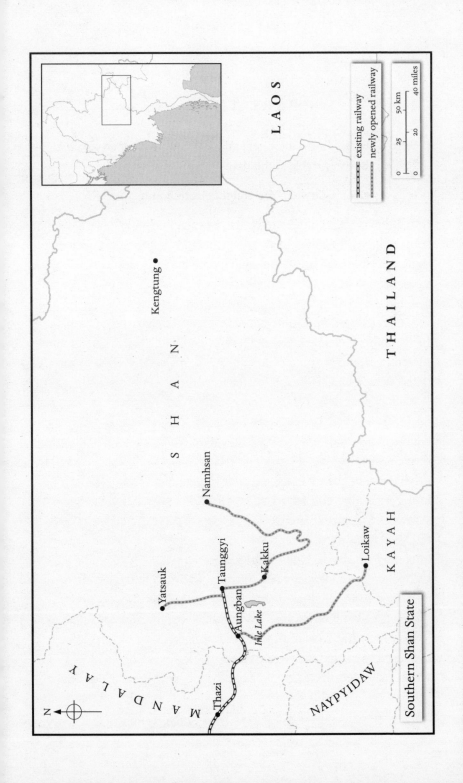

7.

Southern Shan

In southern Shan State, the invisible walls began to appear as soon as I tried to leave the tourist route. At first, I didn't notice they were there. The slow train from Thazi in central Myanmar was a popular part of many itineraries because it stopped at Inle Lake, where tourists could hire a boat to visit the floating villages, pagodas and gardens. The train journey on the British-built railway from the flatlands of central Myanmar took an entire day, and for hours as we ascended into the mountains on switchbacks, past tiny villages that clung to the hillsides, I was free from my usual police guard.

But as soon as we reached the station for Inle Lake, and the backpackers and linen-clad European couples filed out of the train's upper-class carriages to meet the taxis that would drive them to their hotels, the three policemen who had been lounging at one end of my carriage sprang into action.

Two of them sat beside me and the third hurried away to fetch another man, who wore a camouflage jacket, and who introduced himself as the head of the train.

'You will sit in upper class with me,' he said. 'No charge.'

I asked him why I needed to move.

'No problem,' he replied, giving me a steely smile.

The fact that I wanted to travel by train beyond Inle Lake had already caused some confusion. It started the night before, when I showed my map of the railways to the owner of my guesthouse in Thazi, and asked her whether trains were running to a place called Yatsauk, on a branch line that was built by the junta in the 1990s.

She had been making packed lunches for me and the other tourists to take on the train the next day, and when I asked the question, she put down her knife and stared at me.

'A lot of people come here,' she replied. 'Many, many tourists. But you are the only one who is going to Yatsauk.'

She wasn't sure whether I would be able to buy a ticket to the town, because I was a foreigner and there was a large military base there, but she wrote me a note in Burmese, which she told me to give to the stationmaster when I arrived, in case I made it. 'I am looking for a bed,' the note said. 'Please help me.'

When she dropped me off the next morning at Thazi Station with the note and several jam sandwiches, I asked the stationmaster there the same question: were trains running to Yatsauk?

'Yatsauk,' he replied. '*Hote la* – really?' He repeated the word, and looked at me carefully, as if he was trying to work out whether I meant it.

Now, after moving me to an upper-class carriage, the head of the train was quizzing me about my motives for travelling to the town. He wanted to know whether Yatsauk was in my guidebook, and when I said it wasn't, he suggested that I visit Inle Lake instead. It was only when I told him I was writing about Myanmar's railways that he gave in; experience had evidently taught him that Europeans loved trains.

It was another hour before the train left the station, and as dusk set in, I began to understand why everyone had been so confused by my insistence on travelling to Yatsauk. Except for my police guard, the carriage was empty, and the few stations we stopped at were deserted and dimly lit. Later, as we rattled through the darkness, a door swung open and slammed shut, over and over again. It was winter, and unlike in the lowlands, it was very cold. The wind whipped through the carriage, and I wrapped myself in all the clothing I had with me. But still, it was freezing and I would have been miserable, if it weren't for the stars visible through my broken window that were the brightest I'd ever seen.

It was almost midnight by the time we reached Yatsauk, where the stationmaster offered to give me a lift. He drove me through deserted streets to the only guesthouse in town. I was exhausted, so it was a relief when we pulled up outside a warmly lit hotel. Three men wrapped in woollen hats and overcoats were sitting outside, drinking tea, and as the station-master parked his car, they stood up to greet us.

But when the oldest of the men saw me, he froze, and then he said in a loud voice, 'No!' He looked at the other men for support, and then, emboldened, he shouted, 'No foreigners.'

Another man appeared, who had the stiff gait of a soldier.

'They cannot allow you to stay here,' he said, in English.

Was it possible for me to stay anywhere in Yatsauk? I asked.

'No,' he replied, taking out his phone and punching numbers into the keypad. He was calling for a taxi driver, he explained, to take me away. As he spoke quickly into the phone, one of the other men shrugged apologetically.

'Security,' he said, vaguely. 'Military area.'

I asked him if I should come back in the daytime.

'Nothing to see,' the man replied.

Before I could ask any more questions, I was being bundled into a car and waved away. Then we were speeding back through the darkness, away from the military base and the officer training academy on the outskirts of the town, towards

Inle Lake, 50 miles away, where all the other Europeans in this part of the world were contained, sleeping safely in their hotels.

By the time we arrived at the northern edge of the lake, most of the hotels were locked up for the night, but my driver managed to find me a room at a place whose owner he knew. I slept late, and after a large breakfast at a backpacker café of pancakes washed down with an avocado smoothie, I wandered through the bustling town.

This was the Myanmar that tourists saw, a colourful enclave that resembled other tourist towns around the world, but with a Burmese twist. The restaurants and cafés served local food alongside global dishes, the spas were pan-Asian themed, and the souvenir shops were filled with local art and crafts, designed for an international market. There was luxury here, too: many of the hotels built on stilts around the edge of the lake had swimming pools, wellness centres and fine-dining restaurants in their landscaped grounds.

On the lake, the Intha, Shan and Pa-O people who wore traditional clothing and practised pre-industrial industries were the main attraction, to be photographed and bartered with at the markets during the day. In the evening, visitors returned to their hotels for a swim, a massage, and a bottle of wine over dinner.

It was a charming place, a dreamy world of temple bells and floating monasteries and cheerful indigenous people, where Myanmar's military was nowhere to be seen.

It was a fiction, and it was also, as I was beginning to discover, encircled by invisible walls. But this was how it had always worked in Myanmar. When it suited the military to allow foreigners into the country, they were directed to the places that were safe, or almost safe. When they left again, their memories were naturally of the places they had visited.

Later, back at home, they might be troubled by the stories they inevitably heard on the news about the violence that had been taking place nearby. But by the time violence has become a report about violence, its power is weakened, the facts can be contested, and the person listening to the story will never be troubled by it in quite the same way.

All around this charmed place, just out of sight, an immensely complex war was being fought, both in northern Shan State, where I had just been with Ronnie and Sai, and in central and southern Shan, to the east of Inle Lake. The Shan kingdoms had once been a sprawling patchwork of independent territories ruled by hereditary leaders, or *sawbwa*, who paid tribute to the Burmese kings, and they had retained some autonomy under indirect British rule. But at independence in 1948, they were incorporated into the Burmese state. Like many other ethnic groups in the borderlands, the Shan people, who number more than 5 million and inhabit a territory larger than Nepal, had been fighting for autonomy ever since.

That morning, though, there was no sign of the conflict, as I strolled through the narrow streets between the cafés and souvenir shops to a hotel called the Hupin. This was where European railway enthusiasts often stayed when they toured this part of the country. Dieter, the German engineer who was writing a book about Myanmar's railways, had suggested that I visit the hotel's owner, who he knew well.

I wanted to ask her if it was possible to travel on another railway from Inle Lake that was built around the same time as the railway to Yatsauk. It ran east to the nearby Shan capital of Taunggyi, and then through central Shan for hundreds of miles – across what I understood was some of the most militarized territory in the country – to a remote city in the eastern mountains called Kengtung.

I had been trying to find out for months whether it was possible to travel on this railway. But even though this is one of the most basic questions it is possible to ask about a public service, I still had no idea.

In Yangon, I had asked multiple tour agencies, including the one that arranged my permit to visit the Bawdwin mines. Its owner had told me there was 'no connection or schedule' for the railway, and that it would cost me several thousand dollars if I wanted to hire a guide to drive me along the route.

I had asked the guards on the train to Inle Lake the previous day, but most of them said they didn't know anything about the railway further east. The only person who knew anything was a ticket collector called Sunny, who smelled faintly of whisky, and who told me that trains were still running. But they were 'very small trains', he said, cryptically, and he didn't think I would be allowed to travel on them.

'Security problem, no good,' he explained, taking a sip from his flask and offering me a Red Ruby cigarette.

I asked him to explain the problem.

'Gun problem,' he said, with a wry smile.

At the Hupin Hotel, I was pleased to find the owner at the reception desk. She was an elderly woman with a moustache and liver spots like flecks of pepper, wearing a blue blazer that made her look like an old British train conductor. She remembered Dieter well, but she told me she couldn't help me. Her guide who arranged permits for areas that were usually off-limits to tourists was in Yangon, and there was nobody else here who could do it. I asked her if she knew, at least, whether trains were still running on the line.

She told me that the first short section of the railway, to the Shan capital of Taunggyi, was abandoned. The city was built on a plateau, and the 20-mile section of track rose 1,800 feet from Inle Lake.[1] When it opened in 1997, state media announced that it would 'usher in a new era' – connecting the new railway being built across central Shan to the national network[2] – but the incline was so steep that trains travelled at less than 10 miles an hour, and it closed soon afterwards.[3] Whether or not the rest of the railway was still open, she wasn't sure.

'I will call the stationmaster in Taunggyi,' the old woman said. She ushered me into a windowless room, where I sat on a teak throne fitted with a crimson velvet cushion, and waited for her to make the call.

'You cannot go to that area, it is a very remote area, and a very dangerous place,' she said, when she came back. I knew that the land to the east of Taunggyi was militarized, but I had never heard of it being particularly dangerous, at least no more so than other parts of Myanmar's borderlands. I asked her if she could think of anyone in Taunggyi who might help me. Seeing that I was determined, she gave me the stationmaster's phone number, telling me to visit him when I arrived in the city.

That afternoon, I took a minibus to Taunggyi and walked across an open field in the city centre towards a hill cloaked in cherry trees. At the base of the hill, beside a small vegetable market, was the station, a multi-storey concrete block. Just like all the other railway stations built by the junta, it was deserted, but on the other side of the empty concourse there was a raised platform bathed in sunlight, where several men wearing turbans were loading cargo into freight wagons. The stationmaster was overseeing their work, and he told me that he was extremely busy, but that he could spare a minute or two to talk. He clasped both of my hands and bowed deeply, and then he rushed off to give more instructions to his men.

I ran alongside him, first along the platform, and then back and forth through the station buildings, as he told me that trains were still running on this isolated railway. There was a daily passenger service in the afternoon, but I would need permission, if I wanted to travel on it, from an ethnic armed group called the Pa-O National Organization, which controlled the land directly to the east of the city. If I wanted to go further than that, he said, I would need another permission letter, improbably, from Taunggyi's tourism office.

I found the address of the Pa-O's administrative office online, but I had to walk up and down the street several times before I found it. A grey concrete tower block, there was nothing to distinguish it as the urban headquarters of a powerful ethnic armed group except for the flag that flew above the entrance.

The doors were open and I wandered inside to find a spacious lobby that doubled as a small museum. Photographs of Pa-O elders gazed down sternly from the walls at a selection of artefacts, including a replica of a large chunk of jade that the group's mining conglomerate had unearthed in Kachin, and donated to the junta. It was a reminder that the Pa-O were military allies, and their territory was a buffer zone, at the edge of a large area of contested land.

As I looked around the exhibits, several young men and women who were dressed in traditional Pa-O clothing – loose black trousers and jackets – came into the room, and they gathered around me to listen as I explained that I wanted to travel by train through Pa-O territory. At first they laughed, but when they realized I was serious, they told me it would cost me $20 a day to hire a guide, and that we could leave from the station the following afternoon. The only thing left to do before I went was to visit the tourism office across town.

There, standing at the entrance to the single-storey office, as if he had been waiting for me, was a tall, thin man with dark circles around his eyes. Marching me inside, he sat me down at a dark wooden desk, and once I had told him that I wanted to travel by train to Kengtung, he began to ask me questions.

First, he wanted to know what exactly I wanted to do in the region to the east of Taunggyi. Then he wanted to know what type of visa I had, and who I worked for, and how long I had been in the country. As we spoke, another man emerged from a side room to listen. Dressed in a beige suit, he was wearing an earpiece, and for the rest of the time I was in the tourism office, he did not move his amber eyes from my face.

'You cannot travel to Kengtung by land without permission,' the first man said, pressing his long fingers together and giving me a sad smile, as if to apologize that his bureaucracy was designed not to facilitate, but to obstruct. Reaching into a drawer behind him, he pulled out a stack of folders. These were all applications, he said. The top folder, which he held up to show me, contained papers submitted by a group of foreign prospectors who wanted to visit the caves in Mong Nai, a town on the railway route in the centre of Shan. The application contained detailed maps of the places they wanted to visit, as well as extensive information about what they would do there, and their credentials. They had applied months ago, he said, and still they hadn't been granted permits.

Putting the folders back in the drawer, he smiled again.

'It is unstable there,' he said.

Back at my guesthouse that evening, I called a Shan friend who had trained as a military officer before leaving the army to become a businessman.

'It's a military railway,' he told me, bluntly. He said it was built to supply heavy equipment to an airbase at a place called Namhsan. 'They have a huge infantry presence there,' he said. 'I don't know why nobody has blown that railway up.'

He didn't know anything else about it, but he said that once I was in Pa-O territory, he was sure I would be able to find someone to take me further along the route.

'If you run into a major doo-doo and can't bribe your way out, I'll call one of my former coworkers who is the commander's daughter,' he said, before hanging up.

When I arrived at Taunggyi Station the following afternoon, my guide was waiting for me. Like other Pa-O men, Moon believed he was descended from an alchemist, and he dressed as his forefathers had dressed, in a green turban adorned with yellow stars, a black jacket and loose black trousers.

He was an enthusiastic young man with an infectious smile, who had bounced up to the stationmaster to arrange our tickets. Now, he was sitting beside me on a rough wooden bench that ran through the centre of the carriage, and talking me through centuries of Pa-O history.

A succession of wars had scattered the Pa-O people across Myanmar. But half of the Pa-O population, around one million people, now inhabited a small autonomous territory in central Shan, at the heart of a diverse and turbulent region. Like other smaller minorities in this part of the country, including the Wa and the Kokang, Pa-O leaders had protected themselves by signing a ceasefire with the military in return for land, adding another layer of complexity to the struggle for autonomy in Shan.

What Moon didn't tell me was that Pa-O leaders had actively supported the former regime, or that they still fought the Shan over territory and resources, or that opium fields now covered much of their autonomous territory. Perhaps it didn't seem important. After all, Myanmar is the world's second-largest opium producer, and poppies grow across Shan State.[4] Instead,

Moon stuck to safer topics, telling me about the licit crops that were grown in Pa-O: beans, cauliflower, mustard leaf, pumpkin, marrow and gourd.

In the hours that he had been talking, the train had filled up with people. The guard had transformed one end of our carriage into a makeshift bedroom, and was now reclining on a pile of blankets, drinking a can of beer. Outside on the platform, the stationmaster was smoking a cheroot and giving occasional instructions to a group of mechanics who were squatting around the locomotive, trying to fix it.

'Long, long ago there was a female dragon who lived under the water,' Moon was saying, 'and one day she turned herself into a beautiful lady and went out into the forest.' This was the origin story of the Pa-O people: the dragon married an alchemist and laid two giant eggs, which she left in the care of a hermit.

'One of the eggs cracked and inside it was a boy,' Moon told me. 'The other egg could not crack itself, so the hermit had to peel it, and in that egg there was a girl.'

Pa means 'crack' and O means 'peel' – and the boy and the girl became the king and the queen of the Pa-O.

'That's why I wear this dragon badge,' he said, pointing to one of two badges pinned to his jacket. All the women in the carriage with us were wearing traditional Pa-O clothing, too. In the villages, Moon said, the older generations wore traditional clothing even when they slept. It protected them against assimilation, just as the traditional Pa-O stories protected them. But now, he explained, the young people in the cities wore Burmese or Western clothing, and the storytelling tradition that had nourished Pa-O communities for hundreds of years was at risk of fading away.

It was late afternoon by the time we left the station, and as we passed through a succession of small, dusty villages to the south of Taunggyi, Moon told me about his Buddhist faith. There was a lively, communal atmosphere in the carriage, and several of the women were listening attentively to Moon, although they had told us they didn't speak English. A monk was sitting beside us, reading a large book, and soon Moon had pulled it out of his hands and was showing it to me.

'This is the story of our Lord Buddha,' he explained.

The monk turned out to be a useful source of information, and whenever Moon forgot the details of the story he was telling, he would ask the monk, who would produce a small pocketbook, and provide the answer, before tucking it back inside his crimson robes.

By the time we arrived in Kakku, a collection of stupas that form the centre of Pa-O Buddhist worship, it was late and the carriage had almost emptied out. Kakku wasn't the last station on the line, but it was the only place in Pa-O territory where foreigners could stay, and Moon had arranged a room for me to sleep in that night.

We jumped out onto the deserted platform and walked from the station along an earthen track that cut across the surrounding fields, using the torches on our phones to find our way in the dark.

Near the temple complex, two women came out to meet us, and they walked me to a room that was ordinarily used by pilgrims. Made from woven bamboo panels supported by bamboo beams, it was cosy and clean, and after a large meal of fried rice, I slept better than I had slept for weeks.

Early the next morning, I walked barefoot among the stupas, which appeared pale and ghostly in the dawn light. Along the passages of crumbling stone, there were enclaves of newly gilded temples inscribed with the names of donors. Among them I found Moon, who had swapped his traditional clothing for white jeans and a hoodie, and was donating money to a golden statue of a boar.

'For good luck,' he explained, when he saw me.

He had arranged for a car to take us along the roads that shadowed the railway to the eastern edge of Pa-O territory, and we drove later that morning out of Kakku, along a red clay track, and into the countryside.

The Pa-O are farmers and the land here is rich; among the fields of sunflowers, garlic, tobacco and pigeon peas there were small villages, where heaps of cut firewood were stacked outside the houses, and fresh red chillies were spread over the rooftops to dry.

We didn't have a map and there was no phone signal, so we stopped to ask the people we passed for directions. There were men who rode bullock carts, and others who drove tiny diesel-powered tractors that belched clouds of black smoke, and women who walked beside the road and whose red and pink headdresses were accentuated by the deep-blue sky.

Each exchange involved an intense discussion, and after all the talking and gesticulating, we were sent on our way along the tracks that criss-crossed the hills, but only sometimes in the right direction. Eventually we left the villages behind and were bouncing along rough paths between fields filled with weeds and groves of bamboo. There were roadblocks now, formed from heaps of rocks that prevented us from turning along tracks that I imagined led to the opium-poppy fields.[5]

Instead, we veered deeper into the hills, between high banks of red earth. By now the road was almost impassable, but it led us through a cluster of abandoned wooden houses that were sinking into the earth, and beyond the houses – 'Ahh, finally,' said Moon – was the place we had been looking for, the last station in the Pa-O region, before the railway crossed into land that was contested by the Shan.

Beside the station was the stationmaster's house, a single-storey building. Its flimsy front door hung open on its broken hinges, revealing the stationmaster and his wife, who were watching television in their living room. Their television was powered by solar panels attached to large batteries, and when they invited us in, I saw they had little else, except for a few plastic chairs, a bed protected by a mosquito net, a table and a stove.

It was so rare, the stationmaster said, switching off the television and pulling up two chairs for us to sit on, that anyone visited them here. Youthful, with a crop of bouncy black hair, he was clearly pleased to have company. Both he and his wife were ethnic Burmese. They were considered foreigners in what they called Pa-O land, which meant that however hard they tried to integrate, they would never be fully accepted. But then again, that wasn't unusual. Most of Myanmar's stationmasters were Burmese, and they were always considered outsiders when they were posted to remote parts of the country.

In any case, he didn't have time for anything except work, he explained, because he was on duty at all times. He was a station-master, but also an engineer, mechanic and ticket collector. He did everything that needed to be done for the train that arrived each evening, and left again every morning, and all for a monthly salary worth £80.

'I love the train like it's my son,' he said, earnestly. He had worked as a stationmaster for thirty years, and his father had been a stationmaster too. 'I watch out when the train leaves,' he told us, 'making sure it arrives at the next station, and then I wait here every day until it is back home safely.'

The stationmaster's house was at the very edge of the civil

war, but the fighting had never spilled over the invisible border that marked the edge of Pa-O territory, and nobody had targeted the railway. Beyond here, there had been low-level fighting for eight years between the Pa-O and the Shan. It was too dangerous for the stationmaster and his wife to travel to the villages further east, because they were Burmese, but here, he believed they were safe.

It helped that they were Buddhist, he went on, which offered them protection in this isolated house.

'Do you believe that your faith protects you from the fighting?' I asked.

'Yes,' they both nodded.

His wife retrieved a book of blessings from the table and handed it to me.

'We live far from the village, and far from the city. But if we read the blessings and believe in them, then we can also be far from danger,' she said.

But soon, they wouldn't need the blessings any more. This was a dead end, the final station on the line, and even this station was going to close, because there were so few passengers. We were lucky to have found them here, she said. In a few months they would pack up and move away.

When I asked whether the railway further east was still being used, the stationmaster said he didn't think so, at least not by passengers. Was the military using it, I asked.

'You should not go to that place,' he replied gently. 'That place is dangerous for you.'

As we drove back along the track, Moon laid his hand on my arm.

'Our Pa-O government cannot take responsibility for you in Shan territory,' he explained. 'There are terrorists in the jungle.'

I had come as far as I was allowed to go, and it occurred to me as we drove back through the idyllic, peaceful villages towards Taunggyi that just like every other foreigner in Myanmar, I was being shielded from the violence that was playing out everywhere around me.

Everything from the lack of railway timetables, to the ambiguity about permissions, to the officials whose job it was to reroute, and even the division of the countryside into territories controlled by different groups, had the effect of repelling outsiders from a part of the country that was firmly sealed off from the world – even during this brief moment, when more of independent Myanmar was open to outsiders than it had been at any time before or since.

Several months after I visited the stationmaster in Pa-O, I found myself on a reporting assignment that, by chance, took me further along the railway into central Shan, but from the other direction, starting at the railway's eastern terminus at Kengtung.

I still didn't have a permit to travel into this part of the country, and would be staying at safe houses, so I knew that exploring the railway in the central Shan towns beyond the mountains would be impossible. But I had an opportunity, if everything went to plan, to slip behind the military's walls and discover, at last, why there was so much secrecy about the part of Myanmar that the railway was built through.

I flew early one morning from Yangon to Kengtung Airport with my Shan fixer, who I will call S. The airport was a squat white building in the mountains. On the tarmac, groups of lean soldiers in uniform watched us closely as we pulled our luggage from a trolley and climbed into a tuk-tuk, or auto rickshaw. Our driver, a squat man with yellow eyes, dropped us at a motel in the centre of town.

We checked into a room and waited nervously for the arrival of S's uncle, who had agreed to drive us that night along a treacherous mountain pass into central Shan. He was supposed to meet us at 3 p.m., but it was just before midnight when he finally pulled up. He didn't explain why he was late. He wouldn't tell us either how long he thought the journey might take – in Myanmar, this question is widely considered bad luck – nor would he share details of the route.

He was deeply superstitious about the road we would travel on that night, and as we left the city it soon became clear why. Beyond the chain of dark, shuttered villages that extended west from the outskirts of Kengtung, the highway that led into the heart of Shan was a two-lane track carved from the side of the mountains, with a sheer drop to one side.

Our car had no seatbelts and before long we were being flung in every direction, as our driver navigated the highway's innumerable twists and turns. The car flew around hairpin bends, sliding repeatedly across the road to avoid the vehicles that careered towards us, threatening to send us hurtling into the gorge below. I realized, as I gripped tightly onto the seat in front of me, that the section of the junta's railway that was supposed to cut through these mountains into central Shan had only existed, and could only have ever existed, as a line on my map.

S and I had visited Kengtung Station earlier that day and found it occupied by a gang of children, who had scattered their belongings over the platform, and hung out their tiny shirts on a washing line to dry. There was a plaque on the platform that told us this portion of the railway was just 6.6 miles long. The mountains surrounding Kengtung formed part of the same range that Chinese railway contractors were struggling to tunnel through, further north. It wasn't surprising that on the outskirts of the city Aung Min's railway ministry had quietly given up.

There were no streetlights on the highway, and the clouds of dust that obscured our view were at times so thick it was impossible to see more than a few feet ahead. When the dust cleared, it always revealed the same landscape: high banks of red earth, and occasionally an abandoned wreck of a vehicle, a makeshift shrine, or clusters of people squatting in the darkness around the glowing red embers of fires.

These were the labour gangs whose task it was each day to crush rock into gravel and repair the damage that had been done to the road overnight, clearing landslips and replacing the bollards that were supposed to prevent vehicles from skidding into the abyss. Caught in our headlights, these roadside camps appeared ghostly, and their tarpaulin tents looked exceptionally vulnerable, as did the bands of children who leaped out into the road, forcing the cars to stop, and then holding out their hands for money.

I tried to stay awake, but despite myself I was rocked into a half-sleep, which I woke from every few minutes, but could not shake off. I remember those long hours as a nightmare, in which the car streaked through the mountains, punctuated by moments of intense clarity when I was convinced we were going to die.

At 4 a.m. we stopped at a town just off the highway, near a major military checkpoint that closed during the hours of darkness. On the outskirts of the town, groups of travellers warmed their hands around blazing fires as they waited for the gate to open. There was an atmosphere of quiet camaraderie, and as they passed around hot drinks and fried bread for breakfast I imagined they were congratulating one another on surviving another night.

Overwhelmed by the journey and relief that it had ended, and trying not to succumb to exhaustion, I got out of the car to stretch my legs. As someone handed me a cup of sweet tea, I realized that except in the broadest terms I had no idea where we were, nor where we were going. My mobile signal had dropped hours earlier, and I wouldn't pick it up again for several days. Without permission to be here, I was entirely dependent on the people I was with, who until recently had been strangers. But rather than being frightening, there was something strangely calming about the fact that I had given up control.

Soon we were back in the car, and driving along a narrow river valley. As it grew light we joined the queue for the checkpoint. There was a risk that I might be identified as a foreigner here, and sent back, and so I pulled my cap down low and my mask over my face, and pretended to be asleep, with my head against my chest.

It felt subversive to be slipping through a military checkpoint without permission, but S had assured me that nobody here asked for permission to do anything, if they could help it. Until there was genuine representation for the Shan people, he didn't see any problem with ignoring the government's rules.

We drove on, then stopped. Pretending to be asleep, with my hat over my eyes, I listened with trepidation as the driver opened his door to speak to someone, then slammed it shut. We drove on again, then stopped again. Then came the sound of distant voices, and we drove on a little further.

Then, 'Clare, you can wake up,' said S, shaking me gently. We were through the checkpoint and into central Shan, the place that I had been trying to reach from Taunggyi and Pa-O territory. S called it 'the box' because it was sealed off from the outside world.

The horrors of the night were behind us, but there were fresh horrors ahead. As the sun rose, I saw that we were driving along a cracked, earthen road, between parched fields that were bordered by clusters of charred trees. There were women in the fields, with ashen faces and torn clothes, who were collecting piles of twigs, with their small children trailing behind them. More women were walking along the roadside, carrying heavy sacks on their backs. At intervals along the road there were construction gangs, labouring in the dust beside huge piles of stones.

Everything here was pale, grey and dusty. There were soldiers everywhere, riding on motorbikes, driving logging vans, travelling in the back of army trucks, walking through the dust with guns slung over their shoulders, or just sitting by the side of the road, as if the entire region was an open-air prison.

Every so often we came to a military checkpoint. Some of the checkpoints were large and established, where Myanmar soldiers spilled out into the road and S told me to cover my face, as our driver thrust banknotes into their hands. Others were little more than huts and bamboo barricades operated by insurgent fighters, which could be hastily assembled, then moved and reassembled as the front lines shifted, in this interminable war.

S told me that there had always been fighting in this region, and the oldest generations in his family remembered the war when they were children. But he could remember a time when the land had been cloaked in forest. It was a time, he said, when the temperature was cooler, and when Myanmar's military had not yet started the scorched-earth campaigns that Shan human-rights groups would later compare to the 'clearance operations' in northern Rakhine, which would reduce central Shan to a wasteland.[6]

The story that S and members of his family would tell me

over the coming days, and that I would substantiate later,[7] was similar to the stories that I had heard in Myanmar's south and in Kalay. It began in early 1996, when S was still a child. A powerful Shan warlord called Khun Sa had surrendered to the junta, handing over a large swathe of land in central and southern Shan bordering Thailand, where for many years he had controlled the cross-border opium trade. As Myanmar troops moved into Khun Sa's former territory, defectors from his army fought back, launching a guerrilla campaign across the state.

Myanmar's military responded by flooding the patchwork of Shan villages that formed a stronghold in the centre of the state with troops. Within just over two years, the military had cleared out nearly the entire rural population in the centre of the state, forcing around 400,000 people from 1,800 villages to leave their homes, in an area spanning thousands of square miles. When they left, soldiers killed their livestock, destroyed their crops and razed their villages to the ground. Just like the British under Charles Crosthwaite, they patrolled the areas they had cleared, shooting the civilians they saw on sight. Those who refused to leave were detained and tortured, or worse, stabbed to death, or set on fire, or suffocated with plastic bags. There was sexual abuse, and there were massacres, including of women and children, who were rounded up and then machine-gunned down. Shan rights groups allege that over these two years, state security forces killed more than 1,000 people.

Into the razed centre of Shan, towards the end of that decade and into the next, the military built new roads, new barracks, a new airfield and a new railway. The entire region was transformed into a vast labour camp, in which the newly displaced villagers were forced to work under armed guard.

They carried wood from the forests to build new military bases. They spread gravel across new roads that connected the bases, sleeping at the construction sites, beneath shelters built from leaves. They levelled the earth for the new railway, they smashed up stones for ballast, and they built new watchtowers, where they were forced to stand guard, to prevent Shan soldiers from travelling through a land that had, until recently, been their own. Work on the railway was overseen by one of the military's Light Infantry Divisions, elite shock troops with a reputation for brutality who would later spearhead the operations against the Rohingya in Rakhine.[8] In Shan, in the 1990s, their operations went virtually unreported, and they were never held accountable, which can only have emboldened them. The area was sealed off, and the world hardly noticed as an entire region with a rich and complex history was wiped out.

It was the same story that had played out everywhere in Myanmar, of violent clearance operations, followed by infrastructure development, and impunity for military abuses. But there was one important difference. In other parts of the country, the brutal operations had largely crushed the resistance. Once the railways were finished, they had opened to the public, and the sections of track that had survived the intervening years were still accessible, even to tourists. The cities that these railways connected were largely peaceful, too.

But here, it was clear that the regime's attempt to force open this part of the country had gone terribly wrong. I realized as I watched the sun rise over the parched fields that this region wasn't closed to outsiders because the clearance operations had taken place, but because they had failed.

Later, I would read that when a 197-mile section of the railway opened to a town called Mong Nai in central Shan, not far from where we would stay that night, the junta's prime minister Soe Win would claim that the regime's development efforts had resulted in 'remarkable progress'.[9] Surrounded on the platform by an entourage of soldiers, just as Lord Elgin had been in Myitkyina a century earlier, he told the assembled local people that this was a 'friendship railroad of national races' and that the junta was making progress towards building a 'modern and developed nation'. Excerpts from Soe Win's speech were published in state media under the headline, 'For the Nation to Stand Tall among World's Nations, Not to Become Lackey of Others'.

It must have been intensely humiliating for the generals that still, after all these years and all this violence, and despite so much ostentatious pageantry and triumphant messaging, they couldn't defeat even ethnic insurgencies that were small, scrappy and poorly armed.

By the time I travelled across the mountains into 'the box', an estimated 100,000 government troops were stationed across Shan State, about a third of Myanmar's armed forces.[10] But many of the villages that had been cleared when the railway was built were still abandoned, or occupied by Myanmar troops – or insurgent soldiers, because more than two decades after the military had razed a vast area of land and forcibly relocated more than 400,000 people, it was still struggling to consolidate control.

The Shan mountains might have been barriers to state-building, but they didn't stop the movement of people. International borders were so close and so porous that rebel leaders could cross them to regroup and resupply, using their own cross-border networks that long pre-dated the modern state.

At the same time, they drew their own borders within

Myanmar, using improvised landmines or militarized check-points, which government troops couldn't cross. Civilians who were moved to areas under military control often refused to stay in the new settlements, instead returning home, if their homes still existed, or moving to the border towns, or elsewhere in Myanmar, or disappearing into Southeast Asia.

Just like in other parts of the country's borderlands, the military only controlled the places that it physically occupied, including the fragments of railway that were scattered across the countryside, and the barracks that surrounded these broken pieces of track. But even the railway stations were occupied by people they were never meant to serve, like gangs of children, while the tropical climate eroded what remained of the railways themselves.

This was the reality of the military's nation-building project: not a unified Myanmar controlled by the generals, but a complex and diverse landscape of people who constantly undermined them.

Back on the road, our driver came to another checkpoint, and this time S didn't tell me to cover my face. The soldier he paid was Shan. Soon we were slowing down into a village that was decked out in colourful banners. Our view through the windows was blocked by orange Shan jackets and trousers. There were wrists wearing golden watches and fingers adorned with ruby-set rings. As the crowds thinned, I saw the women were dressed in long skirts and jackets embroidered in a dazzling array of colours. Their black plaits flicked from side to side beneath conical bamboo hats that were decorated with sequins and fastened by woollen pom-poms.

Preparations were underway for a Shan festival, said S with a smile. This was his hometown, and it was a Shan town, in the very heart of a region that the military had spent two decades trying to assimilate into the Myanmar state.

It was not just this Shan town. All over Myanmar's eastern borderlands, communities were holding out against integration into the Burmese state.

Leaving southern Shan behind, I took a train to Loikaw, the capital of tiny, landlocked Kayah State, on a railway that meandered south for 100 miles to just beyond the southern tip of Inle Lake. Kayah is Myanmar's smallest state, and it is also distinguished by its unique claim to political sovereignty: this rugged, mountainous territory that borders northern Thailand was never integrated into British Burma. At independence, its people, who are collectively known as Karenni, were among those granted the right to secede after ten years – a promise that was never kept.

In the Kayah capital of Loikaw, I met up with a Karenni man called Clement, who was tall, with a gentle manner and a loping gait. We had been introduced by a friend in Yangon, and he had agreed to work as my translator and guide.

Several days later, I found myself climbing, bleary-eyed, onto the back of Clement's motorbike. It was early, just before dawn, and he was taking me to a Marian festival, which was celebrated each year by more than 10,000 Catholics from every corner of Kayah State.

Clement didn't want to miss the festival, and he had persuaded me to come with him, telling me that it would be a good opportunity to meet farmers from remote villages who had been forced to build the railway to Loikaw that I had just travelled on.

Like other railways in Myanmar's borderlands, this line was built in the 1990s by local people, at gunpoint. It had been open ever since – but unlike in Myanmar's far south, there was still an armed resistance in Kayah. There would be Karenni soldiers at the festival, too, Clement told me, and they could explain why the military's nation-building attempts in Kayah had failed.

Clement handed me a motorbike helmet, and we rode fast out of the city towards a town called Pekon, overtaking pilgrims on the road. As dawn broke for miles in every direction, crowds were amassing at the festival. Some were from seminaries and wore matching jackets, others sung hymns, their bodies rising and falling in unison as the trucks that carried them bumped along the road.

We parked beside hundreds of other motorbikes, and were swept along the road by a sea of worshippers. To the east was a lake, which the inhabitants of remote villages were crossing by boat to reach the festival.

We stopped for breakfast at the house of a Catholic priest who had opened a temporary shop, serving beef porridge, biscuits and hot rice wine on his large, open balcony that overlooked the lake. Since arriving in the Kayah capital of Loikaw several days earlier, I had been offered rice wine at all times of the day.

This was partly because Clement was such an enthusiastic drinker. But then, so was everybody else. As I ate a handful of biscuits, and Clement demolished a bowl of porridge and washed it down with a tankard of wine, most of the other men around us were already drinking glasses of whisky, including the priest himself.

Behind the priest's house there were steps leading up a hill, which we climbed after breakfast, past a nunnery, where dozens of smartly dressed women stood around on the grass.

We pushed on, flanked by hundreds of people, until we came to the top of the hill. On the other side, the view was breathtaking.

Clambering onto a ledge, Clement and I sat cross-legged, looking out over an altar. Immediately below us there were rows of nuns dressed in white, who stood barefoot on colourful mats that were spread out across the mountainside. Beyond them, thousands of people filled the valley, dressed in every colour imaginable. A Catholic mass was underway, and soon everyone had burst into song, including Clement, who kept singing even after the hymn had ended, prompting giggles from some of the nuns.

When the service was over, we walked down the hill to where the congregation had been standing on a platform built into the mountainside. Then we descended a wide flight of crowded steps into a market throng. Beyond rows of stalls selling religious paraphernalia, we came to a vast network of tents formed from colourful tarpaulin sheets that were held up with sticks of bamboo. Each tent contained a stall that was fitted with a kitchen, built around an open fire. Some of the stalls served porridge topped with spicy green sausage, or plates of chopped cows' intestine, or slices of cured dog meat. But above all, these stalls were rice-wine stations.

Dragging me to the nearest one, Clement eagerly ordered us a glass of wine each, and we spent the rest of the morning, the afternoon, and the evening sitting on the floor around a table with his friends and listening to their stories.

The days since I had arrived in Loikaw had all followed a similar pattern, in which Clement took me around the city, and introduced me to his friends and members of his extended family. It was the festive season leading up to Christmas, and in the evenings we traipsed from house to house, singing carols, eating stems of ginger to keep our voices fresh, and sometimes stopping for an hour, while Clement and the older men in the household shared an earthen pot filled with rice wine and talked about the past.

Most people in this community had fled or had been forcibly moved to the city from small, isolated villages in the mountains just a generation earlier, but the tradition of telling stories each evening had endured.

There were stories about how the Karenni here had arrived from Mongolia, via Tibet and Yunnan in southwestern China. There were fables, about the most beautiful bird in the world, and a giant who tricked a young girl into marrying him, and who bore him a child with a tail. There were stories of black magic that was powerful enough to turn a human spirit into a pig or a wild cat, and of old women who ate human souls.

There were photographs of sons and daughters who had died, or who lived a long way from home. There were songs about war and love, which everyone knew the words to, and which they sang late into the nights. During the days, we listened to the stories that I asked people to tell, about life during the decades of military rule, but even these were interspersed with older stories that Clement had heard dozens of times before.

Two days earlier, we had spent an entire day listening to his godmother Bi Pu, a tiny, wizened woman, describe what life had been like here when she was young. She described how she had grown up in the mountains, in a village with just ten houses. The next village was an hour's walk away; there were no cars, no motorbikes, not even any horses. Her family lived in the same way that people had lived here for as long as anyone could remember, growing rice and vegetables to eat, and cotton for clothing, and seeds to make into detergent and shampoo.

Without electricity, when they returned from the fields each evening they would gather around a fire, and listen to the village elders tell stories. They believed, Bi Pu said, that if these stories ever stopped being told, the world would come to an end.

But even when Bi Pu was young, there were outsiders in the community, Italian priests who encouraged them to convert from animism to Christianity. As well as baptizing people they brought Western clothing with them, and foreign ways of thinking. There were new choices to make, and when Bi Pu refused to wear the brass coils that since childhood had lengthened the necks of the older women in her family, her mother accepted her decision.

There were other strangers, too, including soldiers from the Myanmar army. As Karenni soldiers fought to defend their homeland, the war occasionally interrupted Bi Pu's life, but most of the time her family was left alone.

It was only after her eldest sons had grown up that Myanmar soldiers began to appear more often. First, they made requests for taxes, often in the form of bags of rice, or firewood. Then they made demands for labour. Bi Pu's husband came home one day after a meeting with the village chief, and told her that everyone in the village had to leave their homes, to dig holes in the ground and carry soil, for a few days or more.

'Before that, I didn't know what a railway was – I didn't even know what a car was,' Bi Pu said.

She didn't ask questions, because it wasn't her place to ask. It was early 1991, and every day for a month she walked with her husband to the construction site, and they spent the whole day digging. The work was exhausting, she said, stretching her arms above her head to show us the height of the embankment they built.

The 102-mile railway connecting southern Shan with Kayah State wound through the mountains, which meant that many of the people who built it only saw their own camp. Nobody I spoke to in Loikaw could tell me how many people were forced to work on it, with some of them estimating it had been hundreds, and others thousands.

But the junta's newspapers revealed that the scale of mobilization was much greater. In May 1992 the *Working People's Daily* reported that more than 300,000 people in Kayah and southern Shan States had contributed 'voluntary labour' – more than the entire population of Kayah.[11] By the time the railway was finished the following year, the number had risen to almost 800,000.[12] They worked under similar conditions as in other parts of the country, under armed guard, without pay, or food, or shelter.[13] A local rights group would later claim that hundreds or possibly thousands of people had died from beatings, starvation, and disease.[14]

At the same time, there were mass-relocation campaigns just like the ones that were being conducted all across the borderlands around the same time. This created a large pool of displaced people, who could be deployed on infrastructure projects, including the railway.[15]

A spokesperson for the junta's Border Areas Development Programme admitted to Reuters newswire that the people being forced to work on the railway didn't want to leave their homes, but he said it was because they didn't understand the railway was being built for their benefit.

'We are doing it for them. But for the present people must suffer by putting in labour,' he said.[16]

State media reported that the railway was built as part of the Border Areas Development Programme,[17] an ambitious project that was designed to increase food production, diversify the economy and expand infrastructure into ceasefire areas in the borderlands.[18]

Announced in 1989, the year after the junta took power, it was a major departure from the isolationist policies of Ne Win's socialist regime, and it was welcomed by international development institutions, which apparently accepted the junta's claim that it needed external funding to promote social and economic change.

Multiple United Nations agencies allegedly committed to financing parts of the programme, including the UN Development Programme. This was despite the fact that it was being implemented by the same generals who had just brutally suppressed a nationwide uprising and had a long history of atrocities in Myanmar's borderlands. It was also despite protests by ethnic-minority groups, who pointed out that the entire programme was strategic, designed to expand the military's authority.

To these groups, it must have been horrifying that UN agencies were helping the generals to integrate their communities into an abusive, authoritarian state. But UN officials were so accustomed to seeing development as a solution to conflict, rather than its cause, that they failed to interrogate who exactly the beneficiaries would be, or to examine the harms it might cause. Not only were they helping to expand the junta's access into remote areas, they were connecting communities to a global economy that would exploit them, undervaluing their produce and channelling the profits elsewhere.

Those who supported the programme also appear to have believed, just as the British colonial administrators had believed, and the generals had later believed, that development was intrinsically valuable and in the interests of ethnic people; those same people who had protested, because they saw clearly that development by the junta was not in their interests at all.

The idea that these groups, or in fact most people I had met, would have wanted more development by the junta was absurd, with or without UN support. Development by outsiders had always meant dispossession and exploitation here. What ethnic communities wanted, and what they had asked for over and over again, was the freedom to manage their own land and their own resources.

Foreign diplomats including the German ambassador even attended the opening ceremony of the first section of the railway. They accompanied the generals, including Than Shwe's deputy Maung Aye, on a special train to inaugurate the service, as local people waved them along the route. Whether or not they supported the railway's construction, their presence at the opening ceremony legitimized it, and photographs of the event were published in state media the following day.[19]

This was the same route that I had travelled on earlier that week. Trains left from Aungban, a highway town near Inle Lake, whose small houses clung to the hillside, and were cloaked in a permanent cloud of dust. At the station, as I watched women load sacks of cabbages into the train's three small freight carriages, I had assumed the service was now used mostly for trade. There was no public timetable, and there was no platform, either; climbing into the only passenger carriage had required all my upper-body strength.

My companions in the carriage were two dozen men, and most of them fell quickly asleep, as the train snaked through the rolling plains. The villages we passed were monochrome, nestled tightly among the low hills and encircled by bamboo forest. There were no vendors on the train, and the small, sleepy stations were deserted. All afternoon, the patchwork fields rolled on, with the view broken only by rows of eucalyptus trees. As the light shifted and the shadows lengthened, and the train twisted through tunnels and between the hills, I remember this last part of the journey as if it was a dream. My companions only woke up towards evening, and it was almost dark when we began to slow down; to the east was the southern end of the lake, and we were pulling into a town.

The man who had been sitting opposite me pulled on a grey hoodie, and began packing his belongings away.

'I am army,' he said, in English, when he was done. 'Soldier. Pekon Township.'

'Myanmar army?' I asked him, surprised that I hadn't identified him as a soldier.

'Yes. Soldier,' he repeated and just like so many men I had met across the country, he mimed firing a gun.

Another man who had been sleeping beside him was now awake and pulling out an army jacket from beneath his seat. I had noticed it when he boarded the train, but hadn't thought much of it, because civilians in Myanmar often wear camouflage too. I had noticed his gold ring set with jade and diamonds earlier in the afternoon, but because he was wearing a cheap patterned shirt and a scruffy *paso*, I had assumed it was a fake.

'Are you a soldier?' I asked him, and he nodded.

I looked again around the carriage. One by one, the young men who had been dressed in civilian clothing and who I had assumed were traders, stood up and began to pull out green canvas satchels and metal boxes from beneath the seats, and to dress themselves in army jackets and hats.

The train was stopping now at Pekon Station, where there was a large military base.

'I am sergeant clerk,' said the first man, pretending to type on a computer. 'Army, staff.' He pointed at my notebook, which I had been writing in all afternoon.

'You, writing,' he said.

'Yes,' I said, and smiled.

He nodded; he had been watching, and I wondered now whether he had wanted to tell me earlier who he was.

The station was illuminated by small lights strung from the trees. When the train stopped, women emerged from the shadows carrying plates of food, which they offered to the soldiers, who were now passing down their luggage to each other through the windows. Among the last pieces of luggage were several red-and-yellow metal boxes, each around two feet long and a foot wide.

'Sniper,' said the man with the jade ring, pointing at one of the boxes, and he smiled.

For the rest of the journey, I was alone in the carriage with two scruffy children wearing football kits, who had clambered onto the train at Pekon. I wondered how many times on my journey I had been travelling with soldiers and hadn't noticed. I had spent so long now on trains in Myanmar that I hadn't found it strange there was no timetable for this service, or that there were just a handful of people on this train, which ran despite what must have been a huge expense. The railway department was providing a service for the army, but then that shouldn't have surprised me. There was a new government, but nothing about how the railways were run had really changed.

As trains shuttled troops back and forth from the military's bases in southern Shan to its bases in Kayah, the Karenni festival that sprawled across the railway tracks – which I was attending with Clement – was in full swing. When the daily train passed through the festival ground later that night, the vendors would move their stalls to let it through, before setting them up again on the tracks.

These were two separate worlds: while the junta's railways connected places that were deserted, or inhabited by soldiers, just beyond the tracks, community life thrived. This was particularly true in the places that had always resisted centralized rule. Knowing that the state offered them nothing, people here had built what they needed for themselves; as a result, community life in these borderlands was stronger and more resilient than anywhere I had ever been.

Here, all around the railway, there were no Myanmar soldiers to be seen. Instead, at the wine station, I was surrounded by young men who spoke more freely than I had heard anyone in Myanmar speak before. This was a rebel stronghold, and many of them were Karenni soldiers.

Clement and I were joined in the afternoon by a family of eight brothers, who were opium farmers, and several of them had been forced to work on the railway. But this wasn't what they wanted to talk about. Instead, the eldest brother was now describing how Karenni men in the 1990s had been forced to act as porters for the military in its campaigns against Karenni troops.

When the men returned from the battlefield, they looked like animals, he told us.

'They could not eat or talk – they could not even ask for a smoke,' he said. He had been forced to work as a porter himself, for months at a time, carrying bullets and food for the soldiers, surviving on little more than fish paste and a handful or two of rice a day, and sleeping in the jungle in the winter without a blanket.

'Sometimes when an army truck brought fifty or sixty people back to the villages, their clothes were torn, or they had no clothes at all, and they couldn't even walk, they just lay on the side of the road,' he said. After carrying heavy loads for weeks, their shoulders were swollen and covered with welts and open wounds.

Not everyone came home. Two days earlier, Clement's god-mother Bi Pu had told us that her son and his friends had been detained while working in the fields, and forced to act as guides for the military in the mountains. They did as they were told, carrying the soldiers' equipment, until they came across a group of Karenni insurgents.

'They fought,' Bi Pu told us, 'and a bullet hit my son, and there was a lot of blood coming out and he was screaming and crying and asking for help. Nobody dared to help him, even though he did not die straight away.'

She and her husband harnessed their cow to a cart and rode into the jungle to retrieve their son's body, and they carried him back to the house and buried him. After that, she told us, she fell into a deep depression. She was pregnant at the time, and when she gave birth to another boy she couldn't care for him, and he died after an unhappy year.

'I was sick,' she said. 'I couldn't sleep, I didn't want to eat or drink, and I thought of nothing but my son for almost ten years.'

After the soldiers killed her son, Bi Pu said she lost all fear of the army, and of dying, and when she came across soldiers in the village, her other sons had to hold her back, to stop her from attacking them. It wasn't just Bi Pu who had lost her fear. One man had told me that he had been so angry while building the railway that he had thrown handfuls of soil into a soldier's face. Another man, a cow trader, said that when a group of soldiers ordered him to hand over his cows, he ignored them, and when they pointed his guns at him and threatened to kill him, he dared them to go ahead.

The people here were surrounded by stories like this, and strengthened by them. But what did the future hold? Nobody here was optimistic about the political transition. They didn't trust the Burmese people, Clement explained, including Aung San Suu Kyi, whose father after all was the founder of Myanmar's armed forces.

'The army wants to be the father of the country, but we could never call them a father from our hearts,' one of the brothers said. 'We only give them respect because we are afraid.'

Not only this but Aung San Suu Kyi was willing to negotiate with the military, and had made it clear that she saw a place in Myanmar for the armed forces her father had founded. The political transition was, in Clement's eyes, a Burmese struggle, between people with different visions for a Burmese nation.

Here, he said, the leaders were, and had always been, Karenni. It was the Karenni armies who protected the poppy fields in the mountains and who taxed the opium trade, the region's most lucrative business, and it was the Karenni armies who would fight to end the Burmese occupation, when the time inevitably came.

He pointed at a Karenni soldier, a sunburned man in uniform, who was sitting next to me.

'He can do everything,' Clement said, happily, through a fog of wine. 'He is an expert.'

'What kind of things?' I asked him.

'He can dance, a traditional dance that mimics the movement of nature,' Clement said. 'For example, planting the paddy, harvesting the rice. He also has a knife, a sword, 3 feet long. It is a most expensive sword.'

The soldier laughed.

'And,' said Clement, warming to the subject, 'he is very clever and a good man.'

I asked the soldier if he would ever fight again.

'Our local armies are ready to fight,' he replied. 'They are not fighting now, but they could, at any time.'

'What would cause them to fight?' I asked.

'The local armies are watching the government,' Clement interjected. 'Now, the government is making deals with foreign companies and they are coming here to take our land. They talk in Burmese, so we cannot understand what they are saying. If this keeps happening, the fighting will get worse.'

Later that night Clement and I went to find something to eat. Away from the smoke and the clamour of the wine stations, we ordered fried bread and coffee and sat for a while with his oldest friend, who was very drunk and 'very talkative', as Clement put it.

The friend produced two coins and insisted that I take one of them, a silver rupee engraved with the image of King Edward VII, which he had found in the jungle. It had been a week of gifts – Bi Pu had given me a bag that she had woven from cotton, and searching for something to give her in return, I had dug out a 5,000-kyat banknote folded into the shape of an elephant, which she told me she would have placed on her head when she was buried.

I had promised to send her a photograph, too, which Clement took of the two of us standing beneath her jackfruit trees. When she looked at the image on my camera, she had let out a roar of laughter.

'You look like Father Emmanuel,' she told me. 'The eyes, the nose, the hair!'

This, explained Clement, was the Italian priest who had baptized Bi Pu. I asked if he was a handsome man.

'No,' she replied, and she laughed. 'He is ninety-three years old. And he is dead!'

Now, with the rupee coin stowed in my bag, I followed Clement to the edge of the festival site to visit one of his brothers-in-law. Beyond the food stalls, past tattooing stations, and trestle tables where the skins of crocodiles and snakes were displayed for sale, we crossed the railway tracks, and ducked along an alley to the house, which was built around a courtyard. Inside, crowds of people filled the dimly lit rooms. In the largest of the rooms, plastic mats were laid out on the floor, and there was a pile of folded blankets and pillows in one corner.

Several people were asleep in the shadows, and as Clement sprang towards a pot of rice wine and took several large gulps, I slumped, exhausted, against a wall. A woman told me to rest, and as I curled up on one of the mats, she placed a blanket over my body. I fell asleep to the distant clatter of cooking and the low voices of men, and when I woke up, not knowing whether minutes or hours had passed, I was alone.

Outside, I found Clement sitting beside a fire in the courtyard, with a group of Karenni soldiers and four girls who were sitting on a bench and holding hands, and who giggled when they saw me. Someone passed me a pot of wine, and I drank deeply, feeling its warmth flood my body.

Refreshed and feeling more awake than I had for days, I sat with them, and they asked me questions about how to get to England, and about the things that my country was then famous for, like the Queen and Wayne Rooney.

Unlike at Inle Lake, where tourists quizzed local people about their customs, I had become the curiosity here. They wanted to know whether we had tribes in England, and I told them that our tribes had long since disappeared, along with their languages, their histories, their divisions, but also their traditions, and the sense of belonging and community that they offered.

The girls, who evidently felt sorry for me, offered to dress me in their traditional clothing for a photograph. They summoned their grandmother, who helped me to get dressed, and they combed my hair, pulling it off my face and fastening it with a jewelled pin. Their mother fetched a traditional basket, and a flagon of wine for me to hold, and the entire family posed beside me. Then I was photographed again with the soldiers, who flanked me, sombre and proud in their uniforms – the same uniforms that they would wear in 2021, when the military staged another coup, and the Karenni people would fight for their freedom, once again.

8.

Naypyidaw

I gripped the back of Su's motorbike as we drove through the Myaing Galay cement factory compound, past mountains of crushed stone, into a wide, open courtyard that was framed by industrial sheds. The towering factory dwarfed its workers, who zipped around on mopeds, crossing and recrossing the courtyard between the sheds. From a distance, I had been mesmerized by the factory's towers and twisting pipes that rose among the limestone formations on the surrounding plains. But up close, it looked grotesque, and the pipes that formed its exposed belly were stained with dust that contaminated the air and clung to our skin and clothes.

On the other side of the courtyard, we came to a checkpoint that was set into an inner wall, and as we waited there I imagined that every passing worker would send us away. This cement factory was run by Myanmar Economic Corporation, one of the military's two conglomerates, and it was a high-security facility.

But when a moped eventually roared up and screeched to a stop, the hard-faced young man who removed his helmet greeted us with a nod. He was Su's friend, and he cocked his head to indicate that we should follow him. Then he sped off through the gate and into a smaller courtyard that was surrounded by low, administrative buildings.

We parked inside the courtyard, and he ushered us into a

darkened room. On one side was a desk and on the other, half a dozen varnished teak chairs were arranged around a low table. We sat on the chairs, and after twenty minutes, just as I was beginning to wonder whether anyone would show up, a heavy-faced official pushed his way through a side door and sat down at the desk, without looking at any of us.

'Yes,' he barked, in English. His hostility was disconcerting, but I told him that I was interested in the history of the railway that led to his factory.

As I spoke, a soldier strode into the room and stood behind the desk. The air in the room was stifling, and I became suddenly aware that I was thirsty. It is rare in Myanmar not to be offered a drink.

'What do you want to know?' the factory manager said.

That morning, I had scrawled a list of questions in my notepad and I began by asking the most basic one. Were the railway and the cement factories connected? The answer was obvious. The railway terminated in the factory compound. There was nothing else here, and there could have been no other reason for building it.

'There is no connection.' The manager formed each word with care.

I glanced at the soldier, who was studying my response. He nodded in agreement and reached into a pocket for his smartphone, which he raised to take my photograph.

I explained that I had seen from the road that the railway terminated in the compound. Perhaps, I said, it had once been used to transport stones or cement.

'We use the roads. We have always used the roads,' the manager said. 'What else do you want to know?'

I asked him what the railway was used for, if it wasn't used by the factory. He did not know, he said tersely, and as I began to ask another question, he stood up.

'If you have nothing else to ask,' he said, and still avoiding my eyes, he directed us to the door.

In the courtyard as we retrieved the motorbike, Su's friend apologized. The manager hadn't told us the truth, he said; the railway served the factory and trains occasionally still ran.

'What did they have to hide?' I asked.

But he didn't want to say anything more, and he escorted us back through the compound in silence, closing the gates behind us.

I asked Su, who was working as my guide and translator in Hpa-an, if she wanted to go back to the city. But she had been energized by the confrontation, and suggested that we ask at a smaller, older cement factory, run by the same company, which was also connected to the railway. It wasn't far, and soon we were driving along an approach road through the fields towards the factory gates, which were framed with billboards emblazoned with Burmese script.

'Myanmar Economic Corporation Factory, 900 Tonnes of Cement Daily', read one billboard. 'Do Not Enter Without Uniform', read another. 'Former Workers Are Not Permitted Entry'.

Su parked her motorbike beneath one of the billboards. We walked to the gates, where a young security officer wearing a pale-khaki uniform asked to see my letter of permission from the company's head office in Yangon. The idea that I might have one made me smile; I had tried for months in Yangon to arrange a meeting with the company, without success.

When I told him I didn't have a letter, he didn't immediately send me away, so I asked him about the history of the railway. He denied that it was connected to the factories, telling me that it had never been used to transport cement. Frustrated and confused by his answer, I watched as workers spilled from the factory to take their lunch break, streaming past us through the gates. I couldn't figure out why this simple and apparently obvious detail was proving so difficult to establish. Was it possible that I had got it wrong, and that the railway really was built for some other purpose? I was about to turn around and leave with the workers when an elderly guard, who was sitting on a chair beside the gatehouse in the yard, corrected the young official.

'The railway was built to supply the factory,' he said quietly, in Burmese.

The official spun around and asked the old man if his memory was functioning properly.

'The railway and the factory were built in the same year,' the old man went on, apparently untroubled by the insult. 'Before the factory was built, there was a village here.'

In the gatehouse, a clerk looked up from her ledger and nodded.

'The village name was Hla Ka,' she said.

This was too much for the young official.

'Enough,' he said. 'You have talked too much. You are here without permission. You must leave.'

In a large, dusty yard just outside the factory walls, there was a teashop where the workers were now gathering, and Su and I ducked inside. We sat at a long, crowded table, and when a middle-aged woman came over to take our order, we asked her about the village.

She had once lived there, she told us, gesturing towards the yard and the factory beyond it, with her family, in a farmhouse surrounded by an orchard and several acres of paddy fields. When she was young, soldiers from a local battalion had turned up and ordered everyone in the village to dismantle their wooden houses and clear out.

'We had no freedom to protest,' she said.

As for the railway, she confirmed what Su's friend and the elderly guard had told us, that it had served the cement factories, at least until Aung San Suu Kyi's government took office several months earlier, when trains had mostly stopped running. But Hla Ka Railway Station was just down the road, she said. Why didn't we ask there?

Back on the road we stopped to ask directions from a woman who was selling petrol in glass bottles. Her husband, whose arms were scarred by faded green tattoos, watched us from the door of their hut, as Su asked questions in Karen, the local language. The woman pointed along the road, and we drove on for several minutes, until Su stopped again, to ask directions from the owner of a motorbike repair shop.

'Please wait,' he said, and hurried away. When he returned, he was leading a thin old man with yellow eyes, who introduced himself, using a Karen honorific, as Saw Lwin, the stationmaster of Hla Ka Station.

We sat together on a bench in the mechanic's yard and Lwin told us that the railway was still in use but that trains now only ran occasionally. It had been built to connect the older cement factory to the mainline network, and he had moved here in 2001, when the larger factory opened and the railway was extended. Since then, he had been responsible for loading cement onto trains.

When he first moved here, there wasn't much work, he said, but soon more and more factory workers were being assigned to the station. Before long there were seventy people working here, and they loaded cement onto trains continuously, in shifts, all day and all night.

'For many years, we had to work very hard and very quickly,' he said. I asked him why.

'We did not know at that time,' he replied. 'But we knew they must be building something.' In a country where most buildings are made from wood and bamboo, it was clearly something extraordinary.

In November 2005, four years after Lwin started packing cement onto trains at Hla Ka Railway Station, hundreds of military trucks began leaving Yangon, transporting battalions and the staff of government ministries to the shell of a city some 230 miles to the north.[1] On the plains of central Myanmar, crony construction companies had built an interconnected network of highways that linked a number of zones – a military zone, a ministry zone, a hotel zone. This was the foundation of Myanmar's new capital city, Naypyidaw. In the dust and the heat of the plains, it must have looked like a mirage.

There were no hospitals, or schools, or markets. Basic services like electricity and running water were not yet working properly. There was no mobile phone coverage, and private telephone lines were forbidden. Naypyidaw's new residents, who had been ordered to leave their families behind in Yangon, were expected to communicate by walkie-talkie.

It was only after the second convoy left Yangon that foreign diplomats were told that Myanmar's capital city had moved and were given a fax number to contact the government. It took them by surprise: because the entire area had been sealed off, hardly anyone had noticed that the city was being built.

When news reached him that the generals had built a new capital, Lwin immediately understood.

'They were using the cement to build Naypyidaw: its parliament, ministries and roads,' he said.

The realization stunned him. Most of the workers at the cement factories were Karen, the ethnic group that had been closest to the British during the colonial occupation, and whose army, the Karen National Liberation Army, had been fighting Myanmar's military for independence since 1949. For years, he said, the Karen people had been helping to demolish their own sacred limestone hills, to provide their enemies with the materials they needed to build a fortress. But by the time they realized what was happening, it was too late: the seat of power had been moved. As the generals prepared to hold an election that would see the junta step back from power, most of the workers at Hla Ka were dismissed, and Lwin stayed behind to run the station.

Eager to show it to us, he led us behind the mechanic's yard onto the platform, which was hidden among the trees. Across the tracks there was a row of thatch huts, where the women in Lwin's extended family were preparing an evening meal. Stepping onto the tracks, we looked along an avenue of ironwood trees to where, in the distance, one of the cement factories gleamed pale pink in the late afternoon sun.

I asked Lwin where the stone that supplied the factories came from, and he said that he believed it was mined from two local mountains. But another stationmaster, further along the line, would later tell me that the cement factories had been supplied with stone from quarries in Mon State, in Myanmar's south, as well as from a place called Htone Bo near Mandalay.

I happened to recognize the name Htone Bo because I had seen it in a recent investigation by a local publication, which exposed the appalling conditions at Myanmar's prison labour camps. Of the forty-eight prison camps in Myanmar where some 20,000 people worked for free, eighteen were rock quarries, and one of them was at Htone Bo.[2]

Many of the others were located in the south, beside the old British railway through Mon State, not far from where this branch line connected to the mainline network.[3] At the quarries, the report found, prisoners suffered violence and abuse while being forced to smash up granite and limestone boulders, and crush them by hand with sledgehammers into gravel, which was sold to government agencies and private companies for construction.

I was never able to confirm with the stationmaster further along the line whether the materials that supplied the cement factories had been quarried at prison labour camps, because his wife had stormed over to reprimand him before I could ask any more questions, and to warn him, furiously, against sharing official information with strangers.

If it was true, it would have explained the hostile reception that I had received at the cement factories. But regardless of whether the prison camps supplied the factories in Hpa-an, or other factories elsewhere in Myanmar, they formed just another small part of the supply chain that now extended to the far corners of Myanmar, with the military and its new capital city at its centre. Just as British colonial railways had channelled resources and wealth from across the empire back to London, so Naypyidaw appeared to have become the military's metropole.

Back at Hla Ka Station, when the sun began to set, the stationmaster Lwin became uneasy. He had learned to fear the darkness. He asked us to drive back to Hpa-an, and to safety. As we prepared to leave him, Su asked Lwin for his phone number. She had been astonished by his story, and she wanted to talk more to him about it.

As we sped back along the road on her motorbike, Su asked me to wrap my arms around her waist, and she slowed down only after we had crossed the bridge.

'Do you know there is a civil war?' she asked, as we drove through the city's empty streets.

She recalled an evening when she was twelve years old and she had been with her family at a Karen festival to celebrate the harvest. She recalled the singing and the traditional *don* dances and the stalls that sold toys and snacks. It had been a festive, relaxed day. But then, after dark, the stalls began to explode.

'The military bombed the festival,' she said. Her family hid in the grounds until the morning. Her uncles and aunts pretended that it was a game, and made jokes all night, to make the children laugh. But Su had been terrified, and soon afterwards her family packed up and left for Thailand, because they considered it too dangerous to stay.

'Most people left,' she told me. 'My family and friends are still in Bangkok. There is nothing for us here.'

She had returned only as a favour to a Karen community group that funded her studies in Bangkok. Intending to teach English at a village school, she had been shocked to find that the teachers made their students learn English vocabulary by rote, without themselves understanding what it meant. So she rented a room in Hpa-an and opened a private school.

'We must educate our generation,' she said, echoing the words that Min's mother had spoken to him at the railway construction camp in Myanmar's south, all those years ago. 'We have to help our youth.'

Su dropped me at my hostel near the city's central market. Soon afterwards, the power failed and I went outside to find the district in darkness. Shopkeepers along the street were lighting candles outside their stores. As I sat on a step to watch, the hostel's owner fired up her generator, which powered a single bulb in the lobby.

Within minutes, the neighbours emerged from the darkness, one by one, as if they had been drawn to the hostel by its light. They sat on the threadbare sofas in the lobby to talk, and when I joined them, they told me about their hopes for the new government, the peace process that Aung San Suu Kyi was leading, and the prospect that Myanmar might one day become a federal democracy.

None of them could remember a time before the fighting. But now, they explained, there were tourists here, including tall Europeans who came to explore the limestone caves, and to climb the sacred Mount Zwekabin at the edge of the city. For the first time in many years, they said, they were starting to believe in the possibility of peace.

When we pulled into Naypyidaw Railway Station, I was the only passenger in my carriage to get off the train. Looking up and down the platform, I saw that it was deserted. As the train pulled away again, I saw that the adjacent platform was deserted too, and so was the platform beyond that.

I had some time to spare, so I wandered through the station concourse. It was a vast, modernist building fronted with hundreds of panes of reflective glass that resembled an airport terminal, and it was clearly designed for crowds. This was supposed to be the busy centre of Myanmar's national railway network, 'the heart of rail transportation' as the *New Light of Myanmar* called it.

When the station opened, the articles published in state media were filled with hope; the generals were putting the finishing touches to their new capital city, and preparing for elections that would usher in a new era of parliamentary politics. Their new railways and roads connecting the far corners of Myanmar to Naypyidaw were finished, or at least in the world of state media they were finished, and they believed that the new capital would thrive.

But seven years later, there was nobody here. In the cavernous hallways and on the wide flights of stairs, I passed the occasional member of staff. In the entrance hall, a three-storey rotunda featuring an enormous chandelier, there was a soldier in uniform holding the hand of his young son, as he showed him a locomotive on display. But outside the building, the parking bays were empty, and the food stalls and manicured gardens were empty too.

With its abundance of space and light, it was hard to imagine a place more different from the tents that housed thousands of pilgrims after the Marian festival, and the crowded teashops where I had spent so much time across the country, and the displacement camps, whose inhabitants were crammed into squalid longhouses. It was radically different even from the spaces that ordinary soldiers inhabited elsewhere in Myanmar: the sweltering barracks, the dilapidated railway carriages, and the run-down factories.

This railway station, like the city beyond it, was an ostentatious display of wealth and power that was clearly designed to impress. But as I walked again through the empty corridors and along the empty platforms, I wondered who it was all for. The cement produced in Hpa-an and other factories across the country had been transported here to equip Naypyidaw with everything a modern capital might need. Beyond the railway station, there was an international airport, two international conference centres, a multi-use stadium designed to seat up to 30,000 spectators, and an impressive collection of museums, zoological gardens, a safari park, water-fountain gardens, a national landmark garden and even a national herbal park, all connected by miles of concrete highways.

Had it all been built to impress Myanmar's people? Or had it been built to impress the world, when presidents and the owners of multinational companies flocked to the capital, as the generals in Than Shwe's junta anticipated they would? The generals had returned repeatedly in their speeches to the idea that Myanmar needed to 'stand tall' among other nations. Was this really what they believed was required?

In the entrance hall, I found a ticket seller who told me that only a few trains now passed through the city each day. In the seven years since the station had opened, many of the new services connecting Naypyidaw with remote corners of the country had been discontinued. Nobody had a reason to travel here by train, because most people who lived in central Naypyidaw were rich enough to have a car, and there was nothing much in the city that would draw anyone here from elsewhere.

As we spoke, the ticket seller glanced up at a CCTV camera, and I realized that this wasn't a place to be asking difficult questions. Instead, I asked him how to get into the city, and to my surprise he told me that he wasn't sure. There were no public buses running, and there were no taxis outside the station. This was a problem, because Naypyidaw is not designed for pedestrians, either.

The railway station is in the northeast of the city, near the military zone that is set into the foothills of the Shan mountains. The hotel zone, which is the only place in the city where foreigners can stay, was 15 miles away – a five-hour walk, according to Google maps.

The ticket officer conferred with his colleagues, and then asked me to wait outside the deserted terminal. It was half an hour before he came back, this time with another man, who offered to drive me to the hotel zone on the back of his motorbike.

Leaving the station behind us, we cruised along the city's empty streets. The newly planted palms and grey-green ferns that lined the central reservations were all the same height, the curbs were painted with the same red-and-white stripes, and on either side of the roads there were fields filled with pampas grass. Every so often we came to a roundabout that was manicured and empty, and manned by what I began to imagine was the same police officer, who wore the same crisp uniform, and blew the same whistle as he directed us back around the same loop.

The monotony was exhausting because I was trying to make sense of what I was seeing, imagining that we were on the outskirts of the city and always driving towards, but never reaching, its centre.

If Naypyidaw provided a glimpse into the world as the generals wanted it to be, it was clear that what they wanted more than anything else was control. The city's magnitude alone would defeat any uprising: a protest of tens or even hundreds of thousands of people would appear insignificant on its highways, while its political and military targets were so isolated from one another and so heavily fortified that it would be almost impossible to stage an attack.[4]

For the civilian officials appointed by Aung San Suu Kyi's government, who had recently moved into identikit apartment blocks with roofs colour-coded by the ministry, where accommodation was assigned based on department and rank, it must have been terrifying.

When we reached the hotel zone, there was nothing much to distinguish it from other parts of the city, except there were signs outside the vast buildings that identified them as hotels. Each hotel was owned by a different crony company, and each hotel was imposing, surreal, and isolated from the others by more stretches of highway, and more fields filled with pampas grass.

I asked my driver to drop me at a hotel where I had stayed before. Like most other hotels in Naypyidaw, it was an empty, sad place that already had the faded look of an old seaside resort in winter. At the check-in desk, I booked a car to drive me the next day to the military zone, in the city's northeast.

I had come to Naypyidaw to visit the only part of the military zone that is open to the public, the Defence Services Museum, which is also the only place in Myanmar where the military's version of history is on display. The museum was 'a tribute to former dictator Than Shwe', a Reuters report had claimed in 2012, the year it opened.[5] Than Shwe's photograph appeared everywhere in the museum's cavernous halls, the report said, and one of the largest displays was dedicated to his infrastructure projects, including his railways. I still had a long list of unanswered questions about the railways in my notebooks, some of them very basic, and I hoped to find some answers there.

Back at my hotel, the kitchen was closed, and so I walked at dusk to another hotel, a luxury, five-star resort nearby, where I knew there was a restaurant that I could eat in that night.

As I walked along the edge of a deserted highway, surrounded by nothing but concrete and scrubland, I felt as if I was stuck in an unsettling dream. At the entrance to the resort's grounds, I turned through an ornate set of security gates, following a private road through desolate, landscaped gardens, and by the time I had reached the lobby it was almost dark.

The lobby was a huge, ornate pavilion whose ceiling was

painted gold, and just like Naypyidaw Railway Station, it was deserted. At the gilded check-in desk, a receptionist pointed me towards the fine-dining restaurant, where I sat alone in a room that could have seated fifty people.

The waiters were attentive young men and women dressed in pristine uniforms, who had evidently been employed, and trained, in the expectation that this restaurant would be filled with people.

But then, the restaurant hadn't always been empty. As I ordered a glass of wine and a plate of pasta from the international menu, I found myself thinking about the last time I had been here, when every table around me had been packed with foreign investors, diplomats and journalists, who had descended on Naypyidaw to attend a conference hosted by Euromoney Institutional Investor, a British business media group – and I was there to report on the event.

It was 2015, and excitement about Myanmar's political and economic transition was intensifying. It had only been four years since the generals had swapped their fatigues for *taikpon*, traditional jackets worn by civilian officials, but world leaders and chief executives had already flocked to Naypyidaw, just as the generals had anticipated they would.

Euromoney wasn't the only British company that had rushed into the world's newest frontier market. Britain had quickly positioned itself as a leading source of foreign direct investment, a provider of goods and services, and a development partner, which could advise on everything from 'peace issues' to poverty reduction.[6]

The British ambassador and his team had driven 785 miles across the country in a Land Rover painted with the Union Jack flag, on a 'Great Britain Road Show' to promote British business, and British culture. The event was part of 'Great Britain

Week', which was sponsored by British companies and opened with a garden party at the ambassador's colonial-era residence.[7] The message was clear: Britain was back, not as an occupying power, but as a partner in modern Myanmar.

What was less clear was who exactly Britain was partnering with. On the sidelines of the conference, I had watched investors from Britain, as well as from other countries around the world, discuss business opportunities over canapés and drinks with the owners of Myanmar's largest companies. The military had kept such a tight grip on the economy that this mostly meant proxies of the generals, their cronies and their children. This was the same group of people, or their representatives, who had only recently been sanctioned by the West for their role in facilitating the regime's abuses. Now, instead of being held accountable for the violence, they were being rewarded for it, by investors who were willing to enrich them, because their interests were aligned.

There was a lot of talk about responsible business, and there were new aid programmes, but all of this was to some degree a distraction from the main event, which was a rush for profits that was driven by many of the same forces that had once driven British colonial expansion. There was a need, not just in Britain but around the world, for new sources of cheap raw materials and labour, new investments to improve returns, and new markets for manufactured products – all to fuel growth that would fend off unemployment and unrest at home.

Even as Myanmar's generals liberalized parts of the economy, there was immense pressure from international investors for more and faster reforms. Like John Ogilvy Hay, the British businessman who in the 1850s wanted to build a railway across Rakhine, few people at the conference appeared to have questioned the idea that constant and vigorous expansion driven by capital and industry was a force for good.

There was a firmly held belief that everyone in Myanmar would benefit from more investment. But the frenzied way in which deals were being negotiated, and the fact that nobody was looking too hard at where the opportunities had come from, or who precisely would benefit from them, indicated that ordinary people might not benefit quite as much as the conference delegates wanted to believe.

As the archaeologist I had met in Rakhine might have put it, they were living in the 'basket' of the empire, unable to imagine a world that was built any differently. It probably didn't occur to any of the delegates, just as it didn't occur to me at the time, that many of the solutions being proposed at the conference to Myanmar's problems sounded ominously similar to the problems themselves: more large-scale investment that would profit outsiders, and more support for state institutions that were still ultimately controlled by Myanmar's military, despite the transition to partial civilian rule.

After the investment conference, the party had continued back at the hotel where I was now eating in the empty restaurant. The bar that was now deserted had been filled with the sound of laughter, as foreign investors and military cronies ordered bottles of scotch and rounds of cocktails late into the night.

It occurred to me now, as I paid my bill, and walked back alone along the edge of the dark, empty highway, that the hotel had only been packed during the conference because investors had parachuted into the city, but none of them had any reason, let alone desire, to live in Naypyidaw, or work here, or invest here.

Despite everything that Than Shwe's junta had done, or claimed to have done to channel people and resources towards

Myanmar's centre, the life and energy in the country remained where the markets were, which meant in the booming towns along the borders with China and Thailand, and the old colonial capital beside the ports.

Naypyidaw's emptiness revealed that after all this time, Myanmar's main function in the global economy was still to be a cheap source of raw materials and labour, just as it had been under colonial rule.

The driver who picked me up from my hotel the next day was used to shuttling foreigners between the hotel and the ministries, when they came here to do business. He was surprised when I asked him if we could go to the Defence Services Museum. But he agreed to take me there, and soon we were speeding across the city towards the mountains in the northeast.

After a while, a roadblock manned by two soldiers came into view. It was a long way off, but we could see it because like everything else in Naypyidaw the multi-lane highway that led to the military zone was deserted.

'The generals have very big houses inside,' my driver told me, as we approached the roadblock. 'They are very, very rich.'

I asked him, in what I imagined was an offhand way, if we could stop and speak to the soldiers. Before arriving in the city, I had half-entertained the idea of looking for Than Shwe here – or at least of asking the soldiers who would inevitably turn me back to help me arrange an interview with the reclusive former dictator. He was believed to still be alive, though rumours of his ill health and even his death had circulated for years. I even thought I knew where he lived, in a sprawling villa inside the military zone, which had a swimming pool and a tennis court set into its extensive grounds.

But even before I had finished asking the question, I saw my driver's shoulders tense.

'I'm sorry, it's too dangerous,' he replied. 'That area is closed.'

He closed the car windows and asked me not to take any photographs, in case anyone saw me and took down his numberplate. He was trying to impress upon me the danger that we might be in, if we did anything out of the ordinary here. So I said nothing more. It was with visible relief that he turned, just before the roadblock, onto another empty highway that led towards the museum's 600-acre grounds.

At a kiosk at the entrance, I handed my passport to a member of the museum's staff who wrote down my details, and then we drove on into the compound, where we quickly became lost. When we eventually found the museum, which was formed of three enormous wings arranged around a central courtyard, my driver parked and said he would wait for me in the car.

I walked alone towards the courtyard and then past an enormous disused fountain, to the central building, where several young soldiers were lounging near the entrance in the shade. When they saw me, they stood to attention, and as I walked past them, one of them followed me inside.

In the first cavernous room, I became intensely aware of the sound of my shoes squeaking against the polished floor. The soldier shadowed me, as I walked around the exhibits, and held up his phone occasionally to take my photograph. His presence was so distracting that it was only when I had finished looking around the first room and moved onto the next that I realized Than Shwe did not feature in any of the displays. I walked through all the rooms, and then walked through them again. In the entire museum, which I had expected to be a paean to Than Shwe, he was nowhere to be seen.

Not only this, but there were only two small exhibits about

the railways his regime had forced more than a million of Myanmar's people to build. There was a painting of soldiers laying a section of track, and there was an old photograph of the station building in Dawei, the first station that I had visited, in Myanmar's far south. Looking at the photograph, I thought of the stationmaster, standing on the platform and scraping away layers of moss from a plaque to reveal a tribute, not to the people who had sacrificed their lives for the railway, but to the railway itself.

The men and women who had died in the jungle had disappeared without a trace. What did it mean that now, even the dictator who had been responsible for their deaths had been erased from the military's official history?

It seemed to me that while Than Shwe's railways had served an important purpose by helping the military to build itself into a position of power, its new leadership had no incentive to publicly remember the details of how, precisely, the armed forces had become so powerful. Instead, the museum's exhibits now focused on the military's role, as they saw it, as the guardians of Myanmar's sovereignty and its unity under the leadership of Min Aung Hlaing, the general who succeeded Than Shwe in 2011 as commander-in-chief and whose portrait now hung in the place of his predecessor on the museum's walls.

As I walked back through the museum to the car, I stopped in one of the rooms to examine a selection of British-made weapons on display. A guard who was wearing a dark-blue uniform came over to talk to me.

He asked for my name and my occupation, and then he shook my hand.

'My English is poor,' he said apologetically, even though it wasn't bad at all.

He wanted to know when I had arrived in Naypyidaw, which

hotel I was staying at, which country I came from, and whether I was a tourist. When I told him that I lived in Yangon, he wanted to know where it was, exactly, that I lived. When he had finished interrogating me, he told me a little about himself. His name was Moses, and he was a sailor in Myanmar's navy.

'Yangon,' he explained. 'River operations.'

He was a Christian, just like the military veteran I had met on the outskirts of Lashio, which was unusual because non-Buddhists are actively discouraged from joining Myanmar's military, and they are discriminated against within its ranks.[8] But he wasn't devout, he explained, telling me that he often broke the Ten Commandments.

He was also a Karen, the same ethnic minority group as Su, the young woman who had taken me to visit the cement factories in Hpa-an. This also surprised me, because the museum was filled with paintings and other exhibits that glorified the power of the ethnic Burmese and the military's subjection of ethnic people, including the Karen.

But this didn't seem to bother Moses, who was now pointing proudly around the room.

'One foreigner said they thought this was the biggest museum in the world,' he said. Then he pulled me over to a nearby exhibit, a map of Myanmar's coastline, and showed me the place on the map where northern Rakhine meets Bangladesh.

'Little fire to big fire,' he said, showing me what he meant with his hands. 'Growing.'

I had been thinking about the British weapons on display, and I didn't understand immediately what he was talking about.

'Very, very long time, old problem,' Moses went on. 'Everywhere in the world, Osama bin Laden, England, France, Belgium the same.'

He hadn't been thinking about British colonial history, as I had been. He saw me not so much as British, but as a foreigner, which meant that in his view I was likely to sympathize with the Rohingya. Already, this had eclipsed everything else to become the most important difference between people in Myanmar and the outside world, and he seized on the opportunity to explain to me what was really happening.

'I want to explain to you,' he said, earnestly, still pointing at the coastline, 'the Rohingya are not our people. They are Bangladesh people. They want to be, but . . . ', he trailed off. 'Impossible. They are very many population – so many.'

At first he used their name, Rohingya, but once he knew that I understood what he was talking about, then he switched to calling them Bengali.

'First,' he said, 'Bengali 3 per cent, Rakhine 97 per cent. Now, Rakhine 3 per cent, Bengali 97 per cent.'

These views, depressingly, were not extreme; in the years that followed I would hear them echoed by taxi drivers, shop owners, and even some of my closest Burmese friends.

Moses began to pace back and forth and soon I was walking beside him, my shoes still squeaking against the floor, as he rationalized a genocide. Even here, in this vast monument to the military's power, Moses truly seemed to believe that the Rohingya posed a threat to him.

'You know Islamic State, al-Qaeda?' Moses asked. 'Arakan Rohingya Salvation Army is the same. They attack our people. We are a Buddhist people, we want to be peaceful. They want to establish an Islamic state,' he said.

He was impassioned, and he imagined he saw the threat clearly: the Rohingya were foreigners, invaders, there were too many of them, and they had to be pushed out, back to where they came from. It was a chilling lesson in the dangers of erasing history, of forgetting where power comes from, and who holds it, and how it is used.

Listening to him speak, I thought about Anwar, the young Rohingya man I had met in the internment camp on the outskirts of Sittwe, and how afraid he had been of the violence that was engulfing the north of the state.

A fire was blazing – and growing, as Moses said – but it had been ignited by the generals, and when the world did nothing to extinguish it, the military would carry out more massacres in northern Rakhine the following year, on a much larger scale. When the world responded with outrage, but still failed to act in any meaningful way, it would embolden the generals further. By then, they must have known that if they staged a coup, there would be little resistance from anyone outside the country.

The responsibility for maintaining international peace and security lay with the United Nations Security Council, which was controlled by its five permanent members. Two of these five countries, China and Russia, would step in to protect the generals during the Rohingya crisis, and they would be willing to step in again. The other three permanent members, Britain, France and the United States, might have protested, and pulled out some of their investments in Myanmar, or imposed economic sanctions, but they had no interest in upsetting the balance of international power.

When I said goodbye to Moses, he asked if we could take a photograph together. I agreed because I didn't feel like I could refuse, and he took a selfie of the two of us, standing together in a room filled with old British weapons. Beside us was the map showing the 'Western gate' where British soldiers employed by the East India Company had first waged war almost two centuries earlier against an expansionist Burmese Empire.

On my way out of the museum, I passed a group of children

dressed in the white shirts and brown sashes of monastic schools, who were being shown around the exhibits by a group of monks and soldiers. They would learn that afternoon about how Myanmar's military was the only institution capable of protecting Myanmar against its enemies who were intent on tearing the country apart.

Back in the car, I showed my driver a satellite image on my phone of what I believed was Than Shwe's residence, and asked him who lived there. That was Min Aung Hlaing's house, he told me. He didn't know where Than Shwe lived, he said, but he didn't think it was in the military zone. He wasn't even sure, he said, if the former dictator still lived in Naypyidaw at all.

'I told the chairman,' David Abel barked, referring to Than Shwe, 'they were economically not viable – the railway lines he wanted to extend.'

We were sitting together in Abel's office, a small, comfortable room in an office block beside Yangon's Kandawgyi Lake, where the retired Burmese general, who was now in his eighties, ran a consulting business.

'He called me to him,' Abel went on, in an accent that was clipped and English, shaped over three years of training in the 1950s at Sandhurst, the well-known British officer-training school. 'He said, don't look at the economics only, look at the political effect it has, the value to the people.'

Than Shwe had trusted few men, but Abel was one of them. A Roman Catholic of Anglo-Burmese descent, he had overseen three economic ministries at once in the 1990s, and was known as the junta's economics tsar. He also came from a railway family; his father, Alfred Abel, had been an engineer in Maymyo, the summer capital of British Burma.

I asked him what Than Shwe had hoped to achieve by building so many new lines.

'I don't know,' Abel said, shooting me a disarming grin. 'But he did it.'

A year had passed since I had travelled across Myanmar, and I was back at work, but when I found out that one of my colleagues knew Abel's nephew, I had asked my colleague to put me in touch. I wasn't expecting a frank conversation with Abel, but I wanted to ask him the questions I had that were still unanswered, and to give him a chance to respond.

At the time I suspected, and it would turn out I was right, that I wouldn't have another opportunity to speak to any of the men who had served in the 1990s under Than Shwe. Those who were still alive were growing old, and like Than Shwe, they almost never appeared in public. For an outsider like me they were impossible to track down, and even the interview with Abel had taken months to arrange.

His office wasn't far from my apartment, and I had walked there that morning, past Yangon Central Railway Station and through the park that surrounds Kandawgyi Lake, to a compound beside the main road that I drove past almost every day. Inside the compound there was a hot-pot restaurant, and behind it was a Hugo Boss clothing store that marked the entrance to the nondescript office block where Abel now spent his days advising foreign companies on how to do business in Myanmar.

In the lobby, Abel's nephew was waiting for me. He warned me that his uncle had recently been in hospital and that the old general's memory was patchy, and he asked me to take the conversation slowly. Once I had agreed, Abel called me into his office.

As I sat down in a comfortable armchair, the old general

pointed to a flask on the table and asked if I wanted a cup of tea. He grew it for export, he said, to Germany, China, Singapore and Japan.

As I poured myself a cup, he told me he was worried about his health, and he complained about the quality of the local hospitals, telling me he had not been given the right medicine.

His mind darted about, but he knew why I had come to see him. He answered some of my questions and ignored others, and he often returned to the same point, which was that Than Shwe had made all the decisions – or, in other words, that Abel had not been responsible for any of them.

I asked him if he had any power to influence these decisions.

'No,' he replied.

Did anyone in the railway ministry have any power to make decisions? I asked.

'No,' Abel said again, staring at me through his large, steel-framed glasses, as if he was trying to figure out why I hadn't understood him. 'The Chairman made all the decisions.'

Was this the truth? Had Than Shwe really held absolute power? For a long time, I had considered the former dictator to be an enigma, because I had been trying to work out what it was that made him exceptional. He wasn't a leader in the sense that he inspired the people he led. He was described, even by his peers, in language that denoted an absence of character, of ideas and energy: he was reclusive, taciturn, colourless, uncharismatic.[9]

But I had hung on to the idea that there was more to him than that. If there was nothing exceptional about him, how had he held onto power for so many years? How had he been able to direct so much violence, and how had he become so rich? The truth, though, was that Than Shwe was not exceptional. He and his generals had been corrupt, and incompetent, and they had carried out atrocities with shocking callousness. But there was no mystery about what they had done. They had built a modern nation, or something like it, with the same manual that had been used and adapted by other autocrats, all over the world.

Abel had nothing else to say about the decision-making process, and so I asked him to explain why the railways had been built, and he told me the same thing that the junta had always claimed, that they were built for Myanmar's people. But if this was true, I asked him, why had so many people been forced to build them?

At this, Abel stiffened slightly. 'No, no, no,' he replied, sharply. 'They were paid.'

I challenged him, telling him I had met people all across Myanmar who had never been paid. Instead, they had been coerced, threatened and physically abused.

'Then maybe somebody pocketed the money,' he said with a shrug, regaining his composure, as if to suggest that it was hardly important. 'It was budgeted,' he added, and then he thought about it for a moment. 'It was budgeted,' he said, again.

If there was a budget, why did the money never reach the workers? I asked him.

'I don't know about that,' Abel replied. 'There was no complaint about that.'

As we talked on, his answers became increasingly evasive. He didn't know, he said, or he had forgotten. He had nothing to share with me, no data, no official documents. It all happened a long time ago, he might as well have complained, and he was an old man now.

But what incentive did he have to tell me the truth? Why

would he, or any of the other generals who had served under Than Shwe, admit to having done anything wrong, when they knew they had impunity and their lies had always protected them? They were living out their days quietly and privately, and they knew that they would die in peace.

After a while, when it was clear that Abel wasn't going to answer any more of my questions, I asked him if he could think of anyone else who might speak to me, and he laughed.

'The rail people should accept you,' he said, 'the railway ministry.'

I told him I wanted to speak to the railway ministers who had served in the 1990s. 'Most of them are dead,' he replied. 'Pan Aung is dead, he knows the most. Win Sein, dead also. I'm alive, and the chairman is still alive, if you can meet him.'

I asked him if he thought it would be possible to meet Than Shwe.

'I don't think so,' he replied. 'Not easy.'

What was the best way to try, I asked.

'I don't know,' Abel said. 'I tried. He was travelling then, to the Shan States. I could not meet him. Not easy.'

Soon after my conversation with David Abel, he would die of heart failure, at the age of eighty-four.[10] We spoke a little more that day, in his office beside the lake, but his answers to my questions became more repetitive, and before long, there was a knock on the door, indicating that our time was up.

'Oh, more guests,' said the old general, cheerily, and he pointed to my cup on the table. 'Have some tea,' he said.

Afterword

When Myanmar's military seized power again on 1 February 2021, I had recently moved home to London. My husband was still in Yangon. Every evening in the days after the coup, he called me from the balcony of our downtown apartment there. As he stood beneath the *padauk* trees, which are seen as a symbol of strength in Myanmar, the noise on the other end of the line was deafening. From every open window and every balcony on our street, our neighbours were banging pots, pans, buckets and anything else they could find, in an impassioned and unified display of resistance to the return of military rule.

On some nights they sang, and the sound of thousands of voices raised together, each drawing energy and strength from the others, was so powerful that I was often reduced to tears. Night after night, this exorcism of sound grew longer, louder and more demonstrative. Those who had sung their resistance from darkened apartments began to switch on their lights or step out onto the streets.

Within three weeks, millions of people across the country were marching in opposition to the coup, initiating a mass movement that has since become known as the Spring Revolution. They were driven by outrage: a deep, burning anger that had been buried for years beneath hope, but that never went away. The divide between the generals and the people they sought to rule was irreconcilable; with hindsight it now seems obvious that a time of reckoning would come.

At first, my husband described a carnival atmosphere on the

streets. Each day, he told me about the columns of protesters that had streamed past our apartment, decked out in anti-coup T-shirts, headbands, stickers and flags. They called in unison for the release of detained politicians, including Aung San Suu Kyi. They shouted anti-military slogans and held up posters reading 'Fuck the Coup' and other irreverent slogans that were designed to capture the world's attention. They played revolutionary songs, and danced, and handed out roses and bottles of water to police officers.

At the forefront of the protests were striking Myanma Railways staff. An estimated 90 per cent of the country's 30,000 railway employees refused to work after the coup,[1] as part of a nationwide civil disobedience movement. Initiated by medics at state hospitals, the strikes quickly spread to schools, banks, municipal departments and dockyards, bringing much of the government to a grinding halt.[2] It was a powerful statement of ownership: that the state of Myanmar, including its railways, belonged to the people – not the military. To reiterate their point, protesters blocked the railways with stones, logs and iron bars.[3] Striking workers and other civilians even lay down on the tracks, demonstrating their readiness to give up their lives for this cause.[4]

As train services were brought to a standstill, the military's response was swift and violent. To the generals, the railways were critical supply lines, which had to be kept open at all costs. At Mandalay Station, security forces fired rubber bullets at protesters who were trying to prevent an army supply train from leaving.[5] Armed police raided railway housing compounds and ordered staff to return to work, threatening to evict them if they refused.[6] Reports circulated that workers were being forced at gunpoint to drive the trains, and that soldiers would be brought in to replace striking employees.[7]

The violence against railway workers was an early-warning sign. By the end of the month, security forces were shooting to kill.[8] My Facebook feed was soon filled with horrifying content: videos of soldiers opening fire on peaceful demonstrators, police viciously beating civilians, bloodied bodies on hospital trolleys, anguished mothers attending candlelit memorials to honour the dead.

Independent newsrooms, including the magazine where I had worked until the previous summer, closed their offices. My former colleagues stopped reporting under their own names, but still braved gunfire and arrest to cover the protests. These were young men and women who were woefully unprepared to report from the front lines of a dangerous, urban war. Yet, day after day, they packed their notebooks and cameras, and went out to document the violence that was tearing through their streets.[9]

For me in London, the weeks after the coup passed in a blur of panicked messages and private grief. To anticipate more violence felt like an act of betrayal, yet I steeled myself for it. It was surreal to listen to dispatches from Myanmar in the safety of my London home, while friends and colleagues were arrested, or went into hiding, or packed their bags to join the resistance, or fled across Myanmar's borders, some of them as refugees.

My husband packed up our apartment and flew back to London, with our three cats in tow. Most of the other British expats in Myanmar also crowded onto departing planes, less than a decade after they had all arrived. Who could blame them for leaving? They could escape to another country, where their friends and families were safe, and where their government played a basic protective role.

In Britain, media coverage of the violence soon waned. It

wasn't considered an important news story: even when Myanmar was a British colony it was seen as a backwater, and I still regularly meet people in London who have never heard of the country. There has been no collective reflection in Britain on our colonial past in Myanmar and so there's little interest in its aftermath, particularly now that Aung San Suu Kyi, with her long-standing ties to Britain, is no longer considered a human-rights icon. She was Myanmar's news hook; without her, the country is slipping again from international view.

But even as outside interest dwindles, local journalists and citizen reporters are still risking their lives to report the news. Hundreds of new guerrilla groups have sprung up all over the country: small bands of civilians who have armed themselves mostly with home-made weapons. These men and women are not hardened fighters. They are ordinary people, just like the people who I met all over Myanmar, who now feel they have no choice but to fight. Many of these groups are known as People's Defence Forces and are allied with the government-in-exile, which is formed of elected lawmakers and other civilian leaders. Others are independent, or they fight alongside established ethnic armed groups.[10]

More than two years after the coup, Myanmar's railways remain bitterly contested, reflecting the broader struggle for control of the state. In the north, armed groups have prevented train services from resuming on the entire network north of Mandalay,[11] including in Kachin, where the Kachin Independence Organization has been training former railway workers to fight.[12] Elsewhere, People's Defence Forces and ethnic armed groups have been bombing military supply trains, blowing up bridges, and shooting railway police.[13]

The junta led by Min Aung Hlaing is struggling to establish control. But unlike the resistance, which has received almost no foreign backing, Myanmar's military is being supported by governments, corporations and institutions from around the world.

With Japanese development funding, the generals are upgrading the railway between Yangon and Mandalay, the country's two largest cities, which will enable them to run high-speed trains through the capital, Naypyidaw. A Spanish firm is supplying the junta with hundreds of new trains, and Japanese companies are helping it to improve the tracks, stations, bridges, signalling and communications.[14]

China has signed an agreement with the junta to restart work on its high-speed railway across central Myanmar to the Indian Ocean coast, which will cut through multiple conflict zones, and will almost certainly spark more fighting.[15] In Pa-O territory, where I travelled with Moon, the regime is building another new railway, as part of a supply chain developed with Russian support that will enable it to produce more weapons, to crush dissent.[16]

On a mountain in Pa-O territory, near the Shan State capital of Taunggyi, a subsidiary of Russia's state-owned defence company Rostec is preparing to reopen the country's largest iron mine, in partnership with military-run conglomerate Myanmar Economic Corporation.[17] The iron produced in Pa-O territory will be transported across the country, by train, to a steel mill at Myingyan in central Myanmar. A new railway is being built to connect the mine to the national railway network, and 200 miles of connecting track are being upgraded, or reopened in places where they have been abandoned.[18]

I had walked along part of this abandoned track, near Taunggyi. Following the railway into the undergrowth, I had come to a village whose houses were concealed by weeds, and which were identifiable only by the sound of voices inside. I stumbled across a clearing where two old men were sitting either side of a small table, sliding wooden counters across a board. In that moment, they had seemed at peace. Now, I wondered what had happened to them. The villages around the project site are being cleared and Min Aung Hlaing has instructed the railway department to build guard rails beside the tracks 'for ensuring safety' – even the transportation of raw materials must now be protected against attack.[19]

Without legitimacy, the generals must deploy ever more powerful weapons to hold onto power. The tragedy facing Myanmar's people is that they have no shortage of suppliers. In May 2023 the United Nations special rapporteur for human rights in Myanmar published a report entitled 'The Billion Dollar Death Trade'.[20] It found that since the coup, the military had imported at least $1 billion in arms, dual-use goods, equipment and raw materials to manufacture weapons from countries including Russia, China, India, Singapore and Thailand, which it is using to commit atrocities against its own people.

The report accused 'some member states' of outright complicity. This is an extremely serious allegation: at the time of writing in June 2023, Min Aung Hlaing's regime has killed more than 3,700 civilians, while tens of thousands more have died in the ensuing armed conflict.[21] The regime has detained more than 23,000 people on political charges and has tortured thousands of them in detention.[22] It is waging brutal counter-insurgency campaigns, rolling out the same tactics that state forces have used in Myanmar since the British 'pacification' campaigns in the 1880s.[23] Regime troops have set fire to more than 70,000 civilian homes, most of them in the dry zone,[24] and their operations have been shadowed by torture, sexual violence and extrajudicial killings, including decapitations. More than

1.5 million people have been displaced by conflict since the coup, and almost a third of the population is in need of humanitarian assistance.[25]

The United Nations Security Council, the international system's most powerful body, has the power to impose a binding international arms embargo on Myanmar. But it has done nothing except issue empty statements. China and Russia have veto power over resolutions, and both countries insist that the conflict in Myanmar is an 'internal affair' – a claim which their support for the regime renders absurd. Far from challenging them, the other Security Council members including Britain are prioritizing consensus, and their own relations with China and Russia, over their responsibility to keep civilians in Myanmar safe.[26]

But as the international community fails them, people across Myanmar continue to fight. Nothing about their struggle is easy: Myanmar is a traumatized society and it is once again permeated by fear. Depression and other mental-health problems are rife. But while the military deals in terror, the resistance is fuelled by hope. At its core, this is a struggle for basic liberties against institutionalized violence and greed, and it is a struggle that the people of Myanmar are determined to win.

Unlike during the Than Shwe regime, smartphones are ubiquitous in Myanmar now. Despite the regime's efforts to silence the democracy movement, individual stories of courage and tenacity are published online every day. Like the thousands of voices raised in the darkness on my street in Yangon in the days after the coup, these stories serve to strengthen and to inspire. The bravery of civil servants, including railway workers, emboldens others in the resistance. So does the knowledge that most people in Myanmar have no intention of enduring another long period of military rule.

The indomitable spirit of the Spring Revolution has been captured by thousands of songwriters, poets and artists since the coup, but most fittingly by Pandora, one of Myanmar's best-known poets, who imagined the revolution as a train.

There are trains, they are trains

'Every car has its own engine,'
Min Ko Naing* said.
We hear the train a comin'.

Yellow spring leaves lie on the tracks.
Voices curse, making cacophonies.
Are you gonna run us down? Run me down? Run us down!
Trains will roar.

MR** is Myanmar's people.
Bullets rain at midnight
But they won't make our trains kneel.
Hear the trains roar!

Without moving, they move.
Without starting the motor,
revolution's train is starting up,
roaring.

We won't return to the old station,
we'll march to a new future,

* Min Ko Naing is a democracy activist who rose to prominence during the 1988 uprising against military rule.
** Myanma Railways.

with new tickets in our hands.
Then the train will roar.

Do you hear,
can you hear
the roaring train?
Endless cars are linked.
Here comes our train!
Hear the trains. They are our trains.

Pandora (Translated by Ke' Su Thar and Ch. B.), originally
published as part of *Train a Comin': Poems from the Burmese
resistance* in Jacket2 (2021).

Notes

Part One

1 Karen Human Rights Group, 'Ye-Tavoy area update', 5 January 1996.

1. Dawei

1 See Aung Kaung Myat, 'Sit-tat or tatmadaw? Debates on what to call the most powerful institution in Burma', Tea Circle Oxford, 3 October 2022.
2 State media reported that 44,000 people had 'donated' their labour to build the railway on a single day. The representative in Myanmar of the International Labour Organization (ILO) estimated that several hundred thousand people in total were forced to work. See Richard Horsey, *Ending Forced Labour in Myanmar: Engaging a Pariah Regime*, Routledge, 2011, p. 4. Horsey's compelling account of the ILO's efforts since the 1990s to end forced labour in Myanmar informs this chapter throughout.
3 Andrew Selth, *Burma's Armed Forces: Power without Glory*, East-Bridge, 2002, pp. 134–40. See also Thant Myint-U, *The River of Lost Footsteps: A Personal History of Burma*, Faber and Faber, 2007, p. 328.
4 See contemporary reports by human-rights groups, including: 'Total denial: A report on the Yadana Pipeline Project in Burma', EarthRights International and Southeast Asian Information Network, July 1996, and Burma Campaign UK, 'TOTALitarian

oil – TOTAL oil: Fuelling the oppression in Burma', 21 February 2005.

5 Statement by U Ohn Gyaw, Minister for Foreign Affairs, at the 50th Session of the United Nations General Assembly, New York, 3 October 1995.

6 See Karen National Union Foreign Affairs Department, 'Statement by KNU Foreign Affairs Department on Burma–Thailand natural gas pipeline', 24 February 1995.

7 See Human Rights Watch/Asia, 'No safety in Burma, no sanctuary in Thailand', July 1997.

8 'Forced labour in Myanmar (Burma), Report of the Commission of Inquiry appointed under article 26 of the Constitution of the International Labour Organization to examine the observance by Myanmar of the Forced Labour Convention, 1930 (No. 29)', International Labour Organization: ILO, 1998.

9 Ethnic Karen and Mon human-rights groups based in Thailand (the Karen Human Rights Group and the Human Rights Foundation of Monland) also published detailed reports in the 1990s based on refugee testimony. I have drawn on the information contained in these reports, as well as in contemporary reports by the ILO, Amnesty International and Human Rights Watch throughout this chapter. For full details of these reports, see the bibliography.

10 Chapter 14, Article 445, Constitution of the Republic of the Union of Myanmar, Printing and Publishing Enterprise, Ministry of Information, 2008. See International Center for Transitional Justice, 'Impunity prolonged: Burma and its 2008 constitution', September 2009.

11 Asian Development Bank, 'Myanmar Transport Sector Policy Note: Railways', 2016.

12 International Labour Organization, 'Report of the Commission of Inquiry appointed under article 26 of the Constitution of the

International Labour Organization to examine the observance by Myanmar of the Forced Labour Convention, 1930 (No. 29)', 2 July 1998.

13 See Vikram Nehru, 'Myanmar's military keeps firm grip on democratic transition', Carnegie Endowment for International Peace, 2 June 2015.

14 Section 8(1)(g)(n) and (o) of the Village Act (1908), and section 7, sub-section 1(m) and section 9(b) of the Towns Act. Sections 11(d) and 12 of the Village Act and section 9A of the Towns Act, in the words of the International Labour Organization, 'provided for the exaction of labour and services . . . under the menace of a penalty from residents who had not offered themselves voluntarily, that is, the exaction of forced or compulsory labour'. International Labour Organization, 'Report of the Commission of Inquiry appointed under article 26 of the Constitution of the International Labour Organization to examine the observance by Myanmar of the Forced Labour Convention, 1930 (No. 29)', 2 July 1998, p. 46.

15 This archive is held by the Online Burma / Myanmar Library, an invaluable free online research library.

16 Dr Ba Maw, Burma's puppet leader during the Japanese occupation in the Second World War, wrote in his 1968 memoir that two decades after the railway was built, the region was 'once again wilderness, except for a few neatly kept graveyards where many British dead now sleep in peace and dignity'. As for the Burmese who died, he wrote, 'They are now unknown, unhonoured, and unsung, and even unburied in fitting graves. Not even a solitary post stands to this day to tell later generations where their bones lie.' Ba Maw, *Breakthrough in Burma: Memoirs of a Revolution, 1939–1946*: Yale University Press, 1968, pp. 292–97.

17 See *The Kite Tales*, 'Inheritance of silence', December 2016. I stopped in Thanbyuzayat to visit the war cemetery and the museum on my journey by train from Dawei to Yangon.

18 Records WO 325/136–39, held at The National Archives, Kew, London.
19 As cited in Horsey, *Ending Forced Labour in Myanmar*, p. 17.
20 Ibid, pp. 184–85.

2. *The Delta*

1 Aye Min Soe, 'Western Parts of Myanmar Get First Direct Rail Service to Yangon', *New Light of Myanmar*, 25 May 2014.
2 Hlaing Aung, 'Storm-hit Areas Will Have Been Regenerated with Thriving Trees and Crop Plantations by Next Year', *New Light of Myanmar*, 30 May 2008.
3 Human Rights Watch, Letter to Donors on Reconstruction after Cyclone Nargis, 23 July 2008.
4 'Thanks to United Strengths of Government, People and Tatmadaw, Storm-Hit Regions Return to Normalcy within One Year', *New Light of Myanmar*, 6 November 2009.
5 Ibid.
6 Benedict Rogers, *Than Shwe: Unmasking Burma's Tyrant*, Silkworm Books, 2010, pp. 72–76.
7 Maung Maung Htwe, 'Glorious Days in Ayeyarwady Division', *New Light of Myanmar*, 3 August 2010.
8 'May Ayeyarwady Dwellers Serve Interests of Region and Nation with Heart of Gold Like Mighty White Elephant Appeared in the Region: President U Thein Sein Attends Inauguration of Ayeyarwady Bridge (Nyaungdon)', *New Light of Myanmar*, 28 November 2011.
9 Kyaw Ye Lynn, 'Yangon's Railroad to Nowhere', *Frontier Myanmar*, 13 December 2017.
10 Ibid.

11 C. Fyfe, 'Xerox copy of the typescript of Mr Fyfe's railway history of Burma in 14 chapters', Fyfe Papers, Centre of South Asian Studies, University of Cambridge.

12 *The Railway Police Manual, Containing Orders and Rules Made for the Railway Police, Issued with the Sanction of the Government of Burma*: Supdt. Govt. Printing and Stationary, Burma, 1925, pp. 29 and 62.

13 Selth, *Burma's Armed Forces*, pp. 108–23.

14 Gwen Robinson and David Pilling, 'New "Super Cabinet" Drives Rapid Change', *Financial Times*, 4 December 2012; Aung Hla Tun, 'Myanmar president promotes reformers in cabinet shake-up', Reuters, 27 August 2012; Richard Cockett, *Blood, Dreams and Gold: The Changing Face of Burma*: Yale University Press, 2015, p. 211; Evan Osnos, 'The Burmese Spring', *The New Yorker*, 6 August 2012.

15 Asian Development Bank, 'Myanmar Transport Sector Policy Note: Railways', 2016, p. 29.

16 Lindsay Clyde Stubbs, 'The railways of Burma: Their past, present and future', PhD, Macquarie University, Faculty of Business and Economics, Department of Economics, 2018, p. 7.

17 Stubbs, 'The railways of Burma', pp. 77–78 and 114–15. On the network's operating ratio, see Stubbs, pp. 53–58.

3. Magway

1 They even sat in on interviews and provided live reports to their superiors by walkie-talkie, in which they referred to journalists as *gyo thar*, or aliens. See Coconuts Yangon, 'Police in Magway Region refer to journalists as aliens', 2 September 2015.

2 See Htun Khaing, 'Following the Money Trail for Magway's Missing Oil Revenue', *Frontier Myanmar*, 27 February, 2017.

3 See MNA, 'Minbu-Pwintbyu Railroad Section of Kyangin–Pakokku Railroad Construction Project Commissioned into Service', *New Light of Myanmar*, 23 January 2011; 'Kyangin–Pakokku Railroad Linking North and South of Myanmar', *New Light of Myanmar*, 31 January 2012.

4 MNA, 'Transport Network Basic Requirement for Harmonious Progress of Whole Union, Kyangin–Okshitpin Railroad Section Commissioned into Service', *New Light of Myanmar*, 23 March 2009.

5 See Stubbs, 'The railways of Burma', pp. 225–26, 240.

6 As Stubbs has pointed out, the railway was supposed to open in 11 sections, but two of these sections, each around 20 miles long, were never completed, leaving the railway with two large gaps in it. Stubbs, 'The railways of Burma', pp. 231, 241.

7 Reading Stubbs' doctoral thesis, I felt a powerful sense of communion with a fellow traveller. His account of travelling by train along the western bank of the Ayeyarwady River is one of many fascinating episodes in his thesis, which has informed several chapters in my book. See Stubbs, 'The railways of Burma', pp. 221, 245–72.

8 Nay Aung, 'Sesame Farmers Reject Railway Compensation', *Myanmar Times*, 6 October 2015.

9 Nay Aung, 'The Sham Tram', *Myanmar Times*, 4 August 2017.

10 Human Rights Watch, "Nothing for our land": Impact of land confiscation on farmers in Myanmar', 17 July 2018.

11 Christian Wolmar, *Railways & the Raj: How the Age of Steam Transformed India*, Atlantic Books, 2017, pp. 183–87.

12 Michael and Maitrii Aung-Thwin in *A History of Myanmar since Ancient Times: Traditions and Transformations*, Reaktion Books, 2012, pp. 105–6, 148–49 and 252. I have also drawn in the following

paragraphs on other histories of Myanmar, including Robert H. Taylor, *The State in Myanmar*, NUS Press, National University of Singapore, 2009, pp. 44–47, Thant Myint-U, *The River of Lost Footsteps*, pp. 290–97, and Maung Htin Aung, *A History of Burma*, Columbia University Press, 1967, pp. 273–74.

13 Taylor, *The State in Myanmar*, pp. 348–54.

14 Flooding in 2015 because of Cyclone Komen affected more than nine million people across Myanmar. At least 149 people died, 15,000 homes were destroyed, 1.6 million people were temporarily displaced, and more than 840,000 acres of crops were lost. See 'Final report: Myanmar floods, International Federation of Red Cross and Red Crescent Societies', 31 January 2017.

15 See Lawi Weng, 'As Flood Waters Begin to Recede in Pwintbyu, Locals Eye a Slow Recovery', *The Irrawaddy*, 5 August 2015.

16 It wasn't just in Magway. In 2015, flooding destroyed railways in half of Myanmar's administrative divisions. See Kyaw Hsu Mon, '$4.9m Repair Bill for Rail Network after Flood Damage', *The Irrawaddy*, 9 October 2015.

17 Selth, *Burma's Armed Forces*, p. 140.

18 Ibid, pp. 140–45. See also Bertil Lintner, 'Burma's WMD programme and military cooperation between Burma and the Democratic People's Republic of Korea', Asia Pacific Media Services, March 2012.

19 Ibid.

20 'A sourcebook on allegations of cooperation between Myanmar (Burma) and North Korea on nuclear projects', version of 2014-09-22.

21 David Albright, Paul Brannan, Robert Kelley, and Andrea Scheel Stricker, *Burma: a Nuclear Wannabe, Suspicious Links to North Korea and High-Tech Procurements to Enigmatic Facilities*, Institute for Science and International Security, 28 January 2010.

22 Robert E. Kelley and Ali Fowle, 'Nuclear-related activities in Burma', Democratic Voice of Burma, May 2010.

23 'Jane's Intelligence Review examines satellite imagery to collaborate defector's testimony of Myanmar's nuclear programme', 21 July 2010, reprinted in 'A sourcebook on allegations of cooperation between Myanmar (Burma) and North Korea on nuclear projects', version of 2014-09-22, p. 225.

24 Lintner, 'Burma's WMD programme'.

25 Lintner lists the locations of Myanmar's defence industries in an appendix to ibid.

26 Myanmar Statistical Yearbook, 2010–21, Central Statistical Organization, The Government of the Republic of the Union of Myanmar. See also Stubbs, 'The railways of Burma', pp. 120, 127.

27 This is DI-2 or ka-pa-sa 2. See Lintner, 'Burma's WMD programme'.

28 See Zarni Mann, 'Journalists Detained for Reporting Alleged Burmese Chemical Weapons Factory', *The Irrawaddy*, 2 February 2014, and Amnesty International, 'Myanmar: Media workers imprisoned in crackdown on free expression', 10 July 2014. The *Unity Journal* report was published under the headline: 'A secret chemical weapon factory of the former generals, Chinese technicians and the commander-in-chief at Pauk Township'.

29 Catherine Dill and Jeffrey Lewis, 'Suspect defense facility in Myanmar', James Martin Center for Nonproliferation Studies, 9 May 2014.

30 'Kyaw–Zebya Railroad Opens', *New Light of Myanmar*, 10 April 1997.

31 'Senior General Than Shwe Inspects Infrastructural Improvements for Nationwide Development', *New Light of Myanmar*, 18 April 1997.

32 Images Asia, Karen Human Rights Group and The Open Society Institute's Burma Project, 'All quiet on the western front? The situation in Chin State and Sagaing Division, Burma', January

1998. The interview cited in this report was conducted by the Chin Human Rights Organization.

33 MNA, 'Kyaw-Yaymyetni Railroad Section, Ponnyataung Tunnel Opened', *New Light of Myanmar*, 29 January 2007.

34 Min Lwin, 'Burmese Reactors Close to Completion: Military Sources', *The Irrawaddy*, 13 March 2010.

35 Prashanth Parameswaran, 'What's Behind Myanmar Military Chief's Europe Voyage?', *The Diplomat*, 28 April 2017.

36 See 'All quiet on the western front? The situation in Chin State and Sagaing Division, Burma', Images Asia, Karen Human Rights Group and The Open Society Institute's Burma Project, January 1998, and Karen Human Rights Group, 'The situation in North-western Burma', 30 January 1996. On allegations of ethnic cleansing see Martin Smith, *Ethnic Groups in Burma: Development, Democracy and Human Rights*, a report by Anti-Slavery International, 1994, pp. 81–82.

37 Vum Son Suantak, 'How and Why the Burmese Army Murdered Four Chin Christians', Chin Human Rights Organization, *Rhododendron News*, vol. VII, no. II, March–April 2004.

38 'Myanmar policemen killed in Rakhine border attack', BBC News, 9 October 2016.

Part Two

1 New York University Press, 1948.

4. Rakhine

1 I have substantiated Than Myint's account with written histories including Maung Htin Aung's *A History of Burma*, Terence

Blackburn's *The Defeat of Ava: The First Anglo-Burmese War of 1824–26*, and Thant Myint-U's *The River of Lost Footsteps*. Thant Myint-U is Myanmar's leading historian writing in English and I am indebted to his four excellent books (*The Making of Modern Burma*, *The River of Lost Footsteps*, *Where China Meets India* and *The Hidden History of Burma*) for historical details throughout my book, and particularly in this chapter.

2 Kyaw Phone Kyaw, 'NLD Goes It Alone, Raising Ethnic Party Ire', *Frontier Myanmar*, 2 May 2016.

3 See, for example, MNA, 'Railroad to be Constructed to Link Sittway and An and West Bank of Ayeyarwady River: Prime Minister General Thein Sein Tours Townships in Rakhine State', *New Light of Myanmar*, 29 January 2009; 'Sittway–An–Minbu Railroad under Construction to Introduce Rail Service between Sittway and Yangon', *New Light of Myanmar*, 18 March 2010; MNA, 'Kwantaung–Ponnagyun–Yotayok Railroad Section in Ponnagyun Opened', *New Light of Myanmar*, 16 May 2010.

4 Michael and Maitrii Aung-Thwin have written about the impact of colonial railways on the Burmese way of life, influencing my ideas about how railways might have reshaped communities in Myanmar's hinterland. See their *A History of Myanmar since Ancient Times*, pp. 187–96, 205.

5 Anthony Burton, *The Railway Empire*, Cambridge University Press, 1994, p. 50.

6 'National Progress through Regional Development', *New Light of Myanmar*, 29 January 2009.

7 Khin Oo Thar, 'More Land in Arakan State Confiscated for Railway', *The Irrawaddy*, 23 December 2010.

8 See 'Railway Line Rerouted after Arakanese Heritage Site Damaged', *Mizzima*, 30 November 2010.

9 Archibald R. Colquhoun and Holt Samuel Hallett, *Report on the Railway Connexion of Burmah and China*, Allen, Scott & Co. 1888, p. 16.

10 Fyfe, 'Xerox copy of the typescript of Mr Fyfe's railway history of Burma in 14 chapters'.

11 See Thant Myint-U, *The Hidden History of Burma: Race, Capitalism, and the Crisis of Democracy in the 21st Century*, Atlantic Books, 2020, p. 232.

12 See Thant Myint-U, *The River of Lost Footsteps*, pp. 73–76, 81–84.

13 Nearly half of all households in Rakhine at the time had no toilet facilities. See 'How We Live Now: A Survey of Living Standards in Myanmar', *Frontier Myanmar*, 6 August 2018.

14 'Myanmar police shoot dead seven protesters in troubled Rakhine', Reuters, 17 January 2018.

15 For an overview of the military operation against the Rohingya in late 2016, see Amnesty International, 'Myanmar: "We are at breaking point" – Rohingya: persecuted in Myanmar, neglected in Bangladesh', 19 December 2016.

16 'The Jewel of Yangon', Belmond Governor's Residence.

17 See Thomas Richards, *The Imperial Archive: Knowledge and the Fantasy of Empire*, Verso, 1993.

18 John Ogilvy Hay's writing informs this section of my book. Unless otherwise specified, details about his campaign to build a railway and about Rakhine under British rule are taken from his work.

19 Maung Htin Aung, *A History of Burma*, p. 229.

20 For a full (and outraged) account of the Second Anglo-Burmese War, see Richard Cobden, *How Wars Are Got Up in India: The Origin of the Burmese War*, William & Frederick G. Cash, 1853.

21 Ibid.

22 Shashi Tharoor, *Inglorious Empire: What the British Did to India*, C. Hurst, 2017, p. 4.

23 Ibid, pp. 3–4. It was the East India Company, not the British state, that waged and won the first two wars against the Burmese kingdom.

24 Niall Ferguson, *Empire: How Britain Made the Modern World*, Penguin, 2003, p. 169.

25 See Thant Myint-U, *The River of Lost Footsteps*, p. 185.

26 Fyfe, 'Xerox copy of the typescript of Mr Fyfe's railway history of Burma in 14 chapters'. As late as 1945, the *Railway Gazette* was publishing articles that described the proposed connections between India and Burma, and calling for a railway to be built.

27 See (Captain) Alexander Fraser and J.G. Forlong, 'Report on a route from the mouth of the Pakchan to Kraw, and thence across the Isthmus of Kraw to the Gulf of Siam', 1883.

28 See, for example, Colquhoun and Hallett, *Report on the Railway Connexion of Burmah and China*.

29 Thant Myint-U, *The Making of Modern Burma*, Cambridge University Press, 2001, pp. 235–54.

30 Hugh Hughes, *Indian Locomotives Part 3: Narrow Gauge 1863–1940*, Continental Railway Circle, 1994, and Stubbs, 'The railways of Burma', pp. 399–404.

31 'Historical Evidence of a Chittagonian Bengalis Transporter Train: Arakan Light Railway', *Myanmar Informer*, 4 November 2018.

32 Mratt Kyaw Thu, 'Exploring History on the Old Rakhine Railway', *Frontier Myanmar*, 14 December 2016.

33 Ronan Lee, *Myanmar's Rohingya Genocide: Identity, History and Hate Speech*, I.B. Tauris, 2021, p. 33.

34 In 2018, after brutal military operations had driven more than 900,000 Rohingya into Bangladesh, Reuters revealed that Rohingya villages had been razed and replaced by new security infrastructure and new settlements that would be populated with Rakhine Buddhists from elsewhere in the state. See 'Point of no return', Reuters, 18 December 2018.

35 Ibid. See also Mratt Kyaw Thu, 'Forsaken at the "Western gate"', *Frontier Myanmar*, 21 August 2018.

36 For a detailed account of the 2012 violence, see Human Rights Watch, 'The government could have stopped this sectarian violence and ensuing abuses in Burma's Arakan State', 31 July 2012.

37 Myanmar Railways, 'RBE Transport Resumes in Sittway Township', *Global New Light of Myanmar*, 26 January 2015.

38 Aung Hla Tun, 'Myanmar government abolishes direct media censorship', Reuters, 20 August 2012.

39 See Independent International Fact-Finding Mission on Myanmar, 'Report of the detailed findings of the Independent International Fact-Finding Mission on Myanmar' (IIFFMM, Detailed findings), 18 September 2018, A/HRC/39/CRP.2 'V. Emblematic situation 2: Rakhine State, section C.5: Spreading hate'. See also Asia Sentinel, 'Burma's Irresponsible New Media', *The Irrawaddy*, 11 July 2012. By 2018, when I was working as the digital editor of *Frontier*, an investigative magazine, even use of the word 'Rohingya' in our reporting would earn us a torrent of online abuse.

40 Thant Myint-U, *The Hidden History of Burma*, pp. 207–8.

41 Reporters Without Borders, 'Crisis in Arakan State and new threats to freedom of news and information', 28 June 2012.

42 Thant Myint-U, *The Hidden History of Burma*, pp. 207–8.

43 Independent International Fact-Finding Mission on Myanmar, 'Report of the detailed findings of the Independent International Fact-Finding Mission on Myanmar' (IIFFMM, Detailed findings), 18 September 2018, A/HRC/39/CRP.2, 'Summary', p. 1.

44 See Amnesty International, 'Amnesty International withdraws human rights award from Aung San Suu Kyi', 12 November 2018; 'City of Oxford strips Aung San Suu Kyi of human rights award', Reuters, 4 October 2017; and United States Holocaust Memorial Museum, 'Museum rescinds award to Daw Aung San Suu Kyi', 7 March 2018.

45 Padraic Halpin, 'Bob Geldof calls Aung San Suu Kyi "handmaiden to genocide"', Reuters, 13 November 2017.

46 Naaman Zhou and Michael Safi, 'Desmond Tutu Condemns Aung San Suu Kyi: "Silence is too high a price"', *The Guardian*, 8 September 2017.

5. Kachin

1 I knew about Ja Seng Hkawn's railway contract from an *Economist* article. See 'Eager Mindsets', *The Economist*, 30 December 2014. The newspaper's correspondent wrote about his meeting with Ja Seng Hkawn in a subsequent book; Cockett, *Blood, Dreams and Gold*, pp. 234–35.

2 Maran Brang Seng was appointed chairman of the Kachin Independence Organization in 1976 and he led the armed group for almost twenty years, until his death in 1994. See Martin Smith and Larry Jagan, 'Maran Brang Seng: In His Own Words', *Burma Debate*, vol. 1, no. 3, December 1994/January 1995.

3 Thant Myint-U, *The Making of Modern Burma*, pp. 3–8. See also Maung Htin Aung, *Lord Randolph Churchill and the Dancing Peacock: British Conquest of Burma, 1885*, Manohar Publications, 1990, pp. 208–15, and Ni Ni Myint, *Burma's Struggle against British Imperialism, 1885–1889*, Rangoon Universities Press, 1983, p. 157.

4 Thant Myint-U, *The River of Lost Footsteps*, pp. 194–95. See also Aung-Thwin and Aung-Thwin, *A History of Myanmar since Ancient Times*, p. 51.

5 Known as the Panglong Agreement, Aung San's promise to Chin, Kachin and Shan leaders at independence was never fulfilled, and the broken promise continues to haunt the country today.

6 See Selth, *Burma's Armed Forces*, p. 11.

7 See, for example, Nicholas Farrelly, 'Kachin Media War Continues', *New Mandala*, 3 May 2012; and Ba Kaung, 'Kachin Rebels
Blow Up Major Railway', *The Irrawaddy*, 11 November 2011.

8 MNA, 'Rail Sections Partially Damaged by KIA Mines', *New Light
of Myanmar*, 16 January 2013.

9 Transnational Institute, 'The Kachin crisis: Peace must prevail', 8
March 2013.

10 See Katya Cengel, 'Rape Is a Weapon in Burma's Kachin State,
But the Women of Kachin Are Fighting Back', *Time Magazine*, 11
February 2014.

11 For more on the expedition, see F.R. Bagley, 'Mu Valley and
Mogaung railway survey: Report on survey operations north of
Kawlin, during the cold season of 1888–89', British Burma Press,
1889, held at the British Library. See also 'The First Mogaung
Expedition, a Reminiscence of 1886', *The Englishman's Overland
Mail*, 26 January 1899.

12 Maung Htin Aung, *A History of Burma*, p. 263, and Thant Myint-U,
The Making of Modern Burma, p. 192.

13 Some eighteen months after the war, Crosthwaite wrote, 'there
was no district where an Englishman could yet travel safely
without an armed escort'. Charles Crosthwaite, *The Pacification
of Burma*, Edward Arnold, 1912, p. 34. Unless otherwise specified, information relating to Crosthwaite's campaign is drawn
from his report.

14 'At first,' wrote Crosthwaite, 'there were no maps whatever. The
greater part of the country had not been occupied nor even visited by us (*The Pacification of Burma*, pp. 8–9). The landscape's
value to guerrilla fighters was noted by journalist Grattan Geary,
who reported from Burma in the aftermath of the 1885 war.
Quoted in Kwasi Kwarteng, *Ghosts of Empire: Britain's Legacies in
the Modern World*, Bloomsbury, 2011, pp. 174–5.

15 Maung Htin Aung, *Lord Randolph Churchill and the Dancing Peacock*, p. 214. See also Thant Myint-U, *The Making of Modern Burma*, p. 198.

16 Alleyne Ireland, *Colonial Administration in the Far East: The Province of Burma, a report prepared on behalf of the University of Chicago*, Houghton, Mifflin & Co., 1907, p. 183; Fyfe, 'Xerox copy of the typescript of Mr Fyfe's railway history of Burma in 14 chapters'; and Maung Shein, *Burma's Transport and Foreign Trade, 1885–1914*, Department of Economics, University of Rangoon, 1964, pp. 61–63, 73–74.

17 David Baillargeon, '"On the Road to Mandalay": The Development of Railways in British Burma, 1870–1900', *The Journal of Imperial and Commonwealth History*, vol. 48, no. 4, 2020, pp. 654–78. See also Anthony Webster, 'Business and Empire: A Reassessment of the British Conquest of Burma in 1885', *The Historical Journal*, vol. 43, no. 4 (December 2000), pp. 1003–25.

18 Kwarteng, *Ghosts of Empire*, pp. 166–71.

19 Fyfe, 'Xerox copy of the typescript of Mr Fyfe's railway history of Burma in 14 chapters'.

20 'Report on the administration of Burma during 1890–91', Superintendent, Government Printing, 1891, and Crosthwaite, *The Pacification of Burma*.

21 'Mu Valley and Mogaung railway survey: report on survey operations north of Kawlin, during the cold season of 1888–89', British Burma Press, 1889.

22 Shein, *Burma's Transport and Foreign Trade, 1885–1914*, p. 63.

23 Bagley 'Report on the administration of Burma during 1890–91', and *The Homeward Mail*, 24 February 1891.

24 Wolmar, *Railways & the Raj*, pp. 11–12.

25 See Burton, *The Railway Empire*, pp. 142–44; Wolmar, *Railways & the Raj*, pp. 58–61.

26 'Report on the administration of Burma during 1890–91'.

27 'The Fighting in Burmah', *The Western Times*, 28 February 1891, and Collection 205/31, Special operations in Wuntho territory under General Wolseley, February to April 1891, held at the British Library.

28 See Rachatapong Malithong, 'News from "Burmah": The role of the English press in the making of the British Empire in Burma', PhD, University of Manchester, 2018.

29 'Fresh Trouble in Burmah', *Dundee Evening Telegraph*, 24 February 1891; *Madras Weekly Mail/The Pioneer*, 5 March 1891; and 'Another Small War', *London Evening Standard*, 28 March 1891.

30 Thant Myint-U, *The Making of Modern Burma*, p. 204.

31 George Orwell, *Burmese Days*, Penguin Books, 1989, p. 69. *Burmese Days* is based on Orwell's experience working as an officer in the Indian Imperial Police in Burma. It is a work of fiction, but as Orwell wrote in a letter to the novelist and journalist F. Tennyson Jesse, 'much of it is simply reporting of what I have seen'. George Orwell, *The Collected Essays, Journalism, and Letters of George Orwell: Volume 4, In Front of Your Nose, 1945–1950*, Penguin Books, 1970, pp. 141–42.

32 'Report on the administration of Burma during 1890–91', 'Report on the administration of Burma during 1891–92', Superintendent, Government Printing, 1892.

33 See, for example, *The Englishman's Overland Mail*, 9 December 1891.

34 'Another Small War', *London Evening Standard*, 28 March 1891.

35 Dorothy Woodman, *The Making of Burma*, The Cresset Press, 1962, chapter XV: Pacifying the Kachins, pp. 335–79. Woodman notes that the diary of one British lieutenant involved in the punitive expeditions reads 'like that of a professional arsonist', p. 350. See also Ni Ni Myint, *Burma's Struggle against British*

Imperialism, p. 127, and 'Report on the administration of Burma during 1891–92'.

36 Wolmar, *Railways & the Raj*, p. 70.

37 Bagley, 'Mu Valley and Mogaung railway survey'. The annual reports on the administration of Burma for the years 1892–95 all mention the severe sickness among the workers. See also 'Railroad Laying in Burmah', *London Daily News* and *New York Times*, 19 November 1892.

38 Fyfe, 'Xerox copy of the typescript of Mr Fyfe's railway history of Burma in 14 chapters'.

39 'Times' Telegrams, "Lord Elgin in Burma", *The Homeward Mail*, 28 November 1898. See also *The Englishman*, 'The Viceroy's Tour', *The Englishman's Overland Mail*, 1 December 1898.

40 Bagley, 'Mu Valley and Mogaung railway survey'.

41 Myint Maung Soe, 'Bhamo–Katha Railroad Project, a Fruitful Result of Stability and Peace', *New Light of Myanmar*, 7 August 2009.

42 See, for example, MNA, 'Better Transportation Means Positive Signs in Economy and Socio-Economic Life of Nation: MR to Link Mandalay and Bhamo', *New Light of Myanmar*, 22 February 2010.

43 Ba Khaung, Thet Ko Ko and Paul Vrieze, 'A Chronology of Myanmar's Kachin Conflict', *The Irrawaddy*, 20 November 2014.

44 See Kachin Women's Association Thailand, 'Burma's covered-up war: Atrocities against the Kachin people', 4 November 2011.

6. Northern Shan

1 A sample itinerary and pricing for a tour offered by Bernd Seiler's FarRail Tours is available at https://www.farrail.net/pages/touren-engl/burma-mines-railway-steam-in-namtu-2011.php.

2 Kyaw Lin Htoon, 'Fluctuating Fortunes at the Bawdwin Mine', *Frontier Myanmar*, 31 January 2018.

3 Historical details about the Bawdwin mine (where not otherwise referenced) are taken from my conversations with Ronnie and from a short, unpublished history he shared, entitled 'Background History of Bawdwin Mine, Kyaukme District, North Shan State, Myanmar (Burma)'.

4 David Baillargeon, ' "A Burmese wonderland": British world mining and the making of colonial Burma', PhD, UC Santa Barbara, 2018.

5 Ibid.

6 Taylor, *The State in Myanmar*, pp. 69–70. In a 1938 review of *Trials in Burma* by Maurice Collis, George Orwell applauds Collis for having recognized 'that the Burman has profited very little from the huge wealth that has been extracted from his country'. George Orwell, *The Collected Essays, Journalism, and Letters of George Orwell*: Volume 1, *An Age Like This, 1920–1940*, Nonpareil Books, 2000, pp. 306–7. See also J.S. Furnivall, *An Introduction to the Political Economy of Burma*, Burma Book Club, 1931.

7 Simon Darvill, *Industrial Railways and Locomotives of India and South Asia*, Industrial Railway Society, 2013, pp. 431–45. Railway-building intensified after 1914, when, in the words of historian Frank McLynn, 'foreign capitalists began to rationalise the Burmese economy on a superefficient basis'. Between 1914 and 1942 foreign investment in the country tripled. Frank McLynn, *The Burma Campaign: Disaster into Triumph*, Vintage, 2011, p. 7.

8 Shein, *Burma's Transport and Foreign Trade, 1885–1914*, pp. 65–66, 78–79.

9 Ferguson, *Empire*, p. 285.

10 Prospectus of the Burma Railway Company, 22 July 1896, held by the British Library. See also Records of the Burma Railways Company, Records of the India Office Relating to the Burma Railways Company and *The Railway Gazette*, London, 1910 and 1913.

11 As cited in Baillargeon, ' "A Burmese Wonderland" '.

12 Thant Myint-U, *The River of Lost Footsteps*, pp. 204–19.

13 McLynn, *The Burma Campaign*, pp. 24–26.

14 Darvill, *Industrial Railways and Locomotives of India and South Asia*, p. 501.

15 McLynn, *The Burma Campaign*, p. 1.

16 On Than Shwe's childhood and experience in the War Office, see Rogers, *Than Shwe*, pp. 22, 58. I have taken details about the fighting between Allied and Japanese forces in Kyaukme from contemporary reporting. See 'Burma Campaign: Japanese 20 Miles from Mandalay', *The Scotsman*, 2 May 1942; 'Many Jap Targets in Burma Bombed', *Londonderry Sentinel*, 11 May 1943; and 'Kyaukse Captured', *Belfast Telegraph*, 31 March 1945.

17 *Railway Gazette*, London, 1947, and 'Annual report of the Burma Railway Board', Rangoon: Government Press, 1946–47.

18 Thant Myint-U, *The River of Lost Footsteps*, pp. 251–55.

19 I have taken the details in these paragraphs from contemporary articles published in the *Railway Gazette*. By 1951–52, the publication was reporting a 'marked improvement in the internal situation of the country', with just 454 cases of railway sabotage, compared to 542 the previous year; *Railway Gazette*, London, 1949–52.

20 Norman Lewis, *Golden Earth: Travels in Burma*, Jonathan Cape, 1952, pp. 226–28.

21 Maung Aung Myoe, *Building the Tatmadaw: Myanmar Armed Forces since 1948*, Institute of Southeast Asian Studies, Singapore, 2009, pp. 25–32, and Selth, *Burma's Armed Forces*, p. 91.

22 Maung Htin Aung, *A History of Burma*, pp. 291–92.

23 Martin Smith, 'Obituary: General Ne Win', *The Guardian*, 6 December 2002. See also contemporary reporting, including 'Burma's "Operation Flush": Dacoit Power Broken', *The Scotsman*, 27 March 1947.

24 See Taylor, *The State in Myanmar*, pp. 317, 342–43, and Selth, *Burma's Armed Forces*, p. 15.

25 Kyaw Lin Htoon, 'Fluctuating Fortunes at the Bawdwin Mine'.

26 Lawi Weng, 'Ethnic Armed Groups Launch Joint Offensive in Northern Shan State', *The Irrawaddy*, 20 November 2016. The attacks were the first by the Northern Alliance of four ethnic armed groups operating in northern Shan State. For details of the attacks and related human-rights abuses, see Amnesty International, 'Caught in the middle: Abuses against civilians amid conflict in Myanmar's northern Shan State', 24 October 2019.

27 See Brian McCartan and Kim Jolliffe, 'Ethnic armed actors and justice provision in Myanmar', The Asia Foundation, October 2016.

28 Dennis Bernstein and Leslie Kean, 'Singapore's Blood Money: Hanging Drug Couriers But Investing with their Suppliers', *The Nation*, 20 October 1997.

29 See Bertil Lintner and Michael Black, *Merchants of Madness: The Methamphetamine Explosion in the Golden Triangle*, Silkworm Books, 2009, pp. 25–27; Rogers, *Than Shwe*, pp. 120–22; and 'Lo Hsing Han', *The Economist*, 27 July 2013.

30 Singapore's investments into Lo Hsing Han's companies were first exposed by journalist Mike Carey on *Dateline*, a programme by Australian television channel SBS, in 1996. The documentary caused outrage, partly because of Singapore's draconian drugs laws, which include a mandatory death penalty for small-time traffickers. Journalists Dennis Bernstein and Leslie Kean, reporting for the American magazine *The Nation*, later alleged that more than half of Singapore's investments in Myanmar since 1988 had been tied to Lo Hsing Han. See Kunda Dixit, 'Exposé on alleged drug links rattles city state', Inter Press Service, 21 November 1996, and Bernstein and Kean, 'Singapore's Blood Money'.

31 See 'Myanmar Moves to Privatize Key State Enterprises', *Wall Street Journal*, 18 February 2010; 'Privatization Linked to Money Laundering', *The Irrawaddy*, 23 March 2011.

32 Shibani Mahtani, 'Cronies of Former Myanmar Regime Thrive Despite U.S. Blacklist', *Wall Street Journal*, 12 August 2015.

33 Kyaw Lin Htoon, 'Fluctuating Fortunes at the Bawdwin Mine'.

34 Shoon Naing, 'Foreign tourist killed in landmine blast in Myanmar hiking region', Reuters, 26 November 2019.

35 Hseng Khio Fah, 'Junta to Start Construction on Lashio–Muse Railroad Project', *Burma Myanmar News*, 23 December 2009.

36 A retired Indian Army officer called Captain Richard Spyre made a proposal to build a railway to China in 1858, marking the start of an obsessive lobbying campaign that rivalled that of John Ogilvy Hay. Like Hay's campaign, it ultimately failed. See Ralph C. Croizier, 'Antecedents of the Burma Road: British Plans for a Burma–China Railway in the Nineteenth Century', *Journal of Southeast Asian History*, vol. 3, no. 2 (September 1962), pp. 1–18.

37 See Chandran Jeshurun, *The Burma–Yunnan Railway: Anglo-French Rivalry in Mainland Southeast Asia and South China, 1895–1902*, Ohio University Center for International Studies, Southeast Asia Program, 1971.

38 Thant Myint-U, *The River of Lost Footsteps*, p. 150.

39 Quoted in Jeshurun, *The Burma–Yunnan Railway*, p. 96, and Stubbs, 'The Railways of Burma', p. 169.

40 The survey report, which was written mostly from memory after the surviving railway staff escaped overland to India, is held at the British Library: Burma China Railway, metre gauge, 116 miles, Lashio to Hsoptap on the Chinese frontier, via the Nam Yau, Nam Ket, Salween, Nam Ting gorges: report & construction estimate, 1941–1942.

41 See Bertil Lintner, 'Same Game, Different Tactics: China's "Myanmar Corridor"', *The Irrawaddy*, 13 July 2015.

42 Renaud Egreteau and Larry Jagan, *Soldiers and Diplomacy in Burma: Understanding the Foreign Relations of the Burmese Praetorian State*, NUS Press, National University of Singapore, 2013, pp. 64–65.

43 David Arnott, the founder of the Burma Library archive, compiled a chronology of China-Myanmar relations until 1999, most of which is sourced from official newspapers including the *Working People's Daily* (renamed the *New Light of Myanmar* in 1993). My own review of state media reports in the 1990s relating to imports of railway materials revealed that the Yunnan Machinery & Equipment Import & Export Company was the largest supplier of railway-related equipment (as well as power plants) to the Than Shwe regime.

44 See Egreteau and Jagan, *Soldiers and Diplomacy in Burma*, pp. 252–60.

45 Sann Oo, 'Govt to Ensure Compensation for Rail Project: Minister', *Myanmar Times*, 5 September 2011.

46 This was an age-old concern. British military planners ruled against a break in gauge on the original railway towards the Chinese border in case troops needed to be deployed in defence of the empire. See Stubbs, 'The railways of Burma', pp. 36, 200–3.

47 Zhang Ye, 'Cross-Border Railway Builds Ties', *Global Times*, 17 August 2016.

48 Patrick Scally, 'Yunnan railway from hell to take at least five more years', GoKunming, 8 June 2017.

49 Patrick Scally, 'After 11 years, Yunnan's railroad from hell sees the light', GoKunming, 27 June 2019.

Part Three

1 George Orwell, 'You and the Atom Bomb', *Tribune*, 19 October 1945.

7. *Southern Shan*

1 Stubbs, 'The railways of Burma', p. 306.

2 'Taunggyi–Shwenyaung Railroad Section Will Usher in a New Era: Entire Work through Harsh Terrain Undertaken Solely by Tatmadawmen', *New Light of Myanmar*, 26 December 1997.

3 Dieter Hettler, *Railways of Burma / Myanmar* (unpublished).

4 United Nations Office on Drugs and Crime, 'Myanmar: Overview'.

5 Yola Verbruggen, 'In Pa-O Zone, No End to Opium Cultivation', *Myanmar Times*, 16 December 2015.

6 Shan community groups, 'The Four Cuts: New video exposes horror of Burma Army "clearance operations" in Shan State', 21 January 2020.

7 My descriptions of the military's operations in Shan State in the 1990s are based on my conversations in Shan as well as on reports by local rights groups, including Karen Human Rights Group, 'Forced relocation in Central Shan State: An independent report', 25 June 1996; Shan Human Rights Foundation, 'Dispossessed: A report on forced relocation and extrajudicial killings in Shan State, Burma', April 1998; Karen Human Rights Group ,'Killing the Shan: The continuing campaign of forced relocation in Shan State', 23 May 1998; and Shan community groups, 'The Four Cuts'. I have also drawn on testimony published by the International Labour Organization in its 'Report of the Commission of Inquiry appointed under article 26 of the Constitution of the International Labour Organization to examine the observance by Myanmar of the Forced Labour Convention, 1930 (No. 29)', 2 July 1998.

8 See, for example, '103-Mile Saikkhaung–Namhsan Railroad Scheduled to Be Completed October Next Year', *New Light of Myanmar*, 19 September 2001. On the involvement of Myanmar's LIDs in

atrocities against the Rohingya, see Simon Lewis et al., 'Tip of the spear: The shock troops that expelled the Rohingya from Myanmar', Reuters, 26 June 2018.

9 MNA, 'Shwenyaung–Taunggyi–Saikkhaung–Namhsan–Mongnai Railroad Inaugurated', *New Light of Myanmar*, 2 January 2006.

10 Shan community groups, 'The Four Cuts'.

11 Martin, *Ethnic Groups in Burma*, p. 84.

12 Myanmar's government told the ILO in October 1993 that 799,447 people had voluntarily worked on the railway. See 'Forced labour in Myanmar (Burma), Report of the Commission of Inquiry appointed under article 26 of the Constitution of the International Labour Organization to examine the observance by Myanmar of the Forced Labour Convention, 1930 (No. 29)', International Labour Organization: ILO, 1998, p. 47.

13 Based on my interviews in Loikaw.

14 Karen Human Rights Group, 'The Ye-Tavoy railway, an independent report', 13 April 1994. The same claim was made by a Karenni MP, see: National Coalition Government of the Union of Burma, Human Rights Documentation Unit, 'Human rights Yearbook', 1994, pp. 83–87.

15 'Forced labour in Myanmar (Burma): Report of the Commission of Inquiry appointed under article 26 of the Constitution of the International Labour Organization to examine the observance by Myanmar of the Forced Labour Convention, 1930 (No. 29)', International Labour Organization.

16 Reuters report published in *The Nation*, 14 October 1992, as cited in Karen Human Rights Group, 'Supplementary report on Karenni State', 15 November 1992.

17 MNA, 'Aungban–Pinlaung Railroad Inaugurated', *Working People's Daily*, 9 January 1993, and Myint Lwin, 'The Aunban–Loikaw Union Railroad', *Working People's Daily*, 10 January 1993, copies held by the Library of Congress.

18 On United Nations funding for the Border Areas Development Programme and local opposition, see Smith, *Ethnic Groups in Burma*; Associates to Develop Democratic Burma, 'United Nations Involvement in the Border Area Development Programme', *Burma Alert*, no. 11, vol. 3, November 1992; and International Commission of Jurists, 'The Burmese way: To where? Report of a mission to Myanmar (Burma)', 1991, p. 86. A local rights group claimed the Aungban–Loikaw railway was originally a UNDP-funded project. See Karen Human Rights Group, 'Karenni State: Forced relocation, concentration camps, and slavery', 10 August 1992.

19 MNA, 'Aungban–Pinlaung Railroad Inaugurated', *Working People's Daily*, 9 January 1993, held by the Library of Congress.

8. *Naypyidaw*

1 Details in this paragraph and the next two paragraphs are based on my own observations of the city, and on Emma Larkin, *No Bad News for the King: The True Story of Cyclone Nargis and Its Aftermath in Burma*, Penguin Books, 2010, pp. 93–95, and Rogers, *Than Shwe*, pp. 163–74.

2 Swe Win, 'Special Report: Abuses, Exploitation Rife in Myanmar's Forgotten Prison Labour Camps', *Myanmar Now*, 1 September 2016.

3 At least three of the prison labour camps beside the British-built railway in Mon State (Taung Zun, Yin Nyein and Zinkyeit) were still being worked by steam trains in 1999, according to one railway enthusiast, who noted that photography at the quarries was forbidden.

4 For a scholarly exploration of why the generals built Naypyidaw, see Dulyapak Preecharush, *Napyidaw, the New Capital of Burma*, White Lotus Press, 2009.

5 Andrew Marshall and Jason Szep, 'At Myanmar military's monument to itself, tributes to a dictator', Reuters, 16 November 2012.

6 Foreign and Commonwealth Office, 'UK activities in Burma', April 2014.

7 British Embassy Yangon, 'Great Britain Week in Burma, 1–7 December', 1 December 2013.

8 Selth, *Burma's Armed Forces*, p. 264, and Maung Aung Myoe, *Building the Tatmadaw*, p. 199.

9 See Rogers, *Than Shwe*, pp. 1–7, and Larkin, *No Bad News for the King*, pp. 92–93.

10 'Obituary: David Abel, Economics Czar Under Myanmar's Military Regime, Dies', *The Irrawaddy*, 21 January 2019.

Afterword

1 'Police, Soldiers Forcibly Evict More Than 1,000 Rail Workers and Their Families', *Frontier Myanmar*, 10 March 2021.

2 Hannah Beech, 'Myanmar Protesters Answer Military's Bullets with an Economic Shutdown', *New York Times*, 19 March 2021.

3 'Protestors Block Railway in Chanayethazan of Mandalay', *Global New Light of Myanmar*, 19 February 2021.

4 See, for example, BBC News, 'Myanmar coup: Aung San Suu Kyi faces new charge amid protests', 16 February 2021.

5 'Myanmar protests focus on junta's economic support', Associated Press, 18 February 2021.

6 'Police, Soldiers Forcibly Evict More Than 1,000 Rail Workers and Their Families', *Frontier Myanmar*, 10 March 2021; 'Despite Pressure, Myanmar Govt Employees Refuse to Work Under Military Rule', 16 February 2021, *The Irrawaddy*; and 'Soldiers and Police Fire into Housing Compound for Mandalay Railway Workers', *Myanmar Now*, 18 February 2021.

7 'Myanmar coup: Mass protests defy military and gridlock Yangon', BBC News, 17 February 2021, and 'Gunfire at Mandalay rail station amid creative Myanmar protests and appeals to civil servants', Radio Free Asia, 17 February 2021.

8 'At least 18 killed in Myanmar on bloodiest day of protests against coup', Reuters, 28 February 2021.

9 See, for example, 'In the Line of Fire: The Deadly Job of Covering Mandalay's Protests', *Frontier Myanmar*, 4 April 2021, and 'A Day of Tragedy and Terror in Hlaing Tharyar', *Frontier Myanmar*, 17 March 2021.

10 See Ye Myo Hein, 'Understanding the people's defense forces in Myanmar', United States Institute of Peace, 3 November 2022.

11 'Over two years with no Myanma Railways train service to Upper Burma', Democratic Voice of Burma, 8 February 2023.

12 'Striking Railway Officers Prepare for Armed Resistance against Junta', *Myanmar Now*, 2 November 2021.

13 The *Global New Light of Myanmar* has published regular reports since the coup about 'terrorist' attacks on the railways. See also 'After a Bold Attack, PDF Fighters Consider Their Next Move', *Myanmar Now*, 31 August 2021; Karen News, 'Military Council's train loaded with weapons hit by landmine explosion wrecking four carriages and killing 24 soldiers in Mon State', 16 December 2022; and 'Bomb kills 3 civilians at Bago region railway station', RFA Burmese, 14 February 2023.

14 'Japan railway projects risk aiding and abetting Myanmar junta atrocities', Justice for Myanmar, 30 May 2023.

15 'China and Myanmar Resume Work on Muse–Kyaukphyu Railway', *Frontier Myanmar*, 27 February 2023.

16 Shan State Frontline Investment Monitor, 'Large-scale coal mining begins in central Shan State for SAC regime's new Pinpet – Myingyan steel production hub', 13 February 2023.

17 Burma News International, 'Pa-O organisation calls for termin-ation of Russia-backed steel plant', 6 October 2022. For more context, see Pa-O Youth Organization, 'Robbing the future: Russian-backed mining project threatens Pa-O communities in Shan State, Burma', June 2009.

18 Shan State Frontline Investment Monitor, 'Large-scale coal mining begins in central Shan State for SAC regime's new Pinpet-Myingyan steel production hub', 13 February 2023.

19 'SAC Chairman PM Senior General Min Aung Hlaing Inspects Progress of Shwenyaung–Taunggyi Railway upgrading project', *Global New Light of Myanmar*, 8 March 2023.

20 UN News, 'UN rights expert exposes $1 billion "death trade" in arms for Myanmar military', 17 May 2023.

21 https://acleddata.com/acleddatanew/wp-content/uploads/2023/02/ACLED_2022-Year-in-Review_Report_Jan2023.pdf.

22 Data compiled by the Assistance Association for Political Prison-ers, which is the definitive source on civilian deaths and arrests in Myanmar since the coup. Accessed on 13 June 2023.

23 See Shona Loong, 'The Dry Zone: An existential struggle in cen-tral Myanmar', The International Institute for Strategic Studies, 5 July 2022.

24 Data compiled by Data for Myanmar, as of 31 May 2023, presented as an interactive map at https://www.datawrapper.de/_/sFXWD.

25 United Nations Office for the Coordination of Humanitarian Affairs, Myanmar Humanitarian Update No. 30, 13 June 2023.

26 See Chris Sidoti, 'It is high time for the UK to take action on Myanmar at the UNSC', Al Jazeera, 18 April 2022.

Bibliography

Books

Ali, Muhammad Shamsher, *The Beginnings of British Rule in Upper Burma: A Study of British Policy and Burmese Reaction, 1885–1890*, University of London, 1976

Andrews, Kehinde, *The New Age of Empire: How Racism and Colonialism Still Rule the World*, Bold Type Books, 2021

Aung-Thwin, Maitrii, *The Return of the Galon King: History, Law, and Rebellion in Colonial Burma*, NUS Press, 2011

Aung-Thwin, Michael, and Aung-Thwin, Maitrii, *A History of Myanmar since Ancient Times: Traditions and Transformations*, Reaktion Books, 2012

Azoulay, Ariella Aisha, *Potential History: Unlearning Imperialism*, Verso, 2019

Ba Maw, *Breakthrough in Burma: Memoirs of a Revolution, 1939–1946*: Yale University Press, 1968

Blackburn, Terence R., *The Defeat of Ava: The First Anglo-Burmese War of 1824–26*, APH Pub. Corp., 2009

Blackburn, Terence R., *Executions by the Half-Dozen: The Pacification of Burma*, APH Pub. Corp., 2008

Burton, Anthony, *The Railway Empire*, Cambridge University Press, 1994

Burton, Antoinette M., *After the Imperial Turn: Thinking with and through the Nation*, Duke University Press, 2003

Callahan, Mary P., *Making Enemies: War and State Building in Burma*, Cornell University Press, 2003

Chachavalpongpun, Pavin, and Thuzar, Moe, *Myanmar: Life After Nargis*, Institute of Southeast Asian Studies, Singapore, 2009

Charney, Michael W., *A History of Modern Burma*, Cambridge University Press, 2009

Charney, Michael W., *Imperial Military Transportation in British Asia: Burma 1941–1942*, Bloomsbury Academic, 2019

Cobden, Richard, *How Wars Are Got Up in India: The Origin of the Burmese War*, William & Frederick G. Cash, 1853

Cockett, Richard, *Blood, Dreams and Gold: The Changing Face of Burma*, Yale University Press, 2015

Colquhoun, Archibald R., and Hallett, Holt Samuel, *Report on the Railway Connexion of Burmah and China*, Allen, Scott & Co., 1888

Crosthwaite, Charles, *The Pacification of Burma*, Edward Arnold, 1912

Darvill, Simon, *Industrial Railways and Locomotives of India and South Asia*, Industrial Railway Society, 2013

Darwin, John, *Unfinished Empire: The Global Expansion of Britain*, Penguin, 2011

Darwin, John, *The Empire Project: The Rise and Fall of the British World System 1830–1970*, Cambridge University Press, 2009

Egreteau, Renaud, and Jagan, Larry, *Soldiers and Diplomacy in Burma: Understanding the Foreign Relations of the Burmese Praetorian State*, NUS Press, National University of Singapore, 2013

Ferguson, Niall, *Empire: How Britain Made the Modern World*, Penguin, 2003

Fredholm, Michael, *Burma: Ethnicity and Insurgency*, Praeger, 1993

Furnivall, J.S., *An Introduction to the Political Economy of Burma*, Burma Book Club, 1931

Furnivall, J.S., *Colonial Policy and Practice: A Comparative Study of Burma and Netherlands India*, New York University Press, 1948

Geary, Grattan, *Burma After the Conquest*, Sampson Low, Marston, Searle & Rivington, 1886

Bibliography

Gildea, Robert, *Empires of the Mind: The Colonial Past and the Politics of the Present*, Cambridge University Press, 2019

Gott, Richard, *Britain's Empire: Resistance, Repression and Revolt*, Verso, 2011

Hantzis, Steven James, *Rails of War: Supplying the Americans and Their Allies in China-Burma-India*, Potomac Books, an imprint of the University of Nebraska Press, 2017

Hay, John Ogilvy, *Papers connected with the improvement of Arakan, and railway communication through Burma; in continuation of the Improvement Committee Report, and 'The "Friend" and our Railway'*, published for private circulation, 1873

Hay, John Ogilvy, *Indo-Burma-China Railway Connections a Pressing Necessity. With a few remarks on communications in and with Burmah past and present*, Blackwood & Sons, 1888

Hay, John Ogilvy, *Arakan, Past, Present, Future: A Résumé of Two Campaigns for Its Development*, William Blackwood, 1892

Hobsbawm, Eric, *Nations and Nationalism since 1780*, Cambridge University Press, 1992

Horsey, Richard, *Ending Forced Labour in Myanmar: Engaging a Pariah Regime*, Routledge, 2011

Hughes, Hugh, *Indian Locomotives*, Part 2: *Metre Gauge 1872–1940*, Continental Railway Circle, 1992

Hughes, Hugh, *Indian Locomotives*, Part 3: *Narrow Gauge 1863–1940*, Continental Railway Circle, 1994

Hughes, Hugh, *Indian Locomotives*, Part 4: *1941–1990*, Continental Railway Circle, 1996

Ireland, Alleyne, *Colonial Administration in the Far East: The Province of Burma: A Report Prepared on Behalf of the University of Chicago*, Houghton, Mifflin & Co., 1907

Jeshurun, Chandran, *The Burma–Yunnan Railway: Anglo-French Rivalry in Mainland Southeast Asia and South China, 1895–1902*, Ohio University Center for International Studies, Southeast Asia Program, 1971

Keck, Stephen L., *British Burma in the New Century: 1895–1918*, Palgrave Macmillan, 2015

Khin Maung Kyi, Ronald Findlay, R.M. Sundrum, Mya Maung, Myo Nyunt, Zaw Oo, et al., *Economic Development of Burma: A Vision and a Strategy*, Olof Palme International Center, 2000

Kratoska, Paul H. (ed.), *The Thailand–Burma Railway, 1942–1946: Documents and Selected Writings*, London: Routledge, 2006

Kwarteng, Kwasi, *Ghosts of Empire: Britain's Legacies in the Modern World*, Bloomsbury, 2011

La Forte, Robert S., and Marcello, Ronald E. (ed.), *Building the Death Railway: The Ordeal of American POWs in Burma*: Scholarly Resources, 1993

Larkin, Emma, *No Bad News for the King: The True Story of Cyclone Nargis and Its Aftermath in Burma*, Penguin Books, 2010

Laurie, William Beatson Ferguson, *Our Burmese Wars and Relations with Burma*, W.H. Allen & Co., 1885

Lee, Ronan, *Myanmar's Rohingya Genocide: Identity, History and Hate Speech*, I.B. Tauris, 2021

Lewis, Norman, *Golden Earth: Travels in Burma*, Jonathan Cape, 1952

Lintner, Bertil, and Black, Michael, *Merchants of Madness: The Methamphetamine Explosion in the Golden Triangle*, Silkworm Books, 2009

MacKenzie, John M., *Propaganda and Empire: The Manipulation of British Public Opinion, 1880–1960*, Manchester University Press, 1984

Mains, A.A., *A Solider with Railways*, Picton, 1994

Marshall, Tim, *Prisoners of Geography: Ten Maps That Tell You Everything You Need to Know About Global Politics*, Elliott & Thompson, 2015

Maung Aung Myoe, *Building the Tatmadaw: Myanmar Armed Forces Since 1948*, Institute of Southeast Asian Studies, Singapore, 2009

Maung Aung Myoe, *In the Name of Pauk-Phaw: Myanmar's China Policy Since 1948*, Institute of Southeast Asian Studies, Singapore 2011

Maung Htin Aung, *The Stricken Peacock: Anglo-Burmese Relations, 1752–1948*, Martinus Nijhoff, 1965

Maung Htin Aung, *A History of Burma*, Columbia University Press, 1967

Maung Htin Aung, *Lord Randolph Churchill and the Dancing Peacock: British Conquest of Burma, 1885*, Manohar Publications, 1990

Maung Shein, *Burma's Transport and Foreign Trade, 1885–1914*, Department of Economics, University of Rangoon, 1964

McLynn, Frank, *The Burma Campaign: Disaster into Triumph*, Vintage, 2011

Molesworth, E.J. (ed.), *Life of Sir Guildford L. Molesworth*, Spon, 1922

Moorhouse, Geoffrey, *India Britannica*, Harvill, 1983

Ni Ni Myint, *Burma's Struggle against British Imperialism, 1885–1889*, Rangoon Universities Press, 1983

Nock, O. S., *Railways of Asia and the Far East*, A&C Black, 1978

O'Dell, Andrew C., *Railways and Geography*, Hutchinson University Library, 1971

Orwell, George, *The Collected Essays, Journalism, and Letters of George Orwell: Volume 1, An Age Like This, 1920–1940*, Nonpareil Books, 2000

Orwell, George, *The Collected Essays, Journalism, and Letters of George Orwell: Volume 4, In Front of Your Nose, 1945–1950*, Penguin Books, 1970

Orwell, George, *Burmese Days*, Penguin Books, 1989

Phayre, Lieutenant-General Sir Arthur P., *History of Burma Including Burma Proper, Pegu, Taungu, Tenasserim, and Arakan, from the Earliest Time to the End of the First War with British India*, Trubner & Co., 1883

Preecharush, Dulyapak, *Napyidaw, the New Capital of Burma*, White Lotus Press, 2009

Puri, Samir, *The Great Imperial Hangover: How Empires Have Shaped the World*, Atlantic Books, 2020

Richards, Thomas, *The Imperial Archive: Knowledge and the Fantasy of Empire*, Verso, 1993

Rogers, Benedict, *Than Shwe: Unmasking Burma's Tyrant*, Silkworm Books, 2010

Said, Edward W., *Culture & Imperialism*, Vintage, 1994

Said, Edward W., *Orientalism*, Penguin, 2003

Satow, Michael, and Desmond, Ray, *Railways of the Raj*, Scolar Press, 1980

Selth, Andrew, *Transforming the Tatmadaw: The Burmese Armed Forces since 1988*, Strategic and Defence Studies Centre, Research School of Pacific and Asian Studies, The Australian National University, 1996

Selth, Andrew, *Burma's Armed Forces: Power without Glory*, EastBridge, 2002

Smith, Martin, *Burma: Insurgency and the Politics of Ethnicity*, Zed Books, 1991

Steinberg, David I., and Fan, Hongwei, *Modern China-Myanmar Relations: Dilemmas of Mutual Dependence*, Nordic Institute of Asian Studies, 2012

Stewart, A.T.Q., *The Pagoda War: Lord Dufferin and the Fall of the Kingdom of Ava 1885–6*, Faber and Faber, 1972

Taylor, Robert H., *The State in Myanmar*, NUS Press, National University of Singapore, 2009

Tarling, Nicholas, *Southeast Asia: A Modern History*, Oxford University Press, 2001

Thant Myint-U, *The Making of Modern Burma*, Cambridge University Press, 2001

Thant Myint-U, *The River of Lost Footsteps: A Personal History of Burma*, Faber and Faber, 2007

Thant Myint-U, *Where China Meets India: Burma and the New Crossroads of Asia*, Faber and Faber, 2012

Thant Myint-U, *The Hidden History of Burma: Race, Capitalism, and the Crisis of Democracy in the 21st Century*, Atlantic Books, 2020

Tin Maung Maung Than, *State Dominance in Myanmar: The Political Economy of Industrialization*, Institute of Southeast Asian Studies, Singapore, 2007

Tharoor, Shashi, *Inglorious Empire: What the British Did to India*, C. Hurst, 2017

Theroux, Paul, *The Great Railway Bazaar*, Hamish Hamilton, 1975

Walker W.K, and Hancock, R.B., *The Burmese Railway Guide, Rangoon and Irrawaddy Valley State Railway*, W.H. Sloan, American Mission Press, 1877

Westwood, John, *Railways of India*, David & Charles, 1974

Westwood, John, *Railways at War*, Osprey Publishing Limited, 1980

Winston, W.R., *Four Years in Upper Burma*, C.H. Kelly, 1892

Wolmar, Christian, *Railways & the Raj: How the Age of Steam Transformed India*, Atlantic Books, 2017

Woodman, Dorothy, *The Making of Burma*, The Cresset Press, 1962

Unpublished Books, Documents, Manuscripts

Background History of Bawdwin Mine, Kyaukme District, North Shan State, Myanmar (Burma)

Burma/Siam Railway: Lushan forced labour camp, statements from Burmese labourers, 1 January 1946–31 December 1947, The National Archives, Kew, ref: WO 325/139

Burma/Siam Railway: Mezali forced labour camp, statements from Burmese labourers, 1 January 1945–31 December 1947, The National Archives, Kew, ref: WO 325/136

Burma/Siam Railway: Shin forced labour camp, statements from Burmese labourers, 1 January 1946–31 December 1947, The National Archives, Kew, ref: WO 325/138

Burma/Siam Railway: Village atrocities by Japanese, statements from Burmese labourers, 1 January 1947–31 December 1947, The National Archives, Kew, ref: WO 325/137

Communications: Railways, Governor's Secretary's Office, Government House, The National Archives, Kew, ref: FO 643/63, 1946–47

Hettler, Dieter, *Railways of Burma/Myanmar*

Fyfe, C., Fyfe Papers, 'Xerox copy of the typescript of Mr Fyfe's railway history of Burma in 14 chapters', Centre of South Asian Studies, University of Cambridge

British Library archive material: official documents,
manuscripts, surveys, reports etc.

Annual report of the Burma Railway Board, Rangoon: Government Press, 1938–39

Annual report of the Burma Railway Board, Rangoon: Government Press, 1940–41

Annual report of the Burma Railway Board, Rangoon: Government Press, 1946–47

Burma China Railway, metre gauge, 116 miles, Lashio to Hsoptap on the Chinese frontier, via the Nam Yau, Nam Ket, Salween, Nam Ting gorges: report and construction estimate, 1941–1942, 1943

'Burma: The new British province.' Delivered before the Royal Scottish Geographical Society in Edinburgh, Glasgow, and Dundee, November 1887, by Sir Charles Bernard

Collection 205/31: Special operations in Wuntho territory under General Wolseley, February to April 1891, IOR/L/MIL/7/9193: 1891–1892

Contracts relating to Burma Railways System, etc. Rangoon, 1916

Correspondence between Captain Richard Sprye, and the Rt. Hon. William-Ewart Gladstone, M.P. for South Lancashire, Chancellor of H.M.'s Exchequer, &c., on the commercial opening of the Shan States, and western inland China, by railway, direct from Rangoon, London: [Printer not identified], 1865

Fifteenth annual report of the Burma State Railway Volunteer Corps. Season 1894–95. Rangoon: Superintendent, Government Printing, Burma, 1895

Fourth annual report of the R&ISR [Rangoon and Irrawaddy State Railway] Volunteer Rifles, Season 1883–84, Rangoon: Superintendent, Government Printing, 1884

Fraser, (Captain) Alexander, and Forlong, J. G., 'Report on a route from the mouth of the Pakchan to Kraw, and thence across the Isthmus of Kraw to the Gulf of Siam', 1883

Lower Burma Railways: Reconnaissance surveys, 2' 6" gauge, Moulmein-Victoria Point Railway: report and estimates. [By Malcolm T. Porter. With maps.] Rangoon, 1913

Maxwell, William Lockhart, 'William Maxwell Papers', 1874–1913, parts 40–50, held by the National Army Museum

Mu Valley and Mogaung Railway survey Report on survey operations north of Kawlin, during the cold season of 1888–89. [F.R. Bagley] Rangoon: British Burma Press, 1889

Papers Relating to a Railway between Rangoon and Prome, in British Burmah, London, H. J. Wicks, 1868

Pegu-Syriam Railway Survey: 1901–2, metre-gauge, 67 miles. reconnaissance report and abstract of cost. [By A. R. Lilley.] Rangoon: Public Works Department, 1902

Prospectus of the Burma Railway Company, 22 July 1896, PW/481

Records of the Burma Railway Company

Records of the India Office Relating to the Burma Railway Company

Report on the administration of Burma, Rangoon: Superintendent Government Printing, 1887–1900

Roberts to Sladen (Mss Eur E290/52, letter dated 3 December 1887)

Southern Shan States Railway Project, 1901–1902: 2' 6" gauge, 112.2 miles. [A. R. Lilley.]. Rangoon: Public Works Department, 1903

The Railway Police Manual, Containing Orders and Rules made for the Railway Police, Issued with the Sanction of the Government of Burma, Rangoon: Superintendent Government Printing and Stationery, Burma, 1925

Articles

Amnesty International, 'Amnesty International withdraws human rights award from Aung San Suu Kyi', 12 November 2018

Associated Press, 'Myanmar protests focus on junta's economic support', 18 February 2021

Aung Hla Tun, 'Myanmar government abolishes direct media censorship', Reuters, 20 August 2012

Aung Hla Tun, 'Myanmar president promotes reformers in cabinet shake-up', Reuters, 27 August 2012

Aung Theinga, 'Cooperation with Understanding of Genuine Goodwill Needed', *New Light of Myanmar*, 26 December 2012

Aye Min Soe, 'Western Parts of Myanmar Get First Direct Rail Service to Yangon', *New Light of Myanmar*, 25 May 2014

Ba Khaung, Thet Ko Ko and Vrieze, Paul, 'A Chronology of Myanmar's Kachin Conflict', *The Irrawaddy*, 20 November 2014

Ba Khaung, Thet Ko Ko and Vrieze, Paul, 'A Chronology of Myanmar's Kachin Conflict', *The Irrawaddy*, 20 November 2014

Ba Kaung, 'Kachin Rebels Blow Up Major Railway', *The Irrawaddy*, 11 November 2011

Baillargeon, David, ' "A Burmese wonderland": British world mining and the making of colonial Burma', PhD, University of California Santa Barbara, 2018

Baillargeon, David, ' "On the Road to Mandalay": The Development of Railways in British Burma, 1870–1900', *The Journal of Imperial and Commonwealth History*, vol. 48, no.4, 2020, pp. 654–78

BBC Burmese, 'Myitnge CDM railway employees have no place to run', 16 September 2022

BBC News, 'Myanmar coup: Mass protests defy military and gridlock Yangon', 17 February 2021

BBC News, 'Myanmar coup: Aung San Suu Kyi faces new charge amid protests', 16 February 2021

BBC News, 'Myanmar policemen killed in Rakhine border attack', 9 October 2016

Beckett, Ian F. W., 'The campaign of the lost footsteps: The pacification of Burma, 1885–95, Small wars and insurgencies', vol. 30, nos. 4/5, 2019, pp. 994–1019

Beech, Hannah, 'Myanmar Protesters Answer Military's Bullets with an Economic Shutdown', *New York Times*, 19 March 2021

Belfast Telegraph, 'Kyaukse Captured', 31 March 1945

Bernstein, Dennis, and Kean, Leslie, 'Singapore's Blood Money: Hanging Drug Couriers but Investing with their Suppliers', *The Nation*, 20 October, 1997

Booth, Robert, 'Boris Johnson Caught on Camera Reciting Kipling in Myanmar Temple', *Guardian*, 30 September 2017

British Embassy Yangon, 'Great Britain Week in Burma, 1–7 December', 1 December 2013

Burma News International, 'Pa-O organisation calls for termination of Russia-backed steel plant', 6 October 2022

Cengel, Katya, 'Rape Is a Weapon in Burma's Kachin State, But the Women of Kachin Are Fighting Back', *Time Magazine*, 11 February 2014

Charney, Michael W., 'Railways and empire', in MacKenzie, John M., (ed.), *The Encyclopedia of Empire*, Wiley Blackwell, 2016, pp. 1722–27

Coconuts Yangon, 'Police in Magway Region refer to journalists as aliens', 2 September 2015

Croizier, Ralph C., 'Antecedents of the Burma Road: British Plans for a Burma–China Railway in the Nineteenth Century', *Journal of Southeast Asian History*, vol. 3, no. 2 (September 1962), pp. 1–18

Democratic Voice of Burma, 'Over two years with no Myanma Railways train service to Upper Burma', 8 February 2023

Dickinson, Rob, 'The Burma Mines Railway 1999', International Steam

Dickinson, Rob, 'Burma Mines in the 1970s', International Steam

Dill, Catherine, and Lewis, Jeffrey, 'Suspect defense facility in Myanmar', James Martin Center for Nonproliferation Studies, 9 May 2014

Dixit, Kunda, 'Exposé on alleged drug links rattles city state', IPS, 21 November 1996

Dundee Evening Telegraph, 'There Is Fresh Trouble in Burmah', 24 February 1891

Farrelly, Nicholas, 'Kachin Media War Continues', *New Mandala*, 3 May 2012

Flora & Fauna International, 'Secret species – camera traps show what lies within Myanmar's lowland forests', May 2020

Frontier Myanmar, 'A Day of Tragedy and Terror in Hlaing Tharyar', 17 March 2021

Frontier Myanmar, 'China and Myanmar Resume Work on Muse–Kyaukphyu Railway', 27 February 2023

Frontier Myanmar, 'How We Live Now: A Survey of Living Standards in Myanmar', 6 August 2018

Frontier Myanmar, 'In the Line of Fire: The Deadly Job of Covering Mandalay's Protests', 4 April, 2021

Bibliography

Frontier Myanmar, 'Police, Soldiers Forcibly Evict More Than 1,000 Rail Workers and Their Families', 10 March 2021

Galache, Carlos Sardiña, 'Rohingya and National Identities in Burma', *New Mandala*, 22 September 2014

Global New Light of Myanmar, 'Protestors Block Railway in Chanayet-hazan of Mandalay', 19 February 2021

Global New Light of Myanmar, 'SAC Chairman PM Senior General Min Aung Hlaing Inspects Progress of Shwenyaung–Taunggyi Railway Upgrading Project', 8 March 2023

Halpin, Padraic, 'Bob Geldof calls Aung San Suu Kyi "handmaiden to genocide"', Reuters, 13 November 2017

Hein Thar, 'Government Seeks to Tame Hlaing Tharyar, Yangon's Wild West', *Frontier Myanmar*, 6 November 2019

Hlaing Aung, 'Storm-Hit Areas Will Have Been Regenerated with Thriving Trees and Crop Plantations by Next Year', *New Light of Myanmar*, 30 May 2008

Hla Oo, 'KIA: The terrorist group from Burma?', 14 January 2013

Hseng Khio Fah, 'Junta to start construction on Lashio–Muse railroad project', Burma Myanmar News, 23 December 2009

Htike Htike Aung, 'Performance of railway transport in Myanmar', Yangon University of Economics, Master of Development Studies Programme, May 2019

Htun Khaing, 'Following the Money Trail for Magway's Missing Oil Revenue', *Frontier Myanmar*, 27 February, 2017

Justice for Myanmar, 'Japan railway projects risk aiding and abetting Myanmar junta atrocities', 30 May 2023

Justice for Myanmar, 'Developing a dictatorship: How governments and international organisations are supporting the illegal Myanmar military junta – and what must be done to stop this', 25 January 2023

Karen National Union Foreign Affairs Department, 'Statement by KNU Foreign Affairs Department on Burma–Thailand natural gas pipeline', 24 February 1995

Karen National Union Information Service, 'Ye–Tavoy Railway Revisited', *Burma Issues*, vol. 5., no. 11, November 1995

Karen News, 'Military Council's train loaded with weapons hit by landmine explosion wrecking four carriages and killing 24 soldiers in Mon State', 16 December 2022

Khin Oo Thar, 'Mrauk U Pagodas Damaged by Railroad Construction', *The Irrawaddy*, 24 November 2010

Khin Oo Thar, 'More Land in Arakan State Confiscated for Railway', *The Irrawaddy*, 23 December 2010

KNG, 'KIO-Burma army clashes erupt along rail line in Southern Kachin state', Burma News International, 12 September 2012

Kyaw Hsu Mon, 'Government to Auction Off 76 Businesses', *Myanmar Times*, 31 January 2011

Kyaw Hsu Mon, 'Minhla–Minbu Railway Section Opens', *Myanmar Times*, 4 October 2010

Kyaw Hsu Mon, 'Plan for Burma–China Train Link Derailed', *The Irrawaddy*, 21 July 2014

Kyaw Hsu Mon, '$4.9m Repair Bill for Rail Network after Flood Damage', *The Irrawaddy*, 9 October 2015

Kyaw Lin Htoon, 'Fluctuating Fortunes at the Bawdwin Mine', *Frontier Myanmar*, 31 January 2018

Kyaw Phone Kyaw, 'NLD Goes It Alone, Raising Ethnic Party Ire', *Frontier Myanmar*, 2 May 2016

Kyaw Ye Lynn, 'Yangon's Railroad to Nowhere', *Frontier Myanmar*, 13 December 2017

Londonderry Sentinel, 'Many Jap Targets in Burma Bombed', 11 May 1943

Larsen, Jensine, 'Crude Investment: The case of the Yadana pipeline in Burma', *Bulletin of Concerned Asian Scholars*, vol. 30, no. 3, 1998, pp. 3–13

Lawi Weng, 'As Flood Waters Begin to Recede in Pwintbyu, Locals Eye a Slow Recovery', *The Irrawaddy*, 5 August 2015

Lawi Weng, 'Ethnic Armed Groups Launch Joint Offensive in Northern Shan State', *The Irrawaddy*, 20 November 2016

Lewis, Simon et al., 'Tip of the spear: The shock troops that expelled the Rohingya from Myanmar', Reuters, 26 June 2018

Lintner, Bertil, 'Same Game, Different Tactics: China's "Myanmar Corridor"', *The Irrawaddy*, 13 July 2015

London Daily News, 'Railroad Laying in Burmah', 19 November 1892

London Evening Standard, 'Another Small War', 28 March 1891

Loong, Shona, 'The Dry Zone: An existential struggle in central Myanmar', The International Institute for Strategic Studies, 5 July 2022

Madras Weekly Mail / The Pioneer, 5 March 1891

Malithong, Rachatapong, 'News from "Burmah": The role of the English press in the making of the British Empire in Burma', PhD, University of Manchester, 2018

Marshall, Andrew, and Szep, Jason, 'At Myanmar military's monument to itself, tributes to a dictator', Reuters, 16 November 2012

Maung Maung Htwe, 'Glorious Days in Ayeyarwady Division', *New Light of Myanmar*, 3 August 2010

McPherson, Poppy et al., 'Point of no return', Reuters, 18 December 2018

Min Lwin, 'Burmese Reactors Close to Completion: Military Sources', *The Irrawaddy*, 13 March 2010

Minorities at Risk Project, Chronology for Karens in Burma, 2004

Minorities at Risk Project, Chronology for Mons in Burma, 2004

Mizzima, 'Railway Line Rerouted after Arakanese Heritage Site Damaged', 30 November 2010

MNA (Myanmar News Agency), 'Aungban–Pinlaung Railroad Inaugurated', *Working People's Daily*, 9 January 1993, copy held by the Library of Congress

MNA, 'Better Transportation Brings About Development of Tourism Industry and More Job Opportunities, Thereby Contributing to Rural Development and Poverty Alleviation', *New Light of Myanmar*, 12 May 2013

MNA, 'Better Transportation Means Positive Signs in Economy and Socio-Economic Life of Nation: MR to Link Mandalay and Bhamo', *New Light of Myanmar*, 22 February 2010

MNA, 'Golden Nut Fixed at First Truss of Ayeyarwady River Bridge (Nyaungdon)', *New Light of Myanmar*, 30 January 2011

MNA, 'Kwantaung–Ponnagyun–Yotayok Railroad Section in Ponnagyun Opened', *New Light of Myanmar*, 16 May 2010

MNA, 'Kyangin–Pakokku Railroad Linking North and South of Myanmar', *New Light of Myanmar*, 31 January 2012

MNA, 'Kyangin–Pakokku Railroad to Link Ayeyarwady West Bank with Delta, Central Myanmar, Northern Sagaing Div and Rakhine State', *New Light of Myanmar*, 14 June 2010

MNA, 'Kyaw–Yaymyetni Railroad Section, Ponnyataung Tunnel Opened', *New Light of Myanmar*, 29 January 2007

MNA, 'Kyunchaung–Daungtha Section of Kyangin-Pakokku Railroad Project Commissioned', *New Light of Myanmar*, 27 February, 2011

MNA, 'May Ayeyarwady dwellers serve interests of region and nation with heart of gold like mighty white elephant appeared in the region: President U Thein Sein attends inauguration of Ayeyarwady Bridge (Nyaungdon)', *New Light of Myanmar*, 28 November 2011

MNA, 'Minbu–Pwintbyu Railroad Section of Kyangin-Pakokku Railroad Construction Project Commissioned into Service', *New Light of Myanmar*, 23 January 2011

MNA, 'Pathein (Begarat)-Einme Railroad Section Commissioned into Service', *New Light of Myanmar*, 21 March 2011

MNA, 'President U Thein Sein Visits Construction Site of Ayeyarwady Bridge (Nyaungdon): Efforts to Be Made for Parallel

Completion of Motor Road and Railroad on Schedule', *New Light of Myanmar*, 26 April 2011

MNA, 'Railroad to Be Constructed to Link Sittway and An and West Bank of Ayeyarwady River: Prime Minister General Thein Sein Tours Townships in Rakhine State', *New Light of Myanmar*, 29 January 2009

MNA, 'Rail Sections Partially Damaged by KIA Mines', *New Light of Myanmar*, 16 January 2013

MNA, 'Shwenyaung–Taunggyi–Saikkhaung–Namhsan–Mongnai Railroad Inaugurated', *New Light of Myanmar*, 2 January 2006

MNA, 'Sittway–An–Minbu Railroad under Construction to Introduce Rail Service between Sittway and Yangon', *New Light of Myanmar*, 18 March 2010

MNA, 'Thanks to united strengths of government, people and Tatmadaw, storm-hit regions return to normalcy within one year. Government makes utmost efforts for enabling storm-ravaged regions to enjoy new conditions and new life and to stand on their own strengths', *New Light of Myanmar*, 6 November 2009

MNA, 'Transport Network Basic Requirement for Harmonious Progress of Whole Union, Kyangin–Okshitpin Railroad Section Commissioned into Service', *New Light of Myanmar*, 23 March 2009

MR, 'RBE Transport Resumes in Sittway Township', *Global New Light of Myanmar*, 26 January 2015

Mratt Kyaw Thu, 'Exploring History on the Old Rakhine Railway', *Frontier Myanmar*, 14 December 2016

Mratt Kyaw Thu, 'Forsaken at the "Western Gate"', *Frontier Myanmar*, 21 August 2018

Myanmar Informer, 'Historical Evidence of a Chittagonian Bengalis Transporter Train: Arakan Light Railway', 4 November 2018

Myanmar Now, 'Soldiers and Police Fire into Housing Compound for Mandalay Railway Workers', 18 February 2021

Myanmar Now, 'Striking Railway Officers Prepare for Armed Resistance against Junta', 2 November 2021

Myanmar Now, 'After a Bold Attack, PDF Fighters Consider Their Next Move', 31 August 2021

Myint Lwin, 'The Aunban–Loikaw Union Railroad', *Working People's Daily*, 10 January 1993, copy held by the Library of Congress

Myint Maung Soe, 'Bhamo–Katha Railroad Project, a Fruitful Result of Stability and Peace', *New Light of Myanmar*, 7 August 2009

Myo Min, 'The socio-economic struggles of Cyclone Nargis' migrants in Yangon', Tea Circle Oxford, 30 March 2020

Nadi Hlaing and Haack, Michael, 'Myanmar Railway Workers Stay Defiant Even After Junta Evicts Them from Homes', *South China Morning Post*, 24 April 2021

Nang Mya Nadi, 'One dead, four hurt in Kachin train explosion', Democratic Voice of Burma, 11 January 2013

Narinjara, 'Ancient Arakanese city walls destroyed for Sittwe-Rangoon road', Burma News International, 23 April 2012

Nay Aung, 'Sesame Farmers Reject Railway Compensation', *Myanmar Times*, 6 October 2015

Nay Aung, 'The Sham Tram', *Myanmar Times*, 4 August 2017

Nehru, Vikram, 'Myanmar's military keeps firm grip on democratic transition', Carnegie Endowment for International Peace, 2 June 2015

New Light of Myanmar, 'General Maung Aye Inspects Construction Tasks for Saikkhaung–Namhsan Railroad Project', 25 October 2001

New Light of Myanmar, 'General Maung Aye Inspects Construction of Saikkhaung–Namsang Railroad', 13 May 2002

New Light of Myanmar, 'Kyaw–Zebya Railroad Opens', 10 April 1997

New Light of Myanmar, 'Minister for Rail Transportation Inspects Taunggyi–Banyin–Saikkhaung–Mogni–Namhsan Railroad', 25 December 2000

New Light of Myanmar, 'More Railroads, Roads Being Built in Shan State (South) for Regional Progress: General Maung Aye Discusses Transport and Economy in Taunggyi', 1 July 2001

New Light of Myanmar, 'National Progress through Regional Development', 29 January 2009

New Light of Myanmar, 'Progress of Infrastructures Across the Nation in the Time of the State Peace and Development Council', 1 January 2011

New Light of Myanmar, 'Senior General Than Shwe Inspects Infrastructural Improvements for Nationwide Development', 18 April 1997

New Light of Myanmar, 'Taunggyi–Shwenyaung Railroad Section Will Usher in a New Era: Entire Work through Harsh Terrain Undertaken Solely by Tatmadawmen', 26 December 1997

New Light of Myanmar, '103-mile Saikkhaung–Namhsan Railroad Scheduled to Be Completed October Next Year', 19 September 2001

Orwell, George, 'You and the Atom Bomb', *Tribune*, 19 October 1945

Osnos, Evan, 'The Burmese Spring', *The New Yorker*, 6 August 2012

Parameswaran, Prashanth, 'What's Behind Myanmar Military Chief's Europe Voyage?', *The Diplomat*, 28 April 2017

Pilger, John, '"Death Railway" Revisited: Rebuilding Myanmar (Burma) with Slave Labor', *South China Morning Post*, 11 May 1996

Radio Free Asia, 'Gunfire at Mandalay Rail Station amid creative Myanmar protests and appeals to civil servants', 17 February 2021

Reporters without Borders, 'Crisis in Arakan State and new threats to freedom of news and information', 28 June 2012

Reuters, 'At least 18 killed in Myanmar on bloodiest day of protests against coup', 28 February 2021

Reuters, 'City of Oxford strips Aung San Suu Kyi of human rights award', 4 October 2017

Reuters, 'Myanmar police shoot dead seven protesters in troubled Rakhine', 17 January 2018

Reuters report published in *The Nation*, 14 October 1992, as cited in Karen Human Rights Group, 'Supplementary report on Karenni State', 15 November 1992

RFA Burmese, 'Bomb kills 3 civilians at Bago region railway station', 14 February 2023

Robinson, Gwen, and Pilling, David, 'New "Super Cabinet" Drives Rapid Change', *Financial Times*, 4 December 2012

Sann Oo, 'Govt to Ensure Compensation for Rail Project: Minister', *Myanmar Times*, 5 September 2011

Scally, Patrick, 'Yunnan railway from hell to take at least five more years', GoKunming, 8 June 2017

Scally, Patrick, 'After 11 years, Yunnan's railroad from hell sees the light', GoKunming, 27 June 2019

Sein Lwin Aung, 'Yangon–Pathein Railway Link Nearing Completion', *New Light of Myanmar*, 31 January 2013

Shan Community Groups, 'The Four Cùts: New video exposes horror of Burma Army "clearance operations" in Shan State', 21 January 2020

Shan Herald Agency for News, 'Forced labour for yet another death railway', 2 November 2001

Shan State Frontline Investment Monitor, 'Large-scale coal mining begins in central Shan State for SAC regime's new Pinpet–Myingyan steel production hub', 13 February 2023

Shoon Naing, 'Foreign tourist killed in landmine blast in Myanmar hiking region', Reuters, 26 November 2019

Sidoti, Chris, 'It is high time for the UK to take action on Myanmar at the UNSC', Al Jazeera, 18 April 2022

Silverstein, Josef, 'Politics and Railroads in Burma and India', *Journal of Southeast Asian History*, vol. 5, no. 1), 1964, pp. 17–28, The National University of Singapore, 1964

Smith, Martin, and Jagan, Larry, 'Maran Brang Seng: In His Own Words', *Burma Debate*, vol. 1, no. 3, December 1994/January 1995

South, Ashley, 'The Dream of a Kayan Homeland', *Frontier Myanmar*, 19 April 2020

Stubbs, Dr Lindsay Clyde, 'The railways of Burma: Their past, present and future', PhD, Macquarie University, Department of Economics, 2018

Smith, Martin, 'Obituary: General Ne Win', *The Guardian*, 6 December 2002

Swe Win, 'Special Report: Abuses, Exploitation Rife in Myanmar's Forgotten Prison Labour Camps', *Myanmar Now*, 1 September 2016

The Economist, 'Eager Mindsets', 30 December 2014

The Economist, 'Lo Hsing Han', 27 July 2013

The Englishman, 'The Viceroy's Tour', *The Englishman's Overland Mail*, 1 December 1898

The Englishman (Special), 'The First Mogaung Expedition, a Reminiscence of 1886', *The Englishman's Overland Mail*, 26 January 1899

The Homeward Mail, 24 February 1891

The Homeward Mail, 'Times' Telegrams, 'Lord Elgin in Burma', 28 November 1898

The Irrawaddy, 'Despite Pressure, Myanmar Govt Employees Refuse to Work Under Military Rule', 16 February 2021

The Irrawaddy, 'Made Homeless by Junta, Myanmar Govt Workers Vow to Continue Strike Till Regime Falls', 31 March 2021

The Irrawaddy, 'Obituary: David Abel, Economics Czar Under Myanmar's Military Regime, Dies', 21 January 2019

The Kite Tales, 'Inheritance of Silence', December 2016

'The Labour Recruitment of Local Inhabitants as Rōmusha in Japanese-Occupied South East Asia, Melber, Takuma', *International Review of Social History*, vol. 61 (December 2016), Supplement 24, pp. 165–85

The Scotsman, 'Burma Campaign: Japanese 20 Miles from Mandalay', 2 May 1942

The Scotsman, 'Burma's "Operation Flush": Dacoit Power Broken', 27 March 1947

United States Holocaust Memorial Museum, 'Museum rescinds award to Daw Aung San Suu Kyi', 7 March 2018

UN News, 'UN rights expert exposes $1 billion "death trade" in arms for Myanmar military', 17 May 2023

Verbruggen, Yola, 'In Pa-O Zone, No End to Opium Cultivation', *Myanmar Times*, 16 December 2015

Vum Son Suantak, 'How and Why the Burmese Army Murdered Four Chin Christians', Chin Human Rights Organisation, *Rhododendron News*, vol. VII, no. II, March–April 2004

Wall Street Journal, 'Myanmar Moves to Privatize Key State Enterprises', 18 February 2010

Webster, Anthony, 'Business and Empire: A Reassessment of the British Conquest of Burma in 1885', *The Historical Journal*, vol. 43, no. 4, December 2000, pp. 1003–25

Yan Pai, 'Privatisation Linked to Money Laundering', *The Irrawaddy*, 23 March 2011

Ye Khaung Nyunt, 'Transportation Between Buthidaung and Maungtaw Has Improved', *Global New Light of Myanmar*, 14 November 2016

Ye Mon, 'In Laiza, Building an "iron spirit"', *Frontier Myanmar*, 19 April 2019

Ye Myo Hein, 'Understanding the people's defense forces in Myanmar', United States Institute of Peace, 3 November 2022

Zarni Mann, 'Journalists Detained for Reporting Alleged Burmese Chemical Weapons Factory', *The Irrawaddy*, 2 February 2014

Zhang Ye, 'Cross-Border Railway Builds Ties', *Global Times*, 17 August 2016

Zhou, Naaman and Safi, Michael, 'Desmond Tutu Condemns Aung San Suu Kyi: "Silence is too high a price"', *The Guardian*, 8 September 2017

Reports and Official Documents

'A sourcebook on allegations of cooperation between Myanmar (Burma) and North Korea on nuclear projects', version of 2014-09-22

All Arakan Students' & Youths' Congress, 'Overview of land confiscation in Arakan State', June 2010

All Burma Students' Democratic Front, 'Burma Focus', vol. 4, no. 9, 15 November 1993

Amnesty International, 'Caught in the middle: Abuses against civilians amid conflict in Myanmar's northern Shan State', 24 October 2019

Amnesty International, Myanmar, 'Conditions in prisons and labour camps', September 1995

Amnesty International, Myanmar, 'Human rights violations against ethnic minorities', August 1996

Amnesty International, Myanmar, 'Portering and forced labour: Amnesty International's concerns', August 1996

Amnesty International, Myanmar, ' "We are at breaking point" – Rohingya: persecuted in Myanmar, neglected in Bangladesh', 19 December 2016

Asian Development Bank, 'Myanmar transport sector policy note: Railways', 2016

Associates to Develop Democratic Burma, 'United Nations Involvement in the Border Area Development Programme', *Burma Alert*, no. 11, vol. 3, November 1992

British Overseas Railways Historical Trust (archive), *The Railway Gazette*, London, 1907–1954

Burma Campaign UK, 'TOTALitarian oil – TOTAL oil: Fuelling the oppression in Burma', 21 February 2005

Coalition on Housing Rights and Evictions, 'Displacement and dispossession: Forced migration and land rights, Burma', November 2007

EarthRights International and Southeast Asian Information Network, 'Total denial: A report on the Yadana pipeline project in Burma', 10 July 1996

EarthRights International, 'Total denial continues: Earth rights abuses along the Yadana and Yetagun pipelines in Burma', May 2000

Fauna & Flora International, 'Myanmar oil palm plantations: A productivity and sustainability review', January 2016

Foreign and Commonwealth Office, 'UK activities in Burma', April 2014

Human Rights Foundation of Monland, 'Destination unknown: Hope and doubt regarding IDP resettlement in Mon State', September–October 2012

Human Rights Foundation of Monland, *Exploitation of Women and Children as Forced Labor on Ye-Tavoy Railway*, 20 May 1996

Human Rights Foundation of Monland, *Human Rights Abuses Related to Total Co. and UNOCAL's Gas Pipeline Project*, Human Rights Report 7/96, 24 November 1996

Human Rights Foundation of Monland, 'The Mon Forum', issues including 2/95, 3/98, 1/99

Human Rights Foundation of Monland, 'Laid waste: Human rights along the Kanbauk to Myaing Kalay gas pipeline', May 2009

Human Rights Watch, 'HRW demands end to forced relocations', 9 July 1996

Human Rights Watch, 'I want to help my own people: Repression impedes civil society and aid: State control and civil society in Burma after Cyclone Nargis', 29 April 2010

Human Rights Watch, 'Letter to donors on reconstruction after Cyclone Nargis', 23 July 2008

Human Rights Watch, ' "Nothing for our land": Impact of land confiscation on farmers in Myanmar', 17 July 2018

Human Rights Watch, ' "The government could have stopped this": Sectarian violence and ensuing abuses in Burma's Arakan State', 31 July 2012

Human Rights Watch/Asia, 'No safety in Burma, no sanctuary in Thailand', July 1997

Images Asia, Karen Human Rights Group and the Open Society Institute's Burma Project, 'All quiet on the western front? The situation in Chin State and Sagaing Division, Burma', January 1998

International Center for Transitional Justice, 'Impunity prolonged: Burma and its 2008 constitution', September 2009

International Commission of Jurists, 'The Burmese way: To where? Report of a mission to Myanmar (Burma)', 1991, p. 86

International Federation for Human Rights, 'Burma, total and human rights: Dissection of a project', FIDH report no. 224/2, November 1996

International Federation of Red Cross and Red Crescent Societies, 'Final report: Myanmar floods', 31 January 2017

International Labour Organization, 'Report of the Commission of Inquiry appointed under article 26 of the Constitution of the International Labour Organization to examine the observance by Myanmar of the Forced Labour Convention, 1930 (No. 29)', Geneva, 2 July 1998

Japan International Cooperation Agency, 'The survey program for the National Transport Development Plan in the Republic of the Union of Myanmar', September 2014

Kachin Women's Association Thailand, 'Burma's covered-up war: Atrocities against the Kachin people', 4 November 2011

Karen Human Rights Group, 'Field reports: Mergui-Tavoy District', 29 July 1995

Karen Human Rights Group, 'Forced relocation in Central Shan State: An independent report', 25 June 1996

Karen Human Rights Group, 'Karenni State: Forced relocation, concentration camps, and slavery', 10 August 1992

Karen Human Rights Group, 'Killing the Shan: The continuing campaign of forced relocation in Shan State', 23 May 1998

Karen Human Rights Group, 'SLORC orders to villages: set 94-E', 2 September 1994

Karen Human Rights Group, 'SLORC orders to villages: set 95-A Ye-Tavoy railway, other labour, & extortion'

Karen Human Rights Group, 'SLORC orders to villages: set 95-C Mon area: Ye-Tavoy railway, other forced labour, etc.'

Karen Human Rights Group, 'The situation in Northwestern Burma', 30 January 1996

Karen Human Rights Group, 'The Ye-Tavoy railway, an independent report', 13 April 1994

Karen Human Rights Group, 'Ye-Tavoy railway area: An update', 31 July 1995

Karen Human Rights Group, 'Ye-Tavoy area update', 5 January 1996

Kramer, Tom et al., 'From war to peace in Kayah (Karenni) State: A land at the crossroads in Myanmar', Transnational Institute, July 2018

Lintner, Bertil, 'Burma's WMD programme and military cooperation between Burma and the Democratic People's Republic of Korea', Asia Pacific Media Services, March 2012

McCartan, Brian, and Jolliffe, Kim, 'Ethnic armed actors and justice provision in Myanmar', The Asia Foundation, October 2016

Ministry of Information, *Constitution of the Republic of the Union of Myanmar*, Printing and Publishing Enterprise, 2008

Ministry of Rail Transportation, *Facts about Myanma Railways*, Myanma Railways, 2008

Mon Information Service, *Forced Labour on the Construction of the Ye-Tavoy Railway*, 1995

Myanmar Statistical Yearbook, 2010–2021, Central Statistical Organization, The Government of the Republic of the Union of Myanmar, 2021

National Coalition Government of the Union of Burma, Human Rights Documentation Unit, 'Human rights yearbooks, 1994–98'

Pa-O Youth Organization, 'Robbing the future: Russian-backed mining project threatens Pa-O communities in Shan State, Burma', June 2009

Smith, Martin, *Ethnic Groups in Burma: Development, Democracy and Human Rights*, a report by Anti-Slavery International, 1994

Sein Htay, *Economic Report on Burma*, Economics and Research Department Federation of Trade Unions-Burma (FTUB), June 2005

Shan Human Rights Foundation, 'Dispossessed: A report on forced relocation and extrajudicial killings in Shan State, Burma', April 1998

Shan Human Rights Foundation, 'The Shan case', 1994

Shan Women's Action Network and Shan Human Rights Foundation, 'Burma army tracks across Shan State', October 2015

Tarkapaw, TRIP NET, Southern Youth, Candle Light, Khaing Myae Thitsar, Myeik Lawyer Network and Dawei Development Association, 'Green desert: Communities in Tanintharyi renounce the MSPP oil palm concession', 2016

Thailand Burma Border Consortium, 'Protracted displacement and chronic poverty in eastern Burma/Myanmar', October 2010

Transnational Institute, 'The Kachin crisis: Peace must prevail', 8 March 2013

United Nations General Assembly, 'Report by the Special Rapporteur on Myanmar, A/51/466', 8 October 1996

United Nations High Commissioner for Refugees South-East Myanmar Information Management Unit, 'Tanintharyi Region profile', June 2014

Acknowledgements

It was in the *Myanmar Times* newsroom that I first began to grapple with Myanmar's modern history, and I have my colleagues there to thank for introducing me to much of the context that informs this book. Thanks to Zay Yar Linn and Aung Myint Ye Zaw for taking me on my first trip to Myanmar's borderlands, which gave me the confidence to travel alone. Thanks also to Aung Shin, Su Phyo Win, Aye Nyein Win and Thiri Min Htun for your (mostly sage) counsel as I prepared to make the journey recorded in this book.

While travelling, I received advice and assistance from dozens of people who collectively made my journey possible. Particular thanks are due to Marcus Allender, Ar Lone and his family, Katie Arnold, Dan Hkung Awng and others at the Humanity Institute, Jan Ford, Dieter Hettler, Htunt Su, Khin Su Wai, Kayleigh Long, Ma Oo, Jeremy Mullins, Nai Aue Mon, Nay Aung, Daniella Ritzau-Reid, Sai Maung Oo, Sai Merng, Sai Nanda Oo, Sai Naw Kham, Soe Moe, Su Hlaing Tun, Sunny, Eve Tasha, Than Htoo, Thein Htaik, Thet Aye, Clement Tysi and journalists based in cities across the country, who were endlessly helpful and shared invaluable contacts. Tracking down sources in remote parts of Myanmar often required multiple intermediaries, many of whom are invisible in this book, but I am grateful to all of them.

I wouldn't have made it far without the patience and good humour of Myanma Railways staff, including the railway police who were my constant companions. Over three months,

Acknowledgements

I spent hundreds of hours travelling alone by train; in another country, this might have been dangerous, but in Myanmar I (almost) always felt safe. Everywhere I went, my fellow travellers provided me with companionship and a supply of fried snacks, fruit, cheroots, betel quids, energy drinks and the occasional swig of whisky.

All of these people made it possible and enjoyable for me to travel to the far reaches of Myanmar. But my greatest thanks are reserved for the men and women who welcomed me into their homes, giving up hours and sometimes days of their time to share their stories with me. These stories form the heart of this book; I have named some of their narrators in the text, but sadly the political climate in Myanmar is such that many others must remain anonymous.

As well as oral histories, this book draws on thousands of secondary sources. The most important of these are articles and human-rights reports published during the Than Shwe era by unnamed journalists and activists. I am indebted to the men and women working for ethnic human-rights groups who took immense risks to compile and publish testimony relating to the junta's railways, including the Karen Human Rights Group, the Human Rights Foundation of Monland and the Shan Human Rights Foundation. Thanks to Richard Horsey and the staff at the International Labour Organization who endured years of harassment while documenting the issue of forced labour – and to Horsey specifically for writing about his experience engaging the regime.

I am grateful to multiple academics and historians, who I have named in my bibliography, but particularly to Lindsay Stubbs at Macquarie University in Sydney. I'm also grateful to the staff of numerous archives and libraries, above all the Online Burma/ Myanmar Library. Thanks to Julian and Dick at the British

Overseas Railways Historical Trust for patiently spending hours pulling down dusty volumes of the *Railway Gazette* for me to pore over, and to the BORHT members who shared ideas and advice. Thanks to the British Library, the British Newspaper Archive, the Centre of South Asian Studies in Cambridge, the Internet Archive for providing access to the Wayback Machine, the National Archives at Kew and the National Army Museum in London. Thank you to Pandora and translators Ke' Su Thar and Ch. B. for giving me permission to reproduce the wonderful poem that appears at the end of my Afterword.

When I returned to Yangon after travelling across Myanmar, I had planned to move home to London, but a great friend gave me a reason to stay. Sonny Swe hired me to work at *Frontier*, an investigative magazine that became my professional home for almost three years while I researched and drafted this book. Sonny and the rest of the small *Frontier* team inspired me every day with their formidable courage and optimism, in what became an increasingly challenging environment for journalism in the years leading up to the coup. Even at the most difficult moments, working at *Frontier* felt like being part of a big family; the office was always filled with laughter, home-cooked food and cold beer. So much of what I learned from my colleagues there has enriched this book, but more than anything I am grateful for the time I spent with all of you.

Without my friends and family there wouldn't be a book at all. I owe a special debt to Libby Burke Wilde for retracing some of my steps with me and capturing the beauty of Myanmar and its railways with spectacular photography, some of which is reproduced in this book – and to Kevin Oliver for coming with us. Thanks to Alison Jones for hosting me in London while I spent two months sifting through the British Library's archives. To Ben Dunant, Gavin Jacobson, Sophia

Acknowledgements

Sednaoui and Thomas Spendlove (and others who have asked not to be named for security reasons) for reading drafts of early chapters, correcting mistakes, and suggesting improvements. To Andrea Malouf for persuading me to attend a writing retreat, to Nick Pelham for hosting it, and to Simon Akam and others for convincing me to stop writing and start looking for a publisher. To Yan and Tom Kean for spending many hours reviewing the manuscript and providing such detailed and thoughtful feedback.

I'm endlessly grateful to my parents Tim and Catherine and my siblings Becca, Kate and James, for keeping my spirits up, reading drafts, and encouraging me to keep writing. To my parents for sharing their home in Sussex, where I finished this book, and to my mother for looking after my daughter Freda (and me), giving me the time I needed to write the final chapters. To Freda who provided much-needed relief during an otherwise intense period of working to a deadline. And to Hen: for coming with me to Yangon; for being completely unfazed when I packed a small bag and disappeared for three months, for reasons that must have been quite unfathomable; for being my reader and sounding board; for your kindness and patience; for the laughter that you fill our home with; and for your love.

Thank you to my agent Angelique Tran Van Sang at Felicity Bryan Associates for believing in the story I wanted to tell and guiding me through the daunting process of finding a home for it. I couldn't have hoped for a better ally. To Juliet Garcia at FBA for seeing potential in the manuscript and for sharing it with Ange. To Ka Bradley at Allen Lane for your infectious enthusiasm, empathetic feedback style and brilliant edits. Knowing this book was in your capable hands gave me the energy I needed to finish it, and it has been a joy working with you.

Acknowledgements

Finally, thanks to everyone at Penguin Press who helped to turn my manuscript into a book, including Katy Banyard, Jeff Edwards, Richard Green, Richard Mason, Peter Pawsey, Simon Smith, Louisa Watson, Anna Wilson, and publicist Pen Vogler.